Covenant of Blood

Chicago Studies in the History of Judaism
A Series Edited by William Scott Green

Lawrence A. Hoffman

Covenant of
Blood

Circumcision and Gender in Rabbinic Judaism

The University of Chicago Press *Chicago & London*

Lawrence A. Hoffman is professor of liturgy at Hebrew Union College–
Jewish Institute of Religion.

The University of Chicago Press, Chicago 60637
The University of Chicago Press, Ltd., London
© 1996 by Lawrence A. Hoffman
All rights reserved. Published 1996
Printed in the United States of America
05   04   03   02   01   00   99   98   97   96   5   4   3   2   1

ISBN (cloth): 0-226-34783-4
ISBN (paper): 0-226-34784-2

Library of Congress Cataloging-in-Publication Data

Hoffman, Lawrence A., 1942–
    Covenant of blood : circumcision and gender in rabbinic Judaism /
Lawrence A. Hoffman.
        p.   cm. — (Chicago studies in the history of Judaism)
    Includes bibliographical references and index.
    ISBN 0-226-34783-4 — ISBN 0-226-34784-2 (pbk.)
    1. Berit milah — History. 2. Blood — Religious aspects —
Judaism. 3. Women in rabbinical literature. 4. Rabbinical
literature — History and criticism.
    I. Title. II. Series.
    BM 705.H63   1996
    296.4'422 — dc20   95-16067
                                                            CIP

Contents

c h a p t e r *1*

Circumcision as Symbol in the Jewish Psyche

A 1993 edition of *The Jerusalem Report* included this remarkable item in its rundown of the news of the month.

> CLIPPING CORPSES: Burial societies all over Israel have been circumcising corpses prior to interment, without permission of the families of the deceased, the Religious Affairs Ministry has disclosed. Most of the dead men have been immigrants from the former Soviet Union. While burial society officials and Sephardi Chief Rabbi Mordechai Eliahu defended the practice, Ashkenazi Chief Rabbi Yisrael Lau said the rabbinate does not force circumcision on live or dead men.[1]

A circumcision watch in the 1990s, if one can imagine such a thing, would have turned up other signs of debate regarding this time-honored Jewish practice. The same year, 1993, for instance, marked the tenth anniversary of the founding of NOAM, The National Association of *Mohalim/ot* [circumcisers, male and female], a body organized to encourage "Jewish medical professionals to demonstrate their commitment to Reform Judaism and to the sanctity of the Jewish family unit . . . our hope [being] that with an increasing number of *Mohalim/ot*, more families will choose to bring their children into the covenant of Judaism through this ancient ritual."[2]

Readers of these two reports, one from Israel and the other from North America, might conclude that not all Jewish parents have been rushing to perform the commandment of circumcising their sons; and they would be correct. Soviet Jews often arrive in either place uncircumcised because men are not normally circumcised in the countries of the former Soviet Union. For Jews to have insisted on it for their own children would have been tantamount to

1

marking them for the rest of their life as Jews, a dangerous gamble with a child's future in countries where Jewish identity has been problematic at best and downright dangerous at worst. But even in the United States and Canada, circumcision had come under attack, as we see from the retrospective musings of two fathers, both rabbis, who duly circumcised their sons and then recorded their reactions.

Shocked by his son's tears, Reform Rabbi Michael Herzbrun, found himself asking, "What about my son's needs? As he struggled in pain, had I somehow abandoned him for the sake of the ceremony? What kept me from aborting the ceremony on his behalf?"[3] Herzbrun's ruminations prompted a debate within the Reform rabbinate that would go on for two years.[4] Just as it died down, the *New York Times Magazine*'s influential "About Men" column published a Conservative rabbi's reflections on his son's circumcision. With the help of the professional *mohel,* he had actually performed the cut himself. When it was over, in stark contrast to Herzbrun, he celebrated for each and every father "this experience, even vicariously, of inflicting upon his child a ritualized blow so intense as to make him shake and recoil, yet so controlled that no damage is done, to signify that this will be the worst the child will ever know from his father's hand."[5]

What makes this glimpse into an age-old ritual and its modern-day dilemma worth reporting is that it is very serious, and it is not new. People agonize over circumcision precisely because it strikes deep roots in the collective Jewish psyche. This chapter explores just how deeply those roots go by rehearsing the classic modern instance of ritual ambivalence over circumcision, which took place exactly 150 years prior to the item in the *Jerusalem Report* with which I began. Later chapters trace the depth of symbolism built up over the years, the meaning circumcision had for biblical Jews and for the Rabbis in the formative period of the Mishnah and Talmud, and the degree to which circumcision (the male rite of initiation par excellence) has symptomatized a deep gender dichotomy in the course of rabbinic Jewish history. In my afterword I will return to North America and the close of the twentieth century. But for now I turn to Germany in 1843.

In August 1843, a group of Frankfurt laymen announced the formation of the Society for the Friends of Reform. Theirs was not the first public outcry for religious reform among Germany's Jewish population; indeed, the society arrived very late on the scene, over a quarter century after emancipated Jewish men and women had begun agitating for the relaxation of premodern Jewish custom and law in the hope of remaining Jewish but being German and modern, all at the same time. In the interim, the rabbinate had been splintered into factions, many remaining unalterably protective of the status quo while others led a movement for rapprochement between tradition and change.[6] In varying degrees advocates of reform gave notice that they would support lay initiatives toward the liberalization of the premodern Jewish condition, in that they would no longer champion the full gamut of Jewish legal principles known as *halakhah*. While not denying the validity of Jewish law per se, they applied a novel evolutionary perspective to its statutes, thus permitting it to remain rooted in talmudic legislation and medieval law codes while still being responsive to the needs of the present.

These liberal rabbis occupied many points on the spectrum of opinion regarding the amount and type of change desired. They ranged from the far left's outright denial of talmudic authority to a variety of more cautious positions in the center and on the right. The Frankfurt society thus holds a unique place in the history of these turbulent times, if only because it managed to unite every single one of those rabbis in virulent opposition to it.

There was more than one reason for this rabbinic unanimity of censure. To begin with, the society was clearly a lay organization daring to make statements on Jewish law and faith, precisely the areas that the rabbis considered their own domain.[7] Much as they may have argued within their own ranks on any given point of interpretation, they were at least all rabbis. They had fought long and hard to overcome the anticlerical spirit of an age in which rabbinism was largely equated with unenlightened obscurantism.[8] After a short period around the turn of the nineteenth century when lay reformers consciously avoided rabbis in favor of preachers, scholars, or almost anyone who might apply sound scholarly exegesis to the sources, rabbis like Abraham Geiger, Zacharias Frankel, and Samuel Holdheim managed once again to assert rabbinic authority. They did so mainly by demonstrating their ability to compromise on issues, and thus to demonstrate their sympathy with those who demanded that Judaism change to meet the times. These rabbis were not now prepared to return the right of Jewish self-determination to the laity.

Aside from their opposition to the Frankfurt society, it is difficult to find much on which these particular three rabbis agreed. Holdheim, who was born in Poland and gradually moved west to Berlin, had mapped out a spiritual odyssey remarkable for its distance from his youthful origins. He had gradually moved away from the highly traditional premodern stance typical of his family upbringing to the point where he championed a radical version of Reform Judaism, one that especially appealed to the ultrarationalists, and even to the assimilationists, in the Prussian capital. Denying to talmudic legislation any inherently binding force for his age, he accused his more moderate colleagues of ingenuously reading their own modern-day views into Jewish legal texts rather than exercising the courage to admit that the spirit of the age, which promoted reason and scientific research, gave them the right to their own Jewish self-determination. On the issues of his day, he was known to go so far as to advocate moving the Jewish Sabbath from Saturday to Sunday. True, he never formally proposed this change among his peers, but only because he knew he would be voted down. On the question of whether worship should continue with the age-old Hebrew rendering of the prayers, he voiced his opposition; let there be German translations instead. At the opposite extreme was Frankel, who eventually walked out of a conference of rabbinic reformers over the very issue of Hebrew, since, in his view, the age-old tongue was an absolute necessity. Straddling the fence on most matters we find Geiger, a consummate politician who often felt one way about an issue but spoke out in favor of another: privately he was often just as radical as Holdheim; publicly he avoided unnecessary controversy by emphasizing moderation.[9] As distant as these three rabbis were from each other on other matters of conscience, however, the proposals published by the Frankfurt Society for the Friends of Reform galvanized them as nothing else had or would, until at last, whether on the right, left, or in the center, they managed to speak out in unanimous opposition.

Rabbis Holdheim, Frankel, and Geiger were not the only ones shocked by the society's manifesto. To consult the list of opponents is to read a sort of "Who's Who" in the world of German Judaism, traditionalists and reformers alike. Rabbis are prominent, of course, but Germany's most prominent layperson, Gabriel Riesser, entered the fray as well, declaring the program retrogressive (this despite the fact that Riesser had hitherto urged reforms of extreme magnitude himself).

Something about the published program of the Frankfurt society must have demanded that Riesser disassociate himself from his erstwhile lay allies. That something must have transcended the rabbi-laity rift such that even this proud lay advocate of reform had no choice but to vote with the rabbis. The Frankfurt laymen had gone too far. Not content to deny theological positions, or even to tinker with worship practices, they did what no other voice for reform could countenance: they declared the age-old Jewish rite of circumcision null and void.

To be sure, their three-paragraph public declaration of principle omitted any reference to circumcision. Had those three platform planks alone emanated from the group, it is possible that despite rabbinic harangues regarding the hubris of the laity, the society might have gotten away with its outspoken stance. Two of them, after all—an affirmation of the evolutionary nature of Judaism, and a repudiation of the age-old hope that God would send a personal messiah to redeem the Jewish People—were in perfect agreement with the position of other reformers, rabbis included; and the third—a denial of the binding power of the Talmud—was no more radical than Holdheim, at least, had been urging. But the published three-point stand was only three-fifths of a larger program that had been cut down so as to avoid the outcry that even the members of the society feared was inevitable. Their earlier full statement had been circulated privately, to Riesser himself, among others, and it had been leaked, so when the shortened version appeared in the public light, it was not just the acknowledged statement that was at stake, but the unacknowledged one as well. One of the planks missing from the former, but known to be included in the latter, was the belief that circumcision should no longer be considered binding in that it was neither a *mitzvah* (a religious act commanded by God) nor even a desirable symbolic act.

Brit milah, the ritual circumcision of a Jewish boy on the eighth day of his life, had been practiced for eons. But for several reasons, this particular rite[10] seemed to clash with the program of Jewish emancipation and acculturation.[11] As an act performed upon the body, circumcision seemed both irrational and physical whereas post-Enlightenment Jews saw their religion as wholly rational and spiritual, a thing for the mind and for the soul, a matter of deep logical appreciation and high aesthetic appeal. "Primitive" tribes practiced circumcision. Did that make Judaism undivested of the custom primitive also? Since Christians in nineteenth-century Germany rarely had their children circumcised, Jewish insistence on doing so had the necessary effect of setting Jewish men apart from non-Jewish men at the very time when Jews wanted to emphasize their similarities rather than differences—how a common Judeo-Christian tradition made all Germans practically the same. Beyond these general objections, however, the issue of circumcision had emerged as a particularly embarrassing point of conflict for the reformers,[12] since the sanitary bureau of Frankfurt had been investigating some cases of infant fatality that were said to be traceable to the operation. It had concluded that insofar as Jewish parents still desired their children to be circumcised, they should employ only those persons licensed by the Frankfurt bureau, not the host of ritual circumcisers (known as *mohalim*) trained in the medieval manner of apprenticeship and recognized informally by the traditional Jewish community.

No wonder the Frankfurt laity wondered aloud whether circumcision really was a necessity for the admission of males to the covenant. But wondering, even aloud, was one thing; doing anything about it was another. Already the group had commissioned one of its community school teachers, Joseph Johlson, to publish a tract attacking the rite, and even to develop an alternative rite that would be appropriately religious in nature and applicable to girls as well as to boys. So even though the society's original plank against circumcision was officially excluded from the final version of the Frankfurt manifesto, its stand against circumcision was sufficiently well known by one and all. The real "sin" of the Frankfurt laymen was that they dared to breach the taboo against questioning the wisdom of circumcision, a sin that was duly punished by the concerted rabbinic attack that we have traced here.

Almost immediately a furor arose, with advocates of circumcision underscoring the absolute necessity of the rite. Rabbi Abraham Trier of Frankfurt invited eighty rabbis to write responsa on the issue. Forty-one answers were received, and twenty-eight were published in a volume entitled *Rabbinical Responses on Circumcision.* The respondents represented the full gamut of positions along the spectrum from orthodoxy to reform, but they were all unreservedly opposed to the Frankfurt society's position.

To be sure, the members of the society were not alone in their opposition to what looked to many like a vestige of a barbarous rite from a distant era that had long been outgrown. The difference was that the others knew better than to say what they believed publicly. Geiger, for example, who was often the epitome of judiciousness, wrote a letter to the renowned scholar Leopold Zunz after the latter had published his own opinion in the case, namely, that circumcision is the very essence of Judaism. Geiger is clear about why the society evoked such public turmoil: "It aroused the greatest antagonism by *attacking at once the rite of circumcision.*" Then Geiger owned up to his own ambivalence, albeit only in his private letter to Zunz. Although, he asserts, "I was not in sympathy with the Reform Society," he confesses:

> I cannot comprehend the necessity of working up a spirit of enthusi-
> asm for the ceremony merely on the ground that it is held in general
> esteem. It remains a barbarous bloody act. . . . The sacrificial idea
> which invested the act with sanctity in former days has no significance
> for us. However tenaciously religious sentiment may have clung to it
> formerly, at present, its only supports are habit and fear, to which we
> certainly do not wish to erect any shrines.[13]

Leave it to Geiger to set the matter straight: the society was guilty of bad tactics, not bad theology. By attacking circumcision, it "aroused . . . antagonism," which is to say, it alienated potential supporters of reform. Theologically, circumcision depended on a doctrine of sacrifice, which Geiger deplored as much as the Frankfurt reformers did. It was a "barbarous bloody act," a medieval vestige rooted in "habit and fear." But Geiger voices his opinion only in a private communication to Zunz. He knew better than to say so in public.

Holdheim, the radical reformer, issued his own public statement one year later, but waffled on the subject. Frankel, the conservative, had already written an article declaring circumcision to be a sine qua non of a boy's entry into the covenant in that, theologically speaking, only through circumcision is real sanctity conferred on the male child. He had been responding, no doubt, to Johlson's alternative rite of admission to the covenant, since Johlson had called his ceremony Sanctification of the Eighth Day, an elliptical reference to the sanctification of the child rooted in the day on which circumcision normally occurs rather than in the act of circumcision itself. If it is the *day,* not the *rite,* that is formative, says Johlson, then the actual act of circumcision can be replaced by something else as long as the day on which circumcision was practiced is retained. In Frankel's contrary view, even though circumcision must occur on the eighth day, it is the *rite,* not the *day,* that matters. The act of circumcision is itself nothing short of a Jewish sacrament, and as such it is irreplaceable.[14]

But what does this critical rite accomplish? Frankel argues that circumcision can hardly make the child Jewish, since his Jewish identity is dependent on his being born to a Jewish mother. He is Jewish from the womb, and he remains so with or without circumcision. Circumcision must therefore be an objective act that invisibly bestows sanctified status upon an already Jewish but not yet sanctified male. The responsibility is appropriately entrusted to the father in the first instance. If the father fails to carry out the duty, the obligation devolves on the Jewish court, that is, on the all-male representative body of the Jewish People. While Frankel deemed circumcision necessary for fully sanctified Jewish status, Holdheim demurred. Granted that circumcision is required for membership in the Jewish People as a *national* entity—its pre-Enlightenment status, in Holdheim's view—it certainly is not needed to be a Jew by *religion*. But does that mean Jews should or should not circumcise their children? Holdheim stopped short of any practical conclusion.

The liberal rabbis of Germany met three times between 1844 and 1846. They would tackle a host of problems, from Sabbath work prohibitions to the status of women, but they omitted circumcision from consideration. A request to add it to the agenda was unanimously rejected on the grounds that the better wisdom would be to omit all discussion of an issue about which people felt so passionately. Except for a closed session to consider a physician's charge that circumcision caused venereal disease and impotence, the rabbis managed to skirt the topic almost entirely.[15] I say "almost" because delegates to the last of these famous three conferences (Breslau, 1846) were forced to consider at least some specifics and even to hear a resolution by Mendel Hess, the chief rabbi of the grand duchy of Saxe-Weimer. One of the first rabbis to receive a university education, Hess was already noted for his radicalism, best expressed, perhaps, in his insistence in carrying out an 1823 government decree demanding that synagogue services be conducted entirely in German. From 1839 to 1848, he collaborated with Holdheim in coediting a journal to popularize their jointly held views on the religious left. Now, at Breslau, he emerged as the only rabbi, other than Holdheim, to oppose circumcision publicly, as he urged the passage of the following mild ruling:

> Be it resolved by this conference that, although it has learned with pain that some co-religionists observe no longer a command *so universally considered sacred* as circumcision, yet it declares against all external coercion and exclusion as has been demanded by a number of rabbis, and expresses the opinion that those who do not observe the command of circumcision are to be considered members of the Jewish community despite this.[16]

A mild resolution indeed! It declared circumcision "sacred" and "universally considered" so. It supports the Frankfurt society (and others too) only insofar as it prevents the equivalent of moral excommunication being applied to those who do not practice circumcision. But even this suggestion was too close to the raw nerve for the rabbis to consider. The motion was tabled.

Rabbis apparently found it possible to commit nothing less than liturgical surgery on their time-honored prayer book; they could cancel age-old mourning and wedding customs; they even declared the Talmud no longer binding. They had no trouble dispensing with Hebrew and cutting off their ties to a Jewish Land of Israel. They would even think seriously of declaring a marriage with a non-Jew "not forbidden." But they could not even consider abrogating circumcision. Moreover, they could not even agree that males who are not circumcised are still Jews! Nowhere else, to the best of my knowledge, were the reformers so adamantly tied to their past as in the case of circumcision. Why that is the case is the subject of this book.

The period of nineteenth-century Jewish reform was neither the first nor the only chapter in Jewish history where circumcision became a symbolic marker of immense proportion. In the period of the nascent Church, it was circumcision that symbolized the divide between Jew and non-Jew, such that, for example, Peter could be chastised by the Judean Church because he "went to uncircumcised men and ate with them" (Acts 11:3). Classical authors from Strabo (64/63 B.C.E.–21 C.E.) to Tacitus (56 C.E.–early second century) deride the custom as superstitious, even depraved, a deliberate attempt to distinguish Jewish men so that the Jews' regulations against sexual relations with non-Jews could be more easily observed.[17] Even earlier than that, it was circumcision that constituted the visible and therefore dominant sign of Jewishness, to the point where many Jews were ignoring circumcision (Jubilees 15:33–34) or undergoing the operation of epispasm, which undoes its signs, so as to "pass" as non-Jewish. When Antiochus Epiphanes prohibited circumcision (1 Macc. 1:48; 2 Macc. 6:10), he knew he was legislating what Jews would see as a symbolic denial of Judaism. A ban on circumcision some three centuries later was one of the factors involved in the Bar Kokhba War.

The role of circumcision emerges clearly in Josephus's account of the careers of two marginal Jews: Herod the Great (whose father, Antipater, was an Idumean) and Herod's grandson Agrippa, both of whom ruled Judea and consequently had to demonstrate symbolically their Jewish identity. In the first case, we find Herod's sister, Salome, intent on marrying Sylleus, the prime minister of the Arabian king Obodas. Herod agrees, but only if Sylleus will consent to be circumcised.[18] The case of Agrippa is even clearer. The Mishnah portrays him as loath to accept the mantle of Jewish leadership, precisely because of his ancestry. But his subjects call out to him, "Be not aggrieved for you are our brother, Agrippa."[19] Among other things, what is Agrippa remembered for? He marries his daughter to a foreign king, but only if he will be circumcised.[20]

We are concerned here with none of these particular historical incidents in and of themselves, or even with the interesting question of whether their details are actually a true account of what occurred or only a series of apocryphal tales told about various personalities either before or after their death. The fact that they are told is itself sufficient for our purposes. Our concern is the pattern to which they all testify. Persecutors of Jews from Antiochus to Hadrian committed many atrocities, but high on the list of outrages that Jewish history recollects is their banning of that single symbolic hallmark of Jewishness: circumcision. Jewish apostates surely defied much of Jewish law and theology, but the ultimate sin remembered by tradition is their covering up the sign of the covenant. Christianity broke with Judaism over more issues than one, but the mission to the Gentiles—symbolized by eating with the uncircumcised—ranks highest as the index of the rift. And marginal Jews of partial Jewish descent as well as Jewish heroes withstanding the oppression of foes are alike remembered for championing circumcision. Not for nothing do the Rabbis vie with one another to express the greatness of this singular commandment, which stood at the center of their universe:

> The word "uncircumcised" is used only as a name for Gentiles. . . . Rabbi Elazar ben Azariah says, "The foreskin is disgusting, for the word is used in order to refer disparagingly to pagans. . . ." Rabbi Ishmael says, "Great is circumcision, for thirteen covenants are made thereby." Rabbi Yose says, "Great is circumcision, since it overrides the prohibition of the Sabbath [meaning that circumcision is performed on the eighth day of a boy's life even if that day is the Sabbath]." Rabbi Joshua ben Korchah says, "Great is circumcision for it was not suspended even for a moment for the sake of Moses the righteous [a reference to the "bridegroom of blood" narrative, Ex. 4:25]." . . . Rabbi [Judah Hanasi] says, "Great is circumcision, for despite all the commandments that our father Abraham carried out, he was called com-

plete [*shalem*] only with his circumcision. . . ." Another opinion holds, "Great is circumcision, for if it were not for that, the Holy One Blessed be He would not have created this world."[21]

Circumcision has thus remained the sine qua non of Jewish identity throughout time. Among other things, Jews came to believe that it warded off danger and even saved Jews from damnation, that the sign of circumcision was tantamount to carrying God's ineffable name carved in the flesh, that it was a means of attaining mystical unity with the Creator, and that it brought about visionary experience.[22] Socially, too, circumcision was transformed into an attractive event. In medieval Italy, Germany, and North Africa, the circumcision feast was expanded to include dancing, gambling, masquerade, and an all-night vigil, where (eventually) prayer and sermonizing became the norm.[23] No wonder circumcision retained its hold on the Jewish imagination, even during the period of ardent reform, when almost everything was questioned and many things jettisoned. One eternal verity thus endures in Jewish culture: a tenacious grasp on circumcision to the point where opposition to it was declared a taboo. Even today, when feminist concerns and even medical attacks on circumcision are rampant, it still borders on heresy for Jews to suggest giving up the rite.

An old joke relates the tale of a smuggler who crossed the border daily riding a bicycle. The customs official would stop him each time, checking the bicycle handlebars, the tires, the spokes, and other assorted parts in order to ascertain that they contained no contraband, and would permit him clearance. After years of this daily charade, the official retired from duty. Dressed in his new civilian clothes, he proceeded to the border crossing, watching while the smuggler went through his usual routine with the new guard. Then he quickly approached the smuggler with the following plea:

"For ten years I have watched you smuggle something or other over the border, but for the life of me, I cannot figure out what it is or how you do it. Your handlebars are always hollow; the spokes of the bicycle are never silver; the tires regularly carry nothing but air; and the bicycle has no other places to hide anything. Now that I am retired and cannot arrest you, won't you please make my last few years happy by letting me in on the secret? What are you smuggling?

"Bicycles," the smuggler replied, "what else? Just bicycles, one a day for twenty-seven years!"

In our investigation of ritual, we are like border guards, trying to prevent the culture we study from smuggling anything past our attention. How carefully we ferret out old texts, obscure material artifacts, and hazy oral testimony, subjecting them to thorough analysis and unpacking whatever content they may have. Often, however, we fail to notice the obvious, which would tell us a great deal if we were only to look at it with new interest. The rite of circumcision is one such instance of the obvious: it somehow escapes attention even though it turns up at every step along the Jewish people's way through history. Central to the biblical narrative and critical for rabbis throughout time, the rite of circumcision has steadfastly remained the single most obvious boundary issue, marking the limits beyond which Jews felt they could not go without at the same time leaving Judaism. We should like to know why the rite has proved so intransigent to all attempts at eradication or even alteration. Or, putting it another way—since causality in culture is hard to demonstrate—we should at least find out what symbolic baggage circumcision has carried for Jews, such that they have held so strongly to it. This book tries to do just that.

I need to emphasize several introductory caveats, however, having to do with method and with results. First, some considerations of method, each of which I have phrased in terms of a principle that guides this work.

1. Ritual is as much a case of continuity as it is of change.

It is now a truism to note that during the several centuries spanning the changeover to what is variously known as A.D. or C.E. more than a single "Judaism" emerged. Even within "rabbinic Judaism"—the name we apply to the version of Judaism that Jews today consider normative—competing definitions of personal piety, theological orthodoxy, and religious responsibility coexisted. Those who developed rabbinic Judaism, however, did their best to ignore that diversity, presenting themselves as proponents of a tradition that extended all the way back to the return from Babylonian exile in the sixth and fifth centuries B.C.E., and then evolved unilinearly to their own time.

Rabbinic historiography is supported by a literary canon in which each work presents itself as being dependent on what came before. The two Talmuds, one edited in the Land of Israel (c. 400–500 C.E.) and the other in Babylonia (c. 500–600 C.E.), for example, purport to be mere commentaries on the Mishnah (c. 200 C.E.), which is explored as if it were in turn just the logical continuation of Scripture. Precisely because traditional scholarship uncritically accepted these claims, scholars today have made a point of underscoring evolutionary diversity across the centuries. The problem is that neither view is altogether wrong. There is innovation and discontinuity, certainly, but there is also some reality to the rabbinic authors' emphasis on that very continuity that makes tradition what it is—a tradition, not a revolution.[24] To some extent, after all, portrayal is reality.

By analogy, consider modern scholars who explode the putative ancient origins of nineteenth-century nationalistic ritual.[25] All those German oak-leaf ceremonies were unknown until Prussian German unity needed them. Bastille Day may commemorate the French Revolution, but nobody celebrated it until 1880![26] Tell that, however, to schoolboys presenting oak-leaf banners to their German headmaster out of age-old respect for roots in their Teutonic past, or to the Parisian populace dancing in the streets to celebrate their glorious revolution.

Studies of ritual therefore need to stress the equal truth of both perspectives. If we explore only evolution and change, as nineteenth-century *Wissenschaft* scholars insisted, we are really not studying ritual as it is lived among the people who believe and practice it so much as we are forcing ritual into the Procrustean bed of historical causality, exhausting its meaning in an exploration of the historical events that caused it.

The historical model slips easily into being purely literary. Since traditional scholarship had relied on an uncritical reading of the sources to display continuity rather than change, critical historical scholars made a point of applying a hermeneutic of suspicion to everything they read. They were not wrong to do so, and I follow their example here. But they often made a fetish of discriminating sources, especially where tannaitic and amoraic accounts are concerned. Precisely because the Talmud's editors gave the impression that they were merely expanding their mishnaic models, scholarship severed the necessary link between the Mishnah's pre-200 C.E. culture (on the one hand) and the talmudic post-200 situation (on the other). I have no quarrel with source criticism, but again, the study of ritual ought to be just that, the study of ritual—not the study of literary corpora any more than of historical causality. Though Babylonian talmudic thinking circa 550 C.E. may differ from Palestinian mishnaic interpretation some 350 years earlier, it does not follow that in the year 200 actual rabbinic Jews who practiced circumcision greeted the appearance of the Mishnah by abandoning their previous ritual life and starting all over again. We should not proceed as if nothing unified pre- and postmishnaic Judaism. Evolution in rabbinic source compilation should not blind us to the real continuity that people presuppose in their own lives.

This study therefore champions both horns of the traditionalist-historicist dilemma. I will demonstrate the novelty with which different ages interpret the rite of circumcision by pointing out the regular addition of liturgical strata to an earlier core, as well as innovative exegeses of that core. But I will avoid the arbitrary positing of utter discontinuity based simply on a monumental historical event, on one hand, and the appearance of novel literary records, on the other. As much as I posit scientific evolution of texts and cultural agendas, I insist equally on a recognizable continuity of identity across the great divide of the year 200 when authorities presumably metamorphosed from people called Tannaim into others known as Amoraim.[27]

An unanswered question throughout this tannaitic/amoraic core era, however, is how large and how representative our population sample is. To judge by our literary records, everyone was a rabbinic Jew, an estimate that is hardly credible. For all we know, the cultural understanding of circumcision that I explore here was shared by only a tiny percentage of Jews alive at the time. Is rabbinic literature of the second or third century an officially recognized constitution for society as a whole, or is it more akin to interoffice memos holding together the company culture of a small elite of executives? I suspect it is more like the latter. But however unrepresentative it might have been back then, its cultural constructs became the taken-for-granted substratum on which later Judaism was erected. Circumcision as a cultural artifact within this postbiblical rabbinic culture and then within the larger Judaism that it spawned is the focus of this book.

2. The study of ritual as a cultural artifact requires that we go beyond the standard historical/philological investigation of the evolution of a rite.

Consider, for example, circumcision in the Bible, the details of which will concern us in the next chapter. At the outset, we must admit that the agenda of the biblical authors themselves cannot fully be shared by those who study the text that those authors compiled. Even readers motivated solely by sacred concerns have no choice but to refract the contents of the Bible through their own eyes.[28] The same is even more true of university-trained academicians, who come to their task having already adopted sets of questions that have nothing to do with what motivated the biblical writers, but everything to do with the research program or scholarly paradigm that any given scholar adopts as his or her own model of what matters most about Israel's past.

Most of the classic literature on the subject of biblical circumcision was written by philological/historicist scholars trained to understand biblical practices as a reflection of the Bible's surrounding cultural milieu. These authors frequently assumed an evolutionary model of ritual, according to which entities are said to be "understood" when their late manifestations in history are traced back to the cultural environment in which they first arose. James Sanders goes so far as to accuse such scientific biblical scholarship of unintended collusion with fundamentalism:

> Historical criticism has been primarily interested . . . in what was really said and done by the original biblical contributors, through the historian's interest in reconstructing original moments. Those passages that helped such reconstructions have been called genuine or primary, while later additions by editors or scribes have been called spurious or secondary. . . . Biblical criticism, perhaps unwittingly, has subscribed to the same model as fundamentalists. . . . Fundamentalists and liberals, that is, the opponents of biblical criticism as well as its advocates, both attributed authenticity to the original speaker or writer of whatever portion of Scripture was under purview. The only real difference between them was that the one (the conservative) attributed more of the passage to the original individual than did the other (the liberal scholar). The conservative often would claim that every word recorded in the passage stemmed from the first writer or speaker while the biblical critic would distinguish between "genuine" and "spurious" passages, or "original" and "secondary."[29]

This hidden bias in favor of origins can be seen in different ways. On the one hand, we get teleological research, theological treatises that hunt down beginnings in order to show how later instances of growth were contained implicitly within the seed whence the whole institutional plant emerged. This position was once favored by Christian typologists, bent on finding the New Testament prefigured in the Old, and also by Jewish apologists who wanted to demonstrate that the virtues of Israelite religion—monotheism, for example—proceeded along a steady line of thought from a very early point in time until they eventually emerged full blown in "mature" guise. Other scholars eschewed teleology as tendentious, but still operated as if origins mattered

most. Often they took for granted the dubious proposition that a given institution may be perceived in all its innocent purity only at its inception, after
which time it would be corrupted by the ravages of history. They may equally
have assumed the very reverse, that institutions emerge into full-fledged maturity only after evolving from the messy business of syncretistic entanglement
in neighboring cultures, so that by locating their origin in the religiosocial
milieu of the ancient Near East, one could avoid the hubris of misrepresenting
them later as pure inventions of the Israelite mentality. Either way, what we
received from the most capable biblical scholarship was institutional history:
how circumcision (in our case) arose, developed, and grew.

This is a far cry from ritual as a lived cultural entity. Classical scholars
go about their business as if they were IRS agents, auditing sources by tracking
down parallel entries. They ask you to bring in your books, and then they
dismiss you, since the evidence is a set of objective entries in the ledgers. The
agent knows the rules of what to look for and what counts as an acceptable
"story" of income and expenditures. The subjective view of the taxpayer is
utterly irrelevant.

Alternatively, consider a team of public-opinion pollsters sent to find
out how people spend their money. They, too, look through people's bills noting debits and credits, but their tale of the ledger's "meaning" depends on a
running commentary provided by the people who keep it. If their informants
ask to be excused on the grounds that everything they spent is already there
in writing, the pollsters reply that precisely what they need to know is missing,
namely, what each purchase or disbursement meant to the people who spent
it. The IRS may explain a disbursement as a repayment on a loan, mandated
(and therefore explained) by an earlier decision to accrue indebtedness of a
certain magnitude and repayment schedule. The pollsters know all that, but
find it irrelevant to their purpose. They explain the outlay as a sign of confidence in the economy and a managerial tendency to expand into new markets.
Both perspectives would be equally correct.

But polling may necessitate conclusions of which the subjects themselves
are unaware. Again imagine economic pollsters. This time they have deter-
mined that the insecurity of a transient culture threatens an economy that is
dependent on durable goods—a principle derived from their study of people
who have never even heard of durable goods and didn't know they were inse-
cure! Or take an example from medicine. A good doctor combines objective
and quantifiable test data (about which the patient knows nothing) with the

patient's self-evaluation (which tests cannot get at) and arrives at a coherent diagnosis that might surprise the patient very much—as when a psychiatrist hears "I don't sleep well" and writes down "chronic depressive syndrome."

How do pollsters, doctors, and students of ritual know they are right? Nancy Jay puts it well in her study on sacrifice. She knows that she cannot possibly enter fully into the sacrificers' world. Nevertheless, she will have to ask her subjects to explain what they think they are doing, since sacrifice means nothing except in local context—Israelites are not Incas, after all. She comes with her own already-established agenda, however: the desire to link sacrifice to the case of women. She has noted that everywhere she looks sacrifice operates as a symbolic opposition to women in childbirth, and she wants to document that hypothesis and figure out why its holds. So she concludes:

> This will involve a continual negotiation between our perspective and that of the sacrificers themselves, a negotiation that will succeed only if we never uproot sacrificers from their own contexts, and if we do not let what we bring to the study blot out what they say about sacrifice.[30]

Following Peter Winch, she calls this "interpretive sociology." If we want to pursue the study of ritual as Jay the study of sacrifice, we will have to do more than take objective literary measurements of historical origins. To be sure, we cannot deny what those measurements determine—if a prayer did not exist until the eleventh century, for instance, we can hardly use it as evidence for what a rite meant to people who lived a thousand years earlier. I will therefore devote the next few chapters to unraveling what was early and what was late in the evolution of the circumcision liturgy. Once we have the ritual strata in place, however, we will have just begun. Our task then will be to get into the heads of our informants, as it were, as we try to reconstruct the cultural meaning that circumcision had for them.

People in antiquity did not carry our categories around in their heads any more than the pollsters' subjects knew that they were describing insecurity and durable goods. But at least we are asking them about the subjective meaning of the rite in question, and on that subject they are the only acknowledged experts.

3. Of the various kinds of ritual meaning, the one that concerns us most is neither private nor official, but public (either acknowledged or unconscious).

I use the term "public meaning" to designate an agreed-upon value of a cultural action, role, ritual, entity, and so forth. There are private meanings also: idiosyncratic associations that cultural forms evoke for any single individual. These are the concerns of psychoanalysts, who help you come to terms with the most private associations you may have regarding cats, dogs, churches, or Christmas. They may also be the concern of historians intent on knowing why Napoleon or Eisenhower acted one way rather than another, insofar as historical decisions are the outcome of an individual leader's psyche. But private meanings are not my concern here. I am interested in the meanings that people share.

To the extent that people recognize, or act as if they recognize, a shared meaning to what they do, we consider that meaning public.[31] Rites (like circumcision) are artistic constructs of behavior not unlike a literary plot line. The people who go through them are the characters, who must agree on something or they would not show up for the rite in the first place, and would have trouble going through it in the second. What complicates things is that cultures develop official commentaries on what the rite means, so that even as people learn what they are to do they are supplied with the "official" version of what their actions signify. Liturgists have come to recognize, for example, that the theological message said to be implicit within, say, the Eucharist is both public and official; but it does not exhaust the repertoire of public meanings that may exist like an uneasy substratum below the official ones, and may be more presupposed or intuited than actually recognized and verbalized.

If you ask religious experts what their people are doing, you will usually get the official meaning. If you ask people well socialized in the official meaning, they will do their best to appear learned and give you the same thing. Take the example of kindling Sabbath lights.

As an experiment, I have assembled random groups of people with the instructions that they are to bring with them their favorite Jewish symbol, or, if they cannot carry it, they may draw a picture, or even just tell us what it is. Some of the women, especially the older ones, bring candlesticks. I now ask them what the candlesticks mean to them. Invariably someone says, "Light is the symbol of the Divine." That response, however, occurs only in the case of women old enough to have attended Sabbath services prior to the replacement of the old Reform liturgy in 1975. What prompts the response "Light is a symbol of the Divine" is the fact that the old prayer book said so, in the prayer for lighting candles found on page 7![32] Sensing the importance of the rite of lighting candles, these women internalized the official meaning that the liturgy provides. It has now become a public meaning also, insofar as large numbers of women share it.

But it sometimes happens that another woman, someone who has never seen the old liturgy, also brings candlesticks. She listens politely to the official meaning recited by the first speaker, and then she says something else that she read or heard in her upbringing, perhaps something like "Light stands for peace." Now we have two competing official meanings on the floor. Neither woman cares very much that the other one has a different interpretation. I ask one of them, "If you were wrong and the other woman were right, would you still have brought the candlesticks as your favorite symbol?" I always get the same answer: "Of course!" The official meanings are after-the-fact justifications.

Now we see the problem with limiting our inquiry to what the officials tell us, a trap that anthropologists avoid by recognizing that the shaman's explanation, though not wrong, is *official,* and therefore not the sum total of the public meanings people share. It may, in fact, hardly be public at all: it may be a meaning that only the shaman and a few other elite ideologues recognize as real. When we reconstruct biblical or rabbinic liturgical practices we are not unlike anthropologists in the field, except, of course, for the all-important difference that our informants are dead and buried, and cannot talk to us in person. We are limited to the literary, epigraphic, and pictorial communications that they have left behind: the liturgies they recorded, legal data pertaining to how the rituals should be carried out, stories about people who did them, and the like. As readers of cultures, we have to go beyond the officially interpreted cultural remains (like "Light is a symbol of the Divine") to arrive at what the ritual in question meant to people unofficially. It is these unofficial public meanings that we discover in the fragments of literary culture that are not couched *expressly* in authoritative interpretive form: folk tales, for example, or marginal glosses that relate what people say or do. If, for example, you continue probing the women regarding their Sabbath candlesticks, you may find that they always light the candles with their families around them, or with their children there, or at least their daughters. Eventually they may say that whenever they light the candles they do not think at all of the Divine or of peace, but of family: their grandmothers, their mothers, and now themselves and their daughters. We have begun to ferret out a public meaning shared by many women in the room: the chain of women of whom they are a part, symbolized by a traditional women's ritual performed over an object connected with women's spirituality through the years.³³

I do not mean to make a definitive statement here about kindling Sabbath lights, but I do hope the experiment illustrates the approach I want to take in the pages that follow. I will ask what people in antiquity saw in their rites, but I will accept official statements as only part of the answer, insisting on unofficial public meanings as well.

When we study public meanings, we must always ask what public we are talking about.³⁴ Anthropologists in the field can survey several publics; I cannot. By and large, the literature on which I depend is already a biased sample. I am thus largely limited to discovering the public meanings of that class of people called the Rabbis. What follows, then, is the set of public meanings that Rabbis in tannaitic and amoraic times (c. 70–550 C.E.), and therefore their followers as well, saw in circumcision. I emphasize those meanings that are public but not official.

Do people have to be conscious of their public meanings for us to accept them as present? On this perennial question, I ally myself with those who say that they do not.³⁵ My reasons for that decision are rooted in a further understanding of the ways in which rituals can be said to have meaning. To begin with, people can be expected to know their own public meanings—or at least to recognize them when we point them out—only if those meanings are cognitively discrete. I can point to a red light, for example, and expect people to explain, "It means 'stop.'" Or, if I see a dozen people stopping at a red light and I ask whether the red light means "stop," I have reason to predict that they will confirm my insight. If they tell me it means something else, I know I have missed the point. Similarly, I might get the women in my experiment to agree generally that their candle lighting signifies family memories, chains of family tradition, or even family love, but already I can expect much less agreement here than I can with red lights. We may eventually uncover still further public meanings that evoke even less conscious awareness or none at all. Candle lighting is a complex symbol that condenses many meanings, all equally licit, into a single presentation.³⁶

Circumcision is a physical act like lighting candles. Likening it to a cultural vignette or drama being played out before us, we ask the individual actors what they think they are doing. But no single actor can give us the overview we desire. We want to see the whole of which each individual actor sees only a part, the way a drama critic sums up the message of the entire play more cogently than any single character in the play can. For both plays and rituals, we want to observe things about the cultural construct that no single actor or participant can confirm for us; to hypothesize that circumcision, for example, "means" something in terms of how the actors in the rite extrapolate messages about reality, even though, to some extent at least, what they extrapolate goes unrecognized and unstated by them. They simply think that the world is actually composed the way the rite portrays it. It may well even be that the more cogently a rite supports a belief, the less likely the believer is to imagine any alternative and, hence, the less likely also to arrive at a conscious formulation of what the belief is.

Not just anything goes, of course. Our cultural reconstruction is an example of what Susanne Langer called some fifty years ago a "presentational" rather than a "discursive" form of truth. Not enough people remember that she subtitled her book, *Philosophy in a New Key,* "A Study in the Symbolism of Reason, Rite and Art."[37] If Aristotelian reason prefers discursive modes of inquiry, the exploration of rites and art does not. As students of ritual, what we offer in our analysis is a second-level work of art, a critical reading of what the play, the painting, or in our case, the rite is all about. Interpretation here is "imputational" in the sense that it "involves imputing properties which in being imputed actually become intrinsically part of the work."[38] Like other presentational messages, it is either convincing or it is not. Victor Turner's Ndembu were unaware of the whole gamut of symbolic connotations that Turner discovered, and Clifford Geertz's Balinese informants would never have seen a relationship between kinds of bets, social status, and kinship systems. But Turner and Geertz both give us classic presentational interpretations of rituals that many find convincing: they cohere nicely, they seem "right."[39] By contrast, describing *Hamlet* as a farce does not. Nor does Horace Miner's tongue-in-cheek satire entitled, "Body Ritual among the Nacirema," "Nacirema" being "American" written backward, and the paper in question being a detailed "ethnographic" spelling out of how Americans wash their faces and brush their teeth. It's not that we don't do just what Miner says; it's that his parodic reconstruction of what it means is intentionally laughable. His facts are not untrue, but his commentary on them is not compelling; it is not "right."[40]

We are therefore seeking the public and largely unofficial meanings circumcision held for Jews in different times, but particularly in the rabbinic period in the first two or three centuries C.E. These meanings will be recognizable interpretive themes that run deep in rabbinic culture. They fit together with other themes that we discover in other rites and aspects of rabbinic society. They help us to grasp rabbinic culture as a whole, the way a good drama review offers a meaning of the play that exceeds what can be conveyed by any single scene or actor. Our focus is the rite of circumcision. Our topic, however, is nothing less than rabbinic culture as a whole.[41]

Finally, my introductory caveat about results: Researchers may be responsible for choosing a subject in the first place, but they are not responsible for their results, not, that is, if they insist, as I do, on reporting honestly what they find. If you dig under rocks, you may discover some rather unpleasant creatures that you would just as happily put back, preferring to report that all of the earth's species are spanking clean and sunshine fresh. But at least since Freud, we have learned to suspect such laundered reports. And whole peoples, it turns out, are at least somewhat like the individual persons who comprise them, in that cultures, too, speak in ways that reflect deep-seated constructions of reality, not just a two-dimensional map of surface phenomena. On that everyone agrees. No matter how differently researchers decide to proceed to uncover the hidden layers of meaning, we all concur on the fact that there are layers to uncover. That assumption inevitably puts us back under the rocks, not knowing in advance what we will find, but committed to acknowledging the findings. To speak bluntly, what I found in this study surprised me (though perhaps, in retrospect, it shouldn't have). What is more, it made me very uneasy.

Clearly, circumcision is a male rite, and I was prepared to find a good deal of androcentric cultural musings. What I was not prepared for was the centrality of this ritual for Jewish culture as a whole, the very clear way that the symbolism of circumcision marked off the binary opposition between men and women, an opposition that I now take to be very basic to early rabbinic Judaism. For a good while, I deluded myself into thinking that I had two separate entities on my hands: circumcision as a male rite of passage or initiation on the one hand, and a larger independently structured Jewish culture on the other. I forgot that for centuries official Jewish culture was—and still largely is—in the hands of the very men who fashioned the rules of circumcision. Their obsession with circumcision turns ot to have broad implications for the way they spelled out Jewish culture as a whole. I found myself fighting the obvious implications of a male-dominated culture: namely, the fact that Jewish culture, like its dominant symbol of circumcision, traditionally has been far less friendly to the cause of women than I thought it was.

Let me be clear. I am not saying that official rabbinic culture is the sum total of Judaism; obviously, women celebrated their own version of Jewish identity, whether the Rabbis noted it or not. We shall have occasion in later chapters to explore some of their countercultural celebrations. But official rabbinic culture is indeed as male-dominated as feminist critics say it is. My claim here is in direct opposition not only to traditionally minded apologists who have generally held a "separate but equal" doctrine regarding male and female roles in rabbinic culture, but also to sophisticated treatments of the rabbinic textual tradition, the most recent being Daniel Boyarin's description of "Carnal Israel." While I fully agree with much that he has to say, my contribution here can be seen as a ready contrast to his attempt to blunt rabbinic androcentrism. There were, he concludes, "significant oppositional practices to the hegemony of the dominant discourse preserved in the canonical text," by which he means that "at least at the margins of social practice, and maybe even in more central practice, there were important ways in which women were autonomous or participated in highly valued cultural activities, such as studying Torah."[42] As I have already said, and as I shall demonstrate at considerable length with regard to ritual, I concur. Cultures are not monolithic machines that successfully determine universal behavior for all their constituent human "parts" according to preprogrammed sets of operating instructions. I agree also (in part) that "abomination of women, fear of sexuality and of the body . . . are only minor themes in this cultural formation."[43] Boyarin is right to defend rabbinic Judaism as a culture of the body in which sexuality is simply a given, and I do not mean to posit any "abomination of women" at all, much less "fear of sexuality and of the body" per se. But the essence of my argument is that precisely because rabbinic Judaism was a religion of the body, men's and women's bodies became signifiers of what the Rabbis accepted as gender essence, especially with regard to the binary opposition of men's blood drawn during circumcision and women's blood that flows during menstruation. Gender opposition remains absolutely central in my reading of rabbinic texts.

I further part ways with Boyarin's use of the otherwise undisputable claim that "reading texts as only misogynistic can in itself be a misogynistic gesture."[44] Of course it *can be*. But Boyarin seems to suggest that it *must be*, and in my case, anyway, it is not. Boyarin wants his own appropriation of the marginal feminist textual tradition to "constitute and institute" a countervailing feminist voice.[45] So be it. But we should not imagine that an insistence on the fundamental androcentrism of rabbinic culture is "itself . . . a misogynistic gesture," and is therefore any less valid a voice.

Finally, I see no need to agree with Boyarin's assessment that the gender opposition in rabbinic culture can be comprehended only from the perspective of a materialist anthropology, such as "the conditions of human reproduction and child-rearing within hunter-gatherer and later agrarian societies."[46] To begin with, I am unconvinced that such a materialist view is *necessary*. But, more important, even if it is, it is hardly *sufficient* to explain the particular form of male-female binary opposition that rabbinic Judaism displays, and it diverts attention away from rabbinic culture itself and onto some putative universal materialist substratum instead.

So my study of circumcision as a cultural symbol will underscore the gender opposition in rabbinic Judaism. Yet for two reasons I prefer not to call that culture patriarchal: first, because that overused term conjures up theories of prebiblical cults that were somehow made over by Abraham, Moses, and company in a very early time. That may or may not be so—circumcision certainly appears in both of their biographies, after all. But I do not think the debate should be mired in metatheories of putative patriarchalization, and, in any event, I am far more interested in the postbiblical Jewish tale, the period of the Rabbis and beyond, for which the adjective "patriarchal" is both less fashionable and less precise. Second, the categorization of circumcision as "patriarchal" in the biblical sense is often taken to imply that women have to rediscover their prebiblical roots if they are ever to reclaim their share of Jewish tradition. Since I don't think that is a viable or even a desirable strategy for women who want to celebrate full Jewish identity, I want to avoid using the term that is taken to presuppose it. So Jewish culture is not "patriarchal," even though it is just as male-oriented as the most extreme claimants of "partiarchalism" have charged. At least, official rabbinic Judaism is, and it is official Palestinian rabbinic Judaism of the tannaitic and amoraic periods, with its once publicly comprehended meanings, even those under the rocks, that I am describing here.

Let me also be clear that I intend this book neither as a defense nor as an apology. My own bias in favor of gender equality should be evident by now, and will be even more apparent as I proceed. But I undertook this study with no motivations in mind other than a better comprehension of Jewish culture.

It was originally part of a course on life-cycle liturgy that I decided to teach rabbinic students. My goal was to survey all the benchmarks of the traditional rites that mark a Jewish life so as to posit the "shape of a human life" as Jewish ritual imagines it. After a while, however, I found myself doubting that there even is a concept of "life cycle" in Judaism (more on that later), and I was freed to look at the material surrounding life's passages in a different framework. That led to my seeing circumcision as a single focal point in what I will call the "male lifeline." What follows, then, is a description of part of that lifeline from the vantage point of the symbolism of the rite by which it is inaugurated, the most male of all physical rites, circumcision.

As an investigation of the dominant Jewish meaning system, this book need not necessarily present arguments on whether or why Jews should stand firm in favor of circumcision, or be equally bold in terminating it. Yet people will inevitably draw their own lessons from what I have to say, and I owe it to my Jewish conscience, if nothing else, to make some practical observations regarding the present time at the end of my analysis. Still, it should be remembered that it is the analysis I was after in the first instance, not whatever lessons it may spawn. The analysis is as objective as scholarship can get. It tells us where we have been. Observations on our present condition anticipate the reactions that readers might have to the analysis and provide a brief survey of the status of circumcision in North America today.

This book was originally going to be called "The Jewish Life Cycle." As I say, however, and for reasons that will be evident as we proceed, I don't believe there is any such thing, except in modern consciousness, which insists on structuring Judaism not as it is and was, but as we wish it were. The most apt substitute would have been "The Jewish Male Lifeline," for that is, in fact, what we have in the sources. But that title would have implied that another book might come out called "The Jewish Female Lifeline," as if rabbinic Judaism gives us both, and we could elect to write a manual for men or for women. In fact, my whole point is that the Rabbis made Judaism inseparable from the male lifeline. Like it or not, they had no idea of a female lifeline. They identify Jewish culture in its fullness only with men's concerns, men's growth, men's maturity; women exist officially only insofar as they enter the orbit of men. What term, I asked, best expresses the Rabbis' equation of "man" and "Jew," and the appendagelike role allotted to women? The answer came to me in a flash. Circumcision, in Hebrew, is *milah.* But *milah* is really a metonymic shorthand of the larger nominal phrase, *brit milah,* meaning "covenant of circumcision." If the physical act of circumcision is the cultural sign of Jewish existence, the cultural construction that it signifies is a covenant between the men being circumcised and God. As we shall see in full detail, the dominant symbol of circumcision is its blood, which the Rabbis juxtapose with menstrual blood as their chief iconic binary opposition to symbolize gender differentiation. Thus I have chosen for my full title: *Covenant of Blood: Circumcision and Gender in Rabbinic Judaism.*

In sum, for the Rabbis of antiquity it is this larger covenantal perspective that the rite of circumcision evoked, a covenant presupposed as existing between men and God, a covenant, moreover, to which women are party only in a secondary way, through their relationship with fathers and then husbands. I repeat: I do not like it that way; I did not expect to find it that way. But that is the only conclusion my evidence will allow. Better to drag this latent cultural presumption out from beneath the rocks to see what else is attached to it than to let it lie undisturbed as if it were not really there. We can work with what we know, not with what we don't. And we know now that traditional rabbinic culture is about a covenant initiated by circumcision. This book explores the fascinating details of how that is so.

chapter 2

Bible and Birth: Some Priestly Public Meanings

The Bible is many things: patriarchal history, law codes in abundance, priestly genealogies, a record of monarchies and prophets, cultic poetry, and wisdom literature, to name just a few. But one unifying strain is a recording of the Jewish People's covenant with God.[1] The Bible thus moves easily from one covenantal concern to another: the rituals God demands and Israel performs; the extent to which Israel's earthly monarchs keep faith with their divine mandate as head over God's people; the Land of Israel, which God has deeded to the People of Israel under the covenant's terms; and circumcision itself. Since circumcision is defined as a "sign" of the covenant (Gen. 17:11), we should not be surprised to find that the Bible constitutes also a sort of logbook chronicling the steadfastness with which the men of Israel saw to it that they were circumcised.

The focus of this book is rabbinic, not biblical. But it will be helpful nonetheless to attend briefly to circumcision in the Bible before exploring it as an expression of rabbinic culture. First, Israelite practice prior to the Rabbis deserves attention in its own right. Moreover, the rabbinic view of the meaning of circumcision stands out in marked contrast to what biblical men and women believed, so that postbiblical interpretation (and innovation) will be foregrounded more sharply once we have ascertained what circumcision constituted for biblical society.

As we saw in chapter 1, the dominant school of biblical scholarship trained a historicist lens on the Bible and sought to reconstruct early Israelite society against the backdrop of its ancient Near Eastern environment. It thus asked when circumcision really began, how the biblical custom differed from the customs of other Semitic peoples, and what meaning circumcision could therefore have had as a rite among the Israelites. With ritual studies yet to be discovered as an academic vocation, the discussion of meaning was hampered by a rather narrow taxonomy of ritual functions—rites of passage or of initiation, for example—but within these basic categories traditional researchers have tried to figure out how the rite in question operated, and in so doing, they have speculated on what biblical Jews may have thought circumcision was all about.

The dominant opinion has been that circumcision was a rite of initiation into a clan or tribe, or that it served as a "rite of redemption, of removal of the taboo thought to rest upon every newborn male child, through the application of the principle that the sacrifice of a part of the tabooed object redeems the remainder."[2] We also find authors emphasizing the official meanings at the expense of the unofficial ones—holding, for instance, that "circumcision as covenant symbol . . . is precisely what it was intended to be."[3] Still other writers have been intent on discovering spiritual or refined religious meaning in Israelite circumcision.[4] In theory, they may all be right. Israelite circumcision may have functioned in several ways that good philological analysis can detect, including the official theological interpretations, which were more than the mere epiphenomena that orthodox Freudian theory supposes by limiting its significance to the realm of the unconscious in culture, such as the father's lingering castration anxiety.[5] Rites are rarely just one thing. Circumcision may thus have been any or all of the things a lot of people say, and still other things as well.

All researchers begin with the recognition that the Pentateuch is a composite document of some sort, though they do not agree on the exact nature of its composition. The traditional documentary hypothesis has held that it contains at least four discrete subtexts that were compiled during a period of time that spanned six hundred years, beginning around the tenth century B.C.E., in the court of David and Solomon. In what follows, I depend to some extent on the validity of that hypothesis, though not necessarily on every detail of its classic formulation, much of which need not be true for my own thesis to hold. I assume the existence of the following: (1) a specific corpus within the Pentateuch that has generally been identified as P and that is the voice of the theocratic postexilic authorities; (2) an earlier corpus normally called D, generally held to reflect pre-exilic monarchical interests as well as the prophets who opposed that very monarchy. Alternatively, if D was finally put together only during the exile (another view that several people have advanced), then

D contains a point of view that extends those interests into a period where landedness and exile from that land take on great interest.[6] Insofar as Israelite kings had always ruled landed entities, however, the right to the land was not something newly discovered only after the Babylonian conquest. It had always been there, and reflections on landed status may therefore be early or late.

Classical theory supposes also a J and an E narrative, these being the two most ancient and independent documents ultimately subsumed under D. The status of these two strands is most in question. They may or may not have existed independently before D. Either way, however, we have a sharp break between D (and including J and E, if they existed independently) and P. Given the uncertainty regarding J and E, it might be easiest to speak simply of two sets of data, pre-exilic and postexilic, understanding that the former (D, plus perhaps J and E) may actually have reached final codification only in exile, and so was not entirely completed prior to the Babylonian captivity. On the other hand, even if J and E are really part of one great pre-exilic or exilic D, it is convenient still to use the J, E, D, P nomenclature, and that is the way my analysis will proceed.

A summary of this chapter's findings will be useful at the outset. Throughout the non-P material, and also including those prophetic books that reflect the same pre-exilic mindset, we shall see that circumcision was a known Israelite custom but that it was not identified as a sign of the covenant. The covenant (or *brit*) was a conditional legal contract with God in which, above all, Israel received a land with its harvest and was assured of protection from enemies beyond the land's borders in return for fealty to God's law. This covenant was not yet seen as arising out of Abraham's circumcision; instead, it was traced to his primeval sacrifice as described in Genesis 15.

Now Genesis 15 is traditionally labeled as J. If it is in fact a separate J document from early monarchical times, then this covenant of law and land goes back to monarchic interests in justifying their dominion. On the other hand, if there is no early and independent J document, but merely an exilic D corpus, then the accent on land reflects exilic thinking as well. My claim for an early dating of Genesis 15 (and for other J fragments where sacrifice and land, not circumcision, are the dominant covenantal associations) presupposes the existence of an early monarchic strand of tales that has been called J. But even if J never existed independently as an actual document, my differentiation of (a) pre-exilic (and perhaps exilic) prophetic and monarchic symbolism of a covenant rooted in land and sacrifice, and (b) post-exilic priestly emphasis of a covenant displayed by circumcision, would still stand. My thesis requires only a pre-exilic covenantal strand where circumcision as covenantal sign is unknown and a postexilic ideology in which circumcision is the priestly sine qua non of the covenant. The prophets and Deuteronomy remain my evidence for the former; the standard priestly documentary fragments, largely Leviticus but also Genesis 17 (which is clearly in opposition to Genesis 15, no matter when we date 15), are my evidence for the latter.

Our step-by-step look at each Pentateuchal text (accompanied also by some prophetic sections) will reveal that even though Jews were practicing circumcision by the time the earliest accounts were penned, it was not until the time of the last author (P), sometime in the late sixth or even fifth century B.C.E., that circumcision became so prominent in Jewish consciousness. But P left his mark on the text as a whole, so that it *seems* to the casual reader that it was always so. Before looking scientifically at the development of circumcision, then, let us read the biblical narratives uncritically and see what a masterful editor P was. How easy it is to get the mistaken impression that circumcision was always as central an institution as P has portrayed it.

We begin with Abraham who circumcised Isaac (Gen. 21:4) after circumcising himself, Ishmael, and all the other male members of his retinue (Gen. 17:23–27). Circumcision is taken for granted in the chapters thereafter as normative for Israelite men. Jacob's sons tell Hamor and Shechem that no Israelite women can have uncircumcised husbands, since an uncircumcised condition for males is "a disgrace among us." But if they are circumcised, Hamor and Shechem will be "as kin" with the Israelites among whom they will live, and whose daughters they can marry (Gen. 34:13–16). When Israel leaves Egypt, God instructs Moses to prepare a Passover offering. "Any slave a man has bought may eat of it once he has been circumcised" (Ex. 12:44). "If a stranger who dwells with you would offer the passover to the Lord, all his males must be circumcised. But no uncircumcised person may eat of it" (Ex. 12:48). The commandment to circumcise every male child on the eighth day is repeated expressly in Leviticus 12:3. Zipporah circumcises Moses' son when his uncircumcised state threatens him with danger (Ex. 4:24–26), and even though the Jews who left Israel were all circumcised, their children born in the desert were not, so that at Gilgal, Joshua has to circumcise them before they can enter the covenanted land (Josh. 5:2–8).

To the uncritical reader of the Bible, it therefore seems that circumcision is the very essence of the covenant. The Deuteronomic author (D), however, writing in the seventh century B.C.E., presents Moses' final charge to Israel as if the covenant that he describes recollects God's deliverance from Egypt and the choice the people now face as to whether they will follow God's will, and thus be prosperous in the land flowing with milk and honey. The only use of the term "circumcise" here is metaphoric, "God will circumcise your heart" (Deut. 30:6), a usage picked up somewhat later by Jeremiah, who admonishes that although "the nations of the earth are uncircumcised," Israel's circumcision counts for little, since Israel is "uncircumcised in the heart" (Jer. 9:25). Circumcised in body or not, therefore, God's People deserves punishment. But God is merciful, so that if Israel only heeds the advice to "circumcise yourselves to the Lord, and take away the foreskins of your heart," God will not let "fury go forth like a fire and burn that none can quench it, because of the evil of your actions" (Jer. 4:4). The uncritical reader of the Bible has to avoid the plain sense of Deuteronomy and Jeremiah; even for the critic, a little imagination can hold out the possibility that for the D author and the pre-exilic prophets, circumcision was central, albeit along with inner conviction, and that it was a lack of this inner conviction that Jeremiah bemoaned.

But the truth is otherwise. Let us now reread the same accounts from the vantage point of what we know from biblical criticism. I said above that the Bible looks like a logbook of circumcision, and I remarked also that it was the postexilic priestly author (P) who emphasized circumcision and made it the central concern that it is. The pre-exilic prophets, like Jeremiah, know nothing of a covenant of circumcision. The only covenant they recall is the Exodus: God took the people out of Egypt and deeded them the land of Israel; they, in turn, must remain loyal to God. The Deuteronomist (D), too, knows only this covenant, which is recalled ritually on the two occasions cited in Deuteronomy 26. But P changes the terms in a radical way. The Pentateuchal circumcision citations listed above are overwhelmingly priestly narratives, or priestly insertions into earlier accounts.

1. The incident between Jacob's sons and Hamor and Shechem (Gen. 34), in which circumcision is cited as an obvious sine qua non for Jewish marriages, is a favorite priestly theme, for it was only after the return from Babylonia that Ezra and Nehemiah enforced endogamy as a major thrust of the priestly ideology (more on that later).[7] S. R. Driver says unequivocally, "In Genesis, as regards the limits of P, there is practically no difference of opinion

amongst critics. It embraces . . . the refusal of his (Jacob's) sons to sanction intermarriage with the Shechemites."[8]

2. Similarly, God's instruction through Moses that only the circumcised may eat the Passover offering, in Driver's opinion, "exhibits throughout the marks of P."[9]

3. The commandment to circumcise every male child on the eighth day is embedded in Leviticus itself, what Driver calls "the priests' code."[10] A closer look reveals that the circumcision discussion is integral to the unit detailing purity regulations, especially those required of women—again a favorite theme for P, and one to which we shall return when we look more closely at the public meanings of circumcision within priestly society.

4. The only two possible exceptions are the episodes when Zipporah circumcises Moses' son (Ex. 4:24–26) and when Joshua circumcises the people at Gilgal (Josh. 5:2–8). Driver assigns the former to J on the grounds of its blatant anthropomorphism and the latter to D because it emphasizes entering the Land of Israel with all of its abundant blessing,[11] one of D's great themes, which, as we saw, forms the essence of the covenant according to Deuteronomy 26 and 30.

Let us look at the possible exceptions first. Even if the Zipporah and Joshua narratives are in fact prepriestly, there is still no reason to believe that the complete doctrine of circumcision as covenant preceded P, for we would still have to contend with the "circumcision of the heart" passages in Jeremiah and Deuteronomy. These are far more reliable indices than the other two texts are, and they are buttressed by a relative ignorance of circumcision as a commandment, as, for instance, in Moses' peroration as Deuteronomy ends.

Take the incident of Zipporah. The only reason to assign it to J is its fragmentary nature, which provides few clues about when it was written, coupled with its anthropomorphism and, therefore, its presumed antiquity. But in fact, no one knows for sure how old it is or, for that matter, what it is even about. If evolutionary presumptions regarding Israelite theology are jettisoned, there is no internal reason for imputing antiquity to the Zipporah account. But assume, for the sake of argument, that it really is a remnant of an old tale embedded in an equally old manuscript that was relayed by J. We would have to grant, at most, what is already granted here: that Jews were practicing circumcision even by the time the first writers, J and E, composed their respective sacred narratives. What is at issue is the further claim I make to the effect that these early authors were relatively unconcerned with the custom, that it was not yet necessarily a sign of the covenant, and that it had yet to be associated with impurity, exogamy, and the host of legal concerns typified by Leviticus. The Zipporah fragment indicates at most that Israelite culture practiced circumcision as a prophylactic against danger—hence Zipporah's rash act in making sure her child was provided with it.

The meaning of circumcision may have been public, but it was hardly official, for it spawned no theological explication. One looks in vain for an indication of its being associated with the covenant. The lack of internal ideological interpretation is precisely why the laconic Zipporah pericope is so hard to fathom.

D's attention is given not to circumcision theology but to covenant-as-land theology. Israel is deeded the land of milk and honey in return for following God's will. The rituals of first fruits and the tithe (Deut. 26) act out the inherent connection between the Temple cult, the centrality of Jerusalem, the promise of material abundance, and the quid pro quo theology wherein Israel gets a harvest in return for doing what God wants. The Land's inhabitants must choose life over death, blessing over curse, says Moses in his final peroration (Deut. 30). Not once does he mention circumcision as the basis of the covenant. Still, Jews were circumcised. The Deuteronomist knew that, as did Jeremiah a century later, so that both writers could use that physical fact to their own advantage by applying circumcision to point metaphorically to what really mattered: inner loyalty to God.

The identification of Joshua 5 as a part of D is, I grant, potentially counterindicative, since it is undeniable that the Gilgal narrative focuses attention on the need for men to be circumcised in order to inherit the land. On the other hand, like Zipporah, the Gilgal story is not necessarily pre-exilic. Driver says it is because it is so land-centered. But P was hardly impervious to claims on the land. Documentary dating is notoriously difficult. Sometimes we can be relatively assured about a source's provenance, sometimes not; and this is a case of the latter. New evidence, in fact, indicates the likelihood that it is a relatively young source that remained questionable very late in Israel's history. It has long been known that Josephus omits mentioning the circumcision at Gilgal.[12] We now have a Targum to the account that does the same thing.[13] All we can say at this stage, then, is that the Gilgal story was part of a polemic regarding the need for physical circumcision before inheriting the land; whether the account as we have it goes back to D or not is uncertain.

It would in any event remain true that we do not find in pre-exilic writings the identification of circumcision as the *essence* of covenant, or even a *sign* of covenant. Though probably a popular custom, perhaps even universally applied to Israelite boys, circumcision does not appear there as a legal mandate, as, for instance, God's instructing Moses to circumcise children on the eighth day. Nor do we find any connection to purity rules between men and women or Jews and non-Jews. These are the additions peculiar to P, who tells us that Shechem and Hamor would have had to be circumcised to marry Jewish women; that newborn boys should be circumcised, but only on the eighth day; and that uncircumcised men may not eat the Passover sacrifice.

It is in this connection that the P author has inserted the Gilgal narrative of Joshua 5:2–9. Whatever the proper date of its original composition, it is canonized here in the context of Joshua 5:10, "The Israelites camped in Gilgal and kept Passover." Their circumcision, then, serves as P's introduction to a Passover story, assuring us that in accordance with Exodus 12:44 and 48, only the circumcised kept the feast.

The P author adds also that mothers should be kept away from men after childbirth, since they are unclean. Making circumcision fall on the eighth day may thus derive from P's belief that mothers are unclean until then, and that, by extension, so are their children, who must wait for that taboo state to pass before being admitted officially to the Israelite society.[14]

A comparison of Genesis 15 and 17 demonstrates the difference between covenant as conceived by J and covenant as conceived by P. The concept has mutated completely between the time the Pentateuch was begun and the time it was completed. Both chapters introduce the reader to God's covenant with Abraham. Because one account follows the other in the text, it seems as if God appeared twice, making one covenant after the other. Actually, chapter 17 portrays the covenant according to P, who added it in order to correct what the earlier account of chapter 15 was lacking.

In both cases, Abraham, who is childless, turns to God for assurance that his line will continue. God duly delivers that promise and notes how mighty Abraham's descendants will someday become. Thereupon God and Abraham enter their covenanted relationship. Having no notion that the covenant has something to do with circumcision, however, J marks it by an elaborate animal sacrifice. By contrast, for P, circumcision is the very essence of the covenant. Whereas for J the sacrificial ritual is merely a secondary event made to serve the primary concern of covenant, P's rival chapter 17 almost makes the covenant secondary to the ritualistic concern for circumcision. It may not be going too far to say that chapter 17 is a veritable aside on the theme of circumcision alone. E. A. Speiser reaches much the same conclusion when he notes, "In the present account by P . . . the overriding feature of the covenant is circumcision." [15]

The theme is established with God's introductory comment to Abraham in the very first two verses: "The Lord appeared to Abram and said to him, 'I am El Shaddai. Walk in My ways and be blameless. I will establish My covenant between Me and you, and will make you exceedingly numerous.'" In this translation, the full import of the chapter is unclear. [16] Why should Abraham be blameless? Is God's covenant dependent on his moral rectitude? If so, this is the first time we hear about it, and it does not surface again in P's account. The Hebrew word for "blameless" is *tamim,* which appears fifteen times in the Pentateuch but in two distinctively different ways. We do find it used to describe moral standing with regard to Noah (Gen. 6:9)—*ish tzaddik tamim hayah bedorotav,* "a righteous man; blameless in his generation." It is used twice in Deuteronomy the same way (Deut. 18:13, 32:4). But in the overwhelming majority of instances, the context is sacrificial. The P author regularly describes the animals due to God as *tamim,* not "blameless" certainly, but "whole, complete, without physical fault." Noah is similarly "whole," though not in a physical way; he is without moral fault perhaps. But what about Abraham? Is he to be morally complete or physically complete? If God really said, "Walk in my ways," referring to ethical behavior, we might presume the former, but the verb here is more specifically *hit-halekh lefanai,* which means "walk before me" in the juridical sense of "coming before God to pass muster." Whether Abraham is to pass muster morally or physically remains open to debate and can be decided only by the context in which the verb appears.

We cannot know for sure, certainly, but the Hebrew allows the following alternative translation, having nothing to do with morality but everything to do with circumcision. (It accords, moreover, with traditional Jewish exegesis of the verse from the Mishnah through the Talmud and on into the twelfth-century circle of German pietists.) [17] "God appeared to Abram and said to him, 'I am El Shaddai. Walk before me *in a state of physical completion,* so that I may establish my covenant between us: namely, I will make you exceedingly numerous.'" That, I believe, is P's official theology in a nutshell: Israelite men must be circumcised to be physically complete, and thus to carry the covenant.

J's version, by contrast, quickly departs from its original problem, Abraham's desire for children, and introduces an allied interest, the justification of Israel's political independence, an issue that faced the Davidic-Solomonic monarchy when J wrote his account. Thus J concludes, "To your offspring I will give this land, from the river of Egypt to the river Euphrates" (Gen. 15: 18–21). But not so P, for whom monarchic interests are absent. In P's day there was no empire save the Persian, to which the newly constituted Judean state (and P) owed fealty. And the monarchy, once represented alongside the priesthood by the joint rulership of Joshua and Zerubbabel, is exactly what P and one hundred years of priestly ancestry have managed to replace with a thoroughgoing theocracy.

For J, then, the covenantal act of sacrifice is the means to fulfill the promise of Israelite hegemony in Canaan. For P, who has no need to establish an ideological basis for that hegemony, the covenantal act that matters is not Abraham's sacrifice but his circumcision, which is never severed from the story's original problematic: his childlessness, which requires for its solution that he complete his own body by paring away his foreskin and then appearing before God *tamim,* "whole." God thus says later in the account, "This is my covenant with you. You are to be a father to a host of nations. . . . You must keep my covenant, you and your sons to follow throughout the ages. This shall be the covenant that you must keep: every male among you shall be circumcised" (Gen. 17:7, 9–10).

Though the equation of covenant with circumcision is missing from the pre-exilic account, it may have its origins as early as exilic Isaiah (56:4). David Sperling surveys the use of the word *brit* in postexilic writing, noting that it has been severed from its earlier sense of law. In pre-exilic passages, God enters into a covenant of law with Israel. It is a conditional thing: Israel's fidelity to God's law entails God's protection of Israel and of Israel's land, which God has deeded to his People. To break the law is to break the covenant. But postexilic writers rarely even use the word *brit,* and when they do it is divorced from its earlier connection to law. By then, says Sperling, it is used in a variety of ways, most of them rather general, but now including the specific sign of circumcision. That is the case with exilic Isaiah who argues (against the exclusivist policies of Ezra/Nehemiah) that Gentiles may be considered a part of God's People as long as they keep two rules: Sabbath observance and (in accordance with Genesis 17) circumcision.[18] Whether Isaiah 56 was composed before or after Genesis 17 is a moot point, though Sperling cites the literature to show that it came later.[19] In either case, both passages reflect the new understanding of *brit:* not as a conditional covenant of law having land entailments but as circumcision, and as a necessity for any man who would consider himself one of God's People.

Indeed, P's daring identification of a man's circumcision as the way in which he becomes perfect retains its hold in Jewish and even in early Christian tradition. Judah Hanasi (c. 200 C.E.) said, "Great is circumcision, for despite all the commandments that our father Abraham carried out, he was called complete (*shalem*) only with his circumcision, as it is written, 'Walk before me and be perfect [*tamim*].'"[20] In Christian Scripture we have John 7:23, where Jesus argues from the rabbinic duty to perform circumcision on the Sabbath to his own right "to heal a man's whole body" on that day.[21]

P's insistence on circumcision as the sine qua non for a Jewish male and his identification of it as the necessary sign of the covenant without which a man could not fully be Jewish thus remained a dominant public meaning in Judaism ever after, as both Jews and non-Jews agreed well into the Roman period. Paula Fredriksen documents the extent to which "circumcision is singled out in Hellenistic, Jewish, pagan, and Christian literature as the premier mark of the Jew."[22] No wonder later readers of Jewish tradition imagine it must always have been so. But it was not.

Circumcision may be old, but it has not been universally outfitted with the same meanings throughout the Bible. J and E (tenth century B.C.E.) are unconcerned with circumcision. They worry about the covenant, but they mean by it a primeval sacrifice made by Abraham so that his offspring—themselves—would inherit the Land of Israel. The author of Deuteronomy (seventh century) and Jeremiah, prior to the Babylonian expulsion (early sixth century), thus emphasize land theology, a covenant that deeds God's chosen land to the chosen people. They know that Jews are circumcised as a sort of national trait, unlike some people, the Egyptians, for example; they explain circumcision as "rolling back the reproach of the Egyptians,"[23] an etiology drawn from the physical act of rolling off the foreskin in the operation itself. But they never mention Abraham's circumcision as the reason behind their own retention of the custom. It is fealty to God's will in general, as symbolized by the circumcision of the heart, that really counts.

P, however, changes all that. As the last redactor, he put the final touch on the Bible as a whole, giving us the false impression that circumcision was always central. As P has glossed the Torah, his own set of priestly meanings predominates, and from then on circumcision really does become basic to

Jewish consciousness. Jews read the Pentateuch as P had left it, after all. When Antiochus Epiphanes banned circumcision, mothers had their children circumcised anyway, even though their action was punishable by death, both their own and that of their children (1 Macc. 1:60–61). By the first century, circumcision was still the norm, practiced by Elizabeth, for example, on her son John (Luke 1:58–59). Eventually, as we shall see in some detail later, although Christians adopted Jeremiah's spiritualized vision of a circumcision of the heart, thus justifying their abandonment of the physical practice, Jews insisted that the age-old physical sign of the covenant be retained throughout the generations. For Jews, then, P's ideological coup proved a brilliant success. *Officially speaking,* circumcision was the sign of the covenant.

But meanings can be public without being official, and an additional, though unofficial, meaning was related to fertility. Thus, Howard Eilberg-Schwartz argues that the covenant was conceptualized as a matter of procreation, so that circumcision was linked to fertility in the first instance and ritualized patrilineal descent in the second.[24]

The evidence is overwhelming, part of it being the fact that the Hebrew word *ot* used by the priestly author to describe the covenant "sign" of circumcision (Gen. 17:11) is used elsewhere iconically.[25] That is to say, "it has properties that make it appropriate for the content which it signifies."[26] Thus, the rainbow, for example, another convenantal *ot* (Gen. 9:15–16), this one standing for God's pact with Noah, is an icon in that rainbows designate the end of a storm and easily come to mark God's promise not to destroy the world through rain. How, then, is circumcision no mere arbitrary sign but an iconic representation of that for which it stands?

A close look at the covenant with Abraham demonstrates how central fertility is to God's promise.

> This is my covenant with you: you shall be the father of a multitude of nations. . . . I will make you exceedingly fertile. . . . You shall keep my covenant, you and your offspring to come throughout the ages. Such shall be the covenant. . . . Every male among you shall be circumcised. . . . An uncircumcised male . . . shall be cut off from his kin; he has broken my covenant. (Gen. 17:4–6, 9–10, 14)

Motivated to the point of obsession by the need for successful human reproduction, the P author regularly weaves into his narrative the history of circumcision, on the one hand, and the issue of fertility, on the other. God sets the stage by giving instructions to Adam and Noah "to be fruitful and multiply" (Gen. 1:28, 8:17), then twice promises Abraham that he will have offspring (Gen. 17:2, 6). But Sarah is barren. So Abraham does what he must to remedy the situation. Accepting the fault as his own, he circumcises his own flesh and that of all the male members of his household, including Ishmael, who thereupon also is promised progeny (Gen. 17). An uncircumcised male is "cut off from his people" (Gen. 17:14), notes Eilberg-Schwartz, because he is infertile, unable to continue the line.

Perhaps the strongest part of the argument linking circumcision to fertility is the Bible's application of circumcision terminology to horticulture. The first three years of a tree's growth are known as its period of uncircumcision, the immature fruit being called uncircumcised and consequently forbidden for use. Trees that reach maturity are said to have entered the time of their circumcision. Immediately thereafter they are expected to bear a maximum yield of fruit, just as Abraham and his male heirs were promised they would. Analogous to pruning fruit trees, their circumcision provides a prophylactic against barrenness. Both acts involve cutting away unwanted growth from a stem or trunk in order to insure fertility.[27]

So circumcision functioned in the Bible as a fertility rite. Why, we should ask, did the priestly interpreters select it to be their primary sign of the covenant as well?

One tempting line of investigation is the political interpretation of circumcision opened up by Karen Ericksen Paige and Jeffrey M. Paige. They argue that economic conditions influence social structure, and that reproductive ritual functions as a sort of "psychological warfare or puffery . . . when opportunities for more direct form of warfare are restricted."[28] Circumcision is a "surveillance ritual" whereby large cohesive kin groups, who are nonetheless potential rivals, monitor the status quo in defense of developments that would disrupt the uneasy truce that holds the social structure in stasis.[29] More specifically, the authors trace circumcision to those societies in which economic factors have caused powerful fraternal interest groups to develop. The members of these groups are nonetheless potential victims of social fission: young men who come of age may become independent clan rulers who break free of the larger group and head out on their own. Clearly, the best protection against such disruption would be the castration of these would-be independent rivals at a time when they are still too young to protest. Circumcision is thus seen as a ritualized form of castration in which the power of the elders is demonstrated publicly, and where the potentially rebellious son's loyalty is evident from his supine agreement to submit to the circumciser's knife.[30]

This is an apt model to apply to Israelite society because of the obvious growth of the priesthood during the postexilic period. For the priesthood is nothing if not an alliance of strong fraternal interest groups, recorded in Nehemiah, Ezra, and Chronicles according to the "father's houses."[31] That the budding theocracy depended on preventing fission within the priestly alliance is clear. Yet, the extent to which the Paiges' ethnographic evidence from preliterate and small-scale societies is transferable to the situation in postexilic Judea is questionable. While the parallels between the socioeconomic infrastructure of postexilic Judea and the Paiges' paradigmatic models from the annals of anthropological research should not be overlooked, other models may be more attractive for our purposes.

The most striking feature of the biblical narratives bequeathed to us by the priestly authors is their obsession with lineage issues. Postexilic society was dominated by the authority of priests and kings. Unlike prophets and judges, whose right to speak derived from their heavenly call, priests and kings held office by virtue of lineage. The postexilic theocracy had effectively transferred the power of Judean kings to the priesthood, for whom lineage lines thus became all important. P therefore intersperses descent lists in telling the story of Israel's history.

The very best index of priestly lineage concerns comes from the twin narratives of Ezra and Nehemiah. Ezra, himself a priest returning from Babylonian exile at precisely the time that P's concerns took shape, begins and ends his book with genealogical lists (chapters 2 and 10); in the middle he assures unblemished lines of descent by putting an end to marriages between Israelite men and foreign women (chapter 12). This is where P's addition of the biblical account of Shechem and Hamor enters in: they had to be circumcised as Jewish kin or else forgo marrying Jews. Nehemiah, Ezra's contemporary, also includes a lineage list (chapters 10–12), and concludes his book with the theme that marked all of his work as governor among the returnees: the threat of exogamy to the purity of the priestly lineage.

> In those days, I saw Jews who had married women from Ashdod, Ammon and Moab. Their children spoke half in the speech of Ashdod and

could not speak in the Jews' language. I contended with them. . . . One of the sons of Joiada, the son of Eliashib the High Priest, was son-in-law to Sanballat the Horonite; therefore I banished him. Remember them, O my God, because they have defiled the priesthood, and the covenant of the priesthood and the Levites. I thus cleansed them from everything foreign. (Neh. 13:23–25, 28–31)

Now the priestly concern with lineage has long been acknowledged. But until Eilberg-Schwartz's work brought it to our attention we failed to notice the intrinsic connection between lineage and circumcision as a symbolic representation of the patrilineal basis for that lineage. Circumcision played three roles for the system, concludes Eilberg-Schwartz. First, it marked a hiatus between Abraham and his male progeny on the one hand, and Abraham's father and male ancestors on the other. The covenant begins only with Abraham and his male heirs, who mark their flesh ever after as a sign of their specificity. Second, and more important, it combined its symbolic reference to male fertility with the priests' need to guarantee that the genealogical line would continue. Finally, and of greatest interest, it demonstrated symbolically the victory of patrilineage over matrilineage as a means of measuring descent.[32]

Eilberg-Schwartz presents considerable evidence regarding the patrilineal system of the priests, which I need not repeat here. But I must explore one tantalizing claim he makes in order to keep my promise to attend to the gender dichotomy inherent in the fact that the central Jewish ritual is the purely male rite of circumcision. To be sure, my primary interest is rabbinic Judaism, but the Rabbis did not change everything. One common thread that appears first in the Bible, and then is creatively elaborated by the Rabbis, is an emphatic dichotomy between men and women, a distinction that is paralleled by a further binary opposition between Jew and non-Jew.

We will understand more clearly what I have in mind once we conceptualize culture as a form of art, akin to such things as the British tradition of portrait painting, romanticism in poetry, and the materialist-idealist debate in Western philosophy. Like painting, poetry, and philosophy, culture, too, provides ongoing themes, tropes, or metaphors by which its adherents negotiate their way through life. The biblical-rabbinic framework for conceptualizing reality thus constitutes a Jewish art tradition, one striking feature of which turns out to be a parallel set of binary oppositions of male/female and Jew/non-Jew, arranged such that male : female :: Jew : non-Jew. Since this pattern emerges from within rabbinic Judaism as a culture, and since culture is like art, we should attend to the way in which artistic traditions develop.

In that context, E. H. Gombrich wonders how artists go about their work. Contrary to the commonsense view that they observe nature objectively and then paint what they see, he suggests that artists see their world as already refracted through the work of prior artists. "So much certainly emerges from a study of portrayal in art: you cannot create a faithful image out of nothing. You must have learned the trick if only from other pictures you have seen." That is to say, "the familiar will always remain the likely starting point for the rendering of the unfamiliar. An existing representation will always exert its spell over the artist, even while he [*sic*] strives to record the truth." [33] Similarly, Harold Bloom asks what we mean by "influence" in poetry. Contending against poetic influence being weighed simply by "source-hunting and allusion-counting, an industry that will soon touch apocalypse anyway when it passes from scholars to computers," he urges us to define influence as follows: "Poetic influence—when it involves two strong authentic poets—always proceeds by a misreading of the prior poet, an act of creative correction that is actually and necessarily a misinterpretation." [34] What Gombrich says of art and Bloom posits for poetry goes for every discipline, even philosophy, where, presumably, dispassionate reason operates. [35]

What is true of art, poetry, and even philosophy is equally true of culture. Generations are born into a world already plotted with themes, myths, roles, and expectations. The creativity of each generation lies in its ability to read its predecessors "strongly." This was never more so than for the Rabbis, who were very creative misreaders of their biblical text. We will see later just how thoroughgoing their revisionism could be. But that very revisionism was postulated on the assumption that their legitimacy and continuity derived from the Scripture that the priestly author had bequeathed them. They accepted its themes, saw the world through biblical eyes. They elaborated an equation by which male : female :: Jew : non-Jew. But they got that theme in the first place from P.

First: male and female. We have seen that the priests underscore patrilineality but not matrilineality. A covenant made with Abraham, but not with Sarah, is sealed with a sign that is itself an iconic reminder that being male, not female, is what matters. [36] It was not always that way. Savina J. Teubel and more recently (and quite spectacularly) Nancy Jay have traced the Pentateuchal stories that deal with descent issues, dividing them according to their authors, J, E, and P, and demonstrated that in the earliest strata, J and E, we have echoes of matrilineality.[37] Ishmael, not Isaac, would have inherited the covenantal promise had it been enough to be born through the patriarchal line; Ishmael had the right father but the wrong mother. Similarly, consider the wife/sister tales (Gen. 12:10–20; 20:1–18; 26:6–11).

> Scholars have long wrestled with these embarrassing wife/sister accounts that appear to portray the patriarchs as either liars or incestuous. E's account states that Sarah was Abraham's actual half-sister. Their marriage would have been impossible in any patrilineal system. Unless we reject E's account (thereby making the patriarchs liars) we must see here a recognition of descent from women so pronounced as to be almost "matrilineal", for if Abraham and Sarah had the same father (20:12) it is only as mothers' offspring that their marriage was not incestuous.[38]

The problem is not simply that an earlier matrilineal system was replaced by a later patrilineal one, but that remnants of the two systems existed side by side. The conflict between the two systems raised problems regarding lines of inheritance and authority. Other societies (ancient Greece, for instance), says Jay, solved the disparity by simply denying the procreative role of the mother. Ancient Israel solved the problem by preferring agnatic endogamy, that is, marriage within the patriline: a man married off his son to his father's brother's daughter. Both son and daughter-in-law would thus come from the same male descent line, and listing their children as coming from their father but ignoring the mother would be functionally equivalent to mentioning the mother too. But the conflict would remain in theory, for even though descent could not be questioned, it would still be "unclear about which is the 'real' parent through whom unilineal descent flows."[39]

The Hebrew Bible solves the theoretical problem with sacrifice, which Jay describes as "indexing" in the sense of "identifying and integrating" the descent line that matters. Jacob, for example, marries his *mother*'s brother's daughter, Rachel. Her father then joins Jacob in a sacrificial meal in which they invoke God as "the God of Abraham" (Jacob's patrilineal grandfather) and "the God of Nahor" (Abraham's brother and Laban's patrilineal grandfather). They are now patrilineal classificatory brothers, and patriarchy is saved.[40] "When membership in patrilineal descent groups is identified by rights of participation in sacrifices, evidence of paternity is created which is as certain as evidence of maternity."[41]

In general, J lives with the ambivalence. E retains both kinds of tales also, but portrays patrilineality as dominant by instituting a sacrificial system whereby those who offer sacrifices are all patrilineal descendants, as in the tale above. By the time you get to P, however, an outright war on the matrilineal system is declared. Since P is unwilling to portray sacrifice not performed by priests, P cannot revert to E's way out of the dilemma. Hence P must imagine that there never was and never could be any matrilineality in Israel's history. Unlike J who tells us that both Adam and Eve had children, P peppers the patriarchal narratives with lists of "begats" where not one woman's name occurs. Now we know how people inherit: only through their fathers. In a sense fathers are all they have. Jay calls P's redaction a "final patrilineal triumph."[42]

This final editor of the Pentateuch has joined forces with Ezra, Nehemiah, and the other priestly books to provide a picture of Israelite society descending from a male-covenanted line going back to Abraham, whose original compact with God had been marked by circumcision. As much as circumcision is a sign of the covenant, it has now become a sign of male descent lines. It is of a piece with P's lengthy male-only genealogies. It is part and parcel of a sacrificial system in which only men are priests, all priests get the right of the priesthood from their fathers who were priests before them, and only priests may sacrifice and receive the emoluments that come with their office. Circumcision is a representation of the very basic cultural dichotomy between men and women.

This male/female antithesis parallels a second opposition: Israelite/foreigner. One cannot but be struck by the particular venom with which Ezra and Nehemiah inveigh against exogamy. The old story told by J or E in Numbers 12 portrays Moses as having married a Cushite. When Miriam speaks out against him for doing so, she is punished with leprosy. This is hardly a tale condemning marriage to foreign women, precisely because men did it all the time without consequence. Nor was Moses alone. Judah married a Canaanite, David a Philistine, and Solomon a whole harem of foreigners. In the Bible, marriage was simply "the non-sacramental private acquisition of a woman by a man."[43] Pre-exilic authors warn against marrying Canaanites, because they might import their idols into the Israelite camp (Ex. 34:16, Deut. 7:1). This is precisely what happens in Number 25:1–2, when "the people profaned themselves by whoring with the Moabite women who invited the people to the sacrifices of their gods. The people ate and worshipped their gods." But to this brief episode, where idolatry, not exogamy, is the obvious concern, the priestly author appended a morality tale to parallel Ezra's dismissal of the foreign wives. His hero is Phinehas son of Eliezer son of Aaron. An Israelite brings a Midianite woman into the camp. Phinehas gives them time to go to bed together; then he storms in on them and stabs them to death. For this bit of zealotry, Phinehas and his descendants are given the priesthood for all time (Num. 25:13).

It is not just men and women, then, who constitute contrasting poles in the priestly system. The concern with lineage purity had twin consequences. Just as women were progressively excluded from convenantal status, non-Jews were separated from Jews. The worst possible case would be a combination of the two negative poles: a non-Jewish woman. Our priestly authors have thus explained their right to the priesthood by recollecting their ancestor's primeval act of murdering a man for bringing a foreign woman into camp (and murdering the woman, too, for coming there). Ezra will eventually follow suit by chasing all such women out of his theocracy. What we have is two boundary lines being established with ever greater severity. In both cases, the threat of ritual purity is used to enforce them.

The issue of ritual purity will crop up more than once in this account, and it deserves an initial discussion now. We should not take it for granted. We saw above that P's demand for circumcision throughout the generations was embedded in precisely the section of the priestly code that also called for the ritual separation of women for a week after bearing sons (two weeks after bearing daughters). Similarly, we have Ezra and Nehemiah's testimony as to the fears of impurity occasioned by marriages of Israelite men and non-Israelite women. "The holy seed has mixed itself with the peoples of the lands" (Ezra 9:2). Why should we find in P exaggerated fears of impurity on the borders that separate Israelites from foreigners and men from women?

Purity rules may arise for a number of reasons, argues Mary Douglas, all of them rooted in social systems with sufficient internal contradictions that ambivalence about rules results, creating what she calls "a system at war with itself."[44] She defines three ways in which this ambivalence can be overcome.

2. *Ambivalence warded off by the threat of male power:* Among Australia's Walbiri, men are given complete control over women. They may do

whatever they wish to them, without fear that they may go too far. As Douglas explains:

> The Walbiri case suggests . . . when male dominance is accepted as a central principle of a social organization and applied without inhibition and with full rights of physical coercion, beliefs in sex pollution are not likely to be highly developed. [That is because] when the threat of physical violence is uninhibited, we can expect the social system to persist without the support of pollution beliefs.[45]

Ambivalence as to descent of progeny is unlikely, since a woman who sleeps with a man not her husband is likely to be disciplined to the point of being beaten or even killed.

2. *Ambivalence denied by an elastic legal system:* Here areas of ambivalence are "explained away" by the development of infinite legal fictions that simply deny the contradictions in theory. Douglas illustrates with the Nuer, whose "political organization is totally unformulated" and whose social structure rests on few absolutely firm principles at all, with the result that "individuals can to some extent follow their personal whims, because the social structure is cushioned by fictions of one kind or another. . . . Nuer display astonishing legal subtlety in the definition of marriage, concubinage, divorce and conjugal separation."[46] A woman may sleep with a man not her husband and then have a child by him, but people will explain away the anomaly by recourse to complex legal fictions that assign the child to her husband and even deny that she slept with the second man altogether.

3. *Ambivalence warded off by fear of impurity:* Consider a legal system that is not highly malleable but where there are limits to the power of men, since women are in the ambivalent position of being subservient to men yet also autonomous agents with their own rights and privileges. These are the social systems that erect purity rules to guard the boundaries where the ambivalences may be played out. Wherever "no softening legal fictions intervene to protect the freedom of the sexes, exaggerated avoidances develop around sexual relations."[47] Here a woman and a man not her husband are warned against sleeping together because of the pollution such behavior brings into the camp.

Combining Douglas's cases of relative male dominance (from the Walbiri) and an elastic legal system (from the Nuer), we can formulate a rule:

Where rules favoring male domination contradict other rules, thus leading to inherent structural contradictions but providing no easy way out, and where the legal system is moving toward rigidity rather than elasticity, we can expect to find purity rules predominating.

That, I maintain, is exactly what we see in the priestly system developed following the return from Babylonian exile. The growing sense of male domination is evident in the circumcision symbolism at every level. But even as the rules of patrilineality increased, the rival matrilineal opposition was not forgotten. P did what he could to deny the underlying matrilineal tales, but he could hardly uproot them altogether from the canon of sacred Scripture that he inherited. The conflict within the system remained. As for a growing and inflexible legal system, one need only consult the priestly codes of Leviticus to see that legalism was precisely what P was establishing. Hence the concern with impurity.

The double impurity of non-Jewish wives is expressly mentioned in Nehemiah's concluding harangue; the threat from within that even Israelite women pose to their men elicits P's legislation against menstrual impurity and the purification rites following childbirth. By themselves, each of these is well enough known as to make further citation redundant. But I wish to claim that, by the time of P, the same social structural changes that required the one (rules against pollution by foreign women from outside the camp) required the other (purity rules against pollution by women from within the camp). We have the following structural equation:

$$\text{men} : \text{women} :: \text{Israelite} : \text{foreigner}$$

In both cases, the impure term threatens to overwhelm its partner. The left-hand term, men (within the class of Israelites) and Israelites (within the class of nations), is the covenanted item, which exists in uneasy tension with a non-covenanted one. Jews returning from Babylonian exile and living within the vast Persian Empire had to deal with non-Jews, just as Jewish men could not avoid dealing with Jewish women, but their relationship is ambivalent and circumscribed by boundary regulations.

We shall see this theme picked up by the Rabbis; they will continue P's lineage concerns, reinforce boundary regulations, pursue the ritual rules that permit boundary crossing (for non-Jews who wish to become Jews), and elaborate the covenantal sign of circumcision into a lengthy ritual from which women as mothers will eventually be eliminated altogether. At the same time, they will alter the public meanings of circumcision, doing away with a focus on fertility. The dominant horticultural metaphor will give way to a symbolism of circumcision blood. This blood will be contrasted with women's menstrual blood as the system comes full circle again, opposing covenanted males with uncovenanted females. But that is the end result of a long investigation to which we now turn.

Interlude from Priests to Rabbis: Origins of a Liturgy

We have seen how the postexilic priestly class made circumcision central to the biblical narrative, and therefore to Judaism. But nowhere in the Bible do we hear of a liturgical ceremony accompanying the rite. The priestly author may have rewritten Israelite history to guarantee circumcision as the means by which men inherit their covenantal status, but he did not stipulate any liturgy to accompany the physical act of circumcision.

Omission of a fixed prayer liturgy in the priestly narratives should not surprise us. Its absence is perfectly in keeping with what we know about the disjuncture between priestly society and what we have been calling, for lack of a better term, the rabbinic era. My purpose here is to survey the changeover of eras, and to provide the institutional backdrop against which rabbinic liturgy in general and its rite of circumcision in particular come into being.

Before the Rabbis, Judaism revolved about a centralized sacrificial cult, which depended on an agricultural economy for its sacrifices. Like the many Greco-Roman cults, its rituals harked back to an era when gentleman farmers like Simeon ben Jeshua Ben Sira were the people who mattered. Prescribed rituals were limited to the official cultic center in Jerusalem, where members of the priestly class who had inherited their status by familial lineage operated the sacrificial system.

When the Temple was destroyed, the hereditary priesthood did not immediately disappear or give up its power and perquisites, but eventually (and *only* eventually) it became an honorific class, its place in society taken by a new elite, the Rabbis, who believed as staunchly in a meritocracy of learning as the ticket to authority as the old priesthood had believed in genealogy as the entrance requirement.

At this point, Jay's theory of sacrifice should be recalled. In agrarian societies, she says, sacrifice "indexes" the priestly descent group, by which she means that it both identifies the group's members and integrates them into a bonded social class.[1] If Jay is correct, the function that sacrifice played of indexing masculine descent lines must have been taken over by some other aspect of religion. This is where circumcision entered. From time to time likened to sacrifice itself (as we shall see), circumcision now indexed descent lines through the male, marking sons as offspring of their father and bonding together generations of males across the ages. The significance of a descent line changes over time, but the idea that generations of men are permanently connected to each other, that what matters about a son is the fact that he will replicate the world-sustaining role of his father, that a masculine subsystem is what sustains the Jewish covenant with God—these are ideas that grow with rabbinic Judaism. If the sacrificial cult had sustained inheritance rules from father to son, including the inheritance of the priesthood, circumcision mirrored the cult by demonstrating the inheritance of covenanted status from one male generation to another.[2]

We saw above how circumcision was connected to the rise of a hereditary postexilic priesthood and its need to symbolize a genealogy of descent through males; how internal contradictions between matrilineal and patrilineal systems evoked impurity rules; how the boundary between men and women, on the one hand, and between Israelites and foreigners, on the other, became hard and fast; and how the dominant metaphors were agricultural—circumcised men likened to properly pruned trees (as the P author puts it in the Genesis narrative, both were expected to "be fruitful and multiply"). Priestly power, patrilineage, agricultural economy, and a functioning centralized Temple cult: these are the bases for the priestly religion of the writer (or writers) we call P.

These elements form what Peter Berger has called a "plausibility structure":

> Worlds are socially constructed and socially maintained. Their continuing reality . . . depends upon specific social processes, namely, those processes that ongoingly reconstruct and maintain the particular worlds in question. . . . Thus each world requires a social "base" for its continuing existence as a world that is real to actual human beings. This "base" may be called its plausibility structure.[3]

To illustrate what he means by "plausibility structure," Berger refers us to the religious world of pre-Columbian Peru before and after its destruction by Spanish conquerors.

> The religious world of pre-Columbian Peru was objectively and subjectively real as long as its plausibility structure, namely, pre-Columbian Inca society, remained intact. . . . When the conquering Spaniards destroyed this plausibility structure, the reality of the world based on it began to disintegrate with terrifying rapidity. . . . When Pizarro killed Atahalpa . . . he shattered a world, [and] redefined reality. . . . What previously had been existence in the nomos of the Inca world, now became, first, unspeakable anomy, then a more or less nomized existence on the fringes of the Spaniards' world—that other world, alien and vastly powerful, which imposed itself as reality-defining facticity upon the numbed consciousness of the conquered.[4]

Berger's widely employed model is useful for both the rise and the fall of the priestly system. If we look back at the priestly redefinition of Judaism, we can see that its success came about in large part because the plausibility structure of pre-exilic society was ruptured by the Babylonian invasion just as Incan society was demolished by Pizarro (though, of course, the Spanish overlords stayed whereas the Babylonian conquerors were gone within two generations). In both cases, however, religiously based social constructions of reality suffered the loss of legitimating social, economic, and political systems. In Israel's case, the monarchy, the Temple with its priests and Levites, and even the "loyal opposition" of the political system, institutionalized prophecy, were eradicated. To be sure, our information on Judean society during the brief Babylonian domination is sparse. We know very little about how it was governed, and who spoke to and for the native population. But there is every reason to believe that the economic, political, and social fabric of the country was as savaged by Babylonia as Peru had been by Spain. The difference was, of course, that within a short space of time Persia had conquered Babylonia and opened the door for the exiles to return. All three power groups—the monarchy, the priesthood, and the prophets—sought to regain a position of authority that was equal to or better than the one they had held in the old order.

In Weberian terminology, the monarchy had been a traditional source of domination while prophecy had been charismatic. In exile, the latter continued with less difficulty than the former, since prophecy depended on no particular locus for its exercise: charismatic authority was just as available to Ezekiel or Second Isaiah in Babylonia as it had been to Amos or Isaiah in the Land of Israel. By contrast, the exiled monarchy in Babylonia practically dropped out of sight, since the traditional basis for its rule included its hereditary landed center in David's capital. At best, it was a monarchy in exile, whereas the prophets, though physically in exile, could claim to hear the voice of God as clearly as ever, and could even point to their predecessors' predictions that had now come true.

Zoroastrian Persian culture, however, granted special status to priests, and it was therefore the Jewish priestly party that won the day. But unlike the monarchy, it enjoyed no traditional Jewish right to rule, so to establish the appropriate nature of its newly won power it promulgated the Pentateuch, which its members had successfully rewritten with themselves at the center. Ezra read the law to the people, and from then on based his and his descendants' right to rule on God's cultic requirements, which only priests could fulfill. Again we see the priests' need to guard their genealogical purity, which constituted the priestly version of royal primogeniture, the justification for passing power down through the generations. Read 1 and 2 Chronicles as opposed to 1 and 2 Kings. Talk about revisionism! Kings is a history of kings; Chronicles is a history of priests, with genealogical lists in abundance—all of them patrilineal.[5]

But the priestly system, too, demanded a stable plausibility structure, and when that fell—as it did, slowly but inexorably, when the Persian world was replaced by successive Hellenistic and Roman empires—the legitimating conceptualizations of priestly Judaism came under attack as well, among them, circumcision. To begin with, Jewish men who never before would have questioned circumcision did so now, many of them electing to remedy their own circumcised status and pass as Greeks. But even those who still practiced circumcision were constrained to rephrase its justification in new terms. Philo, for example, knows the old public meaning, and refers back to the agricultural analogy, citing the "need to be purified and trimmed like plants." Yet he also fishes for new meanings; true to his penchant for allegory, he excuses the practice as an oblique reminder of the soul's search for enlightenment, since what is learning, if not the practice of "shaving off ignorance"?[6] Clearly, Philo is on the way to reconstructing a new Jewish world, one in keeping with Hellenistic philosophy, albeit connected to the Hebrew Bible. The latter demands circumcision; the former newly explains it.

Philo never became the model for a long-term Jewish future. That achievement is attributed to the Rabbis, who, however, faced the same challenge that Philo did, albeit in Jerusalem, not Alexandria. They, too, inherited the priests' Pentateuch along with circumcision, and they, too, had to reinterpret it in keeping with the new plausibility structure of their era.

Toward that end, by the end of the second century, the Rabbis, now called Tannaim, had promulgated a selective version of their accumulated religious reform in a book called the Mishnah. Perhaps a century later, a second collection called the Tosefta made its appearance. By the close of the fourth century, the Yerushalmi (or Palestinian Talmud) reached its final stage of development, and somewhere in the sixth or seventh century the Babli (or Babylonian Talmud) was concluded. Along the way, various exegetical works known as midrash were compiled, each a different collection of rabbinic commentary on Scripture, often assembled with a view toward making theological statements about problems that had newly emerged with the changing times.[7] Contrary to the Rabbis' own claims on the subject, we now know that their several literary products are far from seamless; each has its own purpose, and as a group they are far from homogeneous in their approach or content. But they are not discontinuous either. There is throughout a certain consistency that provides a reasonably coherent worldview that is recognizably "rabbinic," as opposed, say, to Philo's Alexandrian school of thought, or to the more priestly perspective of the Qumran community. While we have to exercise care when citing rabbinic literature, to avoid sloppy attributions that ignore the promulgation date of the document in which the source is carried, it is nonetheless possible to point to a single cultural system that unifies the writings in question. True, various stages of growth are evident as we move from Mishnah to Talmud, but pre-Mishnah and post-Mishnah Judaism are not altogether different. Judaism did not start all over again on the day the Mishnah was promulgated. Some public meanings survived intact.

That claim returns us to chapter 1, where I insisted that studies in ritual breach the gap between traditionalists, who assume that textual evidence from different eras is wholly continuous across time, and their historicist critics, who posit discontinuity between literary strata. That is to say, as much as the study of liturgy as culture cannot ignore the dating of texts, it also should not make the mistake of imagining a total hiatus between historical periods that have been postulated solely on the basis of having given us different docu-ments. As we consider the changeover from the world represented by the late books of the Hebrew Bible on the one hand and the rabbinic works of Mish-nah and Talmud on the other, it becomes evident how much discontinuity is the norm. Yet when we compare Mishnah and Talmud with each other, we should say that despite clear differences in style and agenda, there is more cultural continuity between the two than a purely historicist position is willing to grant. All Rabbis prior to the year 200 did not die on a single day, leaving a tabula rasa for succeeding generations miraculously unaffected by previous ritual practice. We should therefore follow standard historicist wisdom in rec-ognizing something appropriately called rabbinic Judaism that is only loosely continuous with its biblical past; and that is recognizable particularly in a foundational statement known as the Mishnah. Yet favoring the traditionalist pole, we ought to concede that within this culture called rabbinic there are enough shared meanings between tannaitic and amoraic texts as to let us posit relative continuity across the tannaitic-amoraic divide. Rabbinic culture is far from static, there are monumental differences between the ritual world of the Mishnah and that of the codified Babli. Nevertheless, in this single culture we call rabbinic, more is shared across the great literary divide of the year 200 than not.

When it comes to reconstructing circumcision ritual, we therefore need to operate both diachronically and synchronically. From the former perspec-tive, we can array the evidence from the sources chronologically to reconstruct as far as possible what we know of rabbinic interpretations at different points in time, separating out early from late strata. This will save us from sloppy generalizations about *the* rabbinic view, as if there were some universal Jewish attitude. The latter perspective, however, will save us from sterile historicism, reminding us that real live people, for whom a rite like circumcision is part of their lives, do not automatically give up all their public meanings in a day, a year, a lifetime, or (usually) even in the number of generations that memory can recall. If we retain our bird's-eye view of what we can call early rabbinic culture as a whole, we shall see that some cultural themes elucidated in the Mishnah were still the object of thematic variations years later. We shall also find public meanings from the mishnaic or talmudic eras that were lost as European Jews turned to newfound concerns to express what circumcision meant to them. Above all we shall see whole systems at work, socially con-structed worlds of meaning that transcend this or that rabbinic document, making rabbinism not just a set of library entries that can be differentiated as to shelf place, but a culture that we call rabbinic Judaism.

Just when can we assume that the rabbinic, as opposed to the biblical, cultural fascination with circumcision began? No Pentateuchal narrative even suggests a prayer ritual connected with circumcision, and Hasmonean sources are equally silent on the subject, even though circumcision was obviously important to Jews then. Jewish memory recollects the ban on circumcision as Antiochus's symbolic blow at Judaism as a whole, after all. Brave women who saw to it that their children were circumcised anyway are part of the canvas of loyalty and martyrdom that characterizes 1 and 2 Maccabees. So if a liturgical ritual was being practiced at the time, we might have expected some reference to it in those sources. In the absence of such reports, we have to believe that no such ritual existed.

The lack of a liturgy of the word connected to the rite of circumcision is perfectly in keeping with what we know about Hasmonean society in general. The late biblical books of that era indicate that fixed public prayers had yet to be invented, except, perhaps, for the few words recited by priests in the Temple. Even there it is hard to say for sure that the liturgical formulas recalled in the second-century Mishnah (our prime document for the Temple cult) are accurate. They may be more akin to the creative inventions that historians of the time (like Josephus) put into the mouths of their heroes. The Hasmoneans were priests; a conservative force fighting a changing world, they supported the old order passionately. Their foundation myths describe a fight for a purified Temple cult, not the right to communal prayer. Even the later tales invented by Rabbis to identify God's miracles of the time contain stories of miraculous Temple flames that stayed lit for eight days, not a single story of prayer groups outside the Temple. Other Jewish literature of the time mentions neither a synagogue nor a liturgy of the word. Daniel, for instance, is a literary fiction written on the eve of the Hasmonean revolution. With a stroke of its author's pen it could have had its hero going to synagogue, saying a daily communal liturgy, or doing anything at all that we now associate with public Jewish prayer. Yet it is absolutely silent on the subject, with the exception of a brief reference to Daniel's *private* prayer, recited as he looks out through the window, three times every day (Dan. 6:11).

The earliest possible exception is the book of Ben Sira. Ever since the appearance of Joseph Heinemann's highly influential form-critical analysis of liturgy in 1966, it has been common to assume that some form of the Rabbis' paradigmatic synagogue prayer, known variously as the Amidah or the Tefillah, goes back as far as Ben Sira.[8] If Heinemann is correct about the Tefillah, and if circumcision is as central a rabbinic rite as I claim here, it may be that some form of a circumcision liturgy *was* being practiced that early, but that, like the Tefillah itself, it just did not get recorded by rabbinic progenitors who left us no written records from that early date. Our search for the origins of the circumcision rite thus demands that we pause briefly to see what the book of Ben Sira can and cannot tell us about liturgical origins in general, and by extension, about the possibility of an early circumcision liturgy in particular.

Dated somewhere around the second or the third century B.C.E., the book of Ben Sira is the testimony of a gentleman farmer knowledgeable about upper-class Judean society, and therefore a particularly fine witness for the period preceding the Hasmonean revolt. Because it does not appear in the Jewish Bible at all, we are dependent upon the early Church for conveying it to us. As carried by the Roman Catholic canon, even Ben Sira has nothing to say about a synagogue, synagogue liturgy, rabbinic home ceremony, or anything at all that we might identify as akin to the liturgical style that eventually came to characterize the circumcision rite.[9]

Around the turn of this century, however, a Hebrew version of Ben Sira was discovered in the Cairo Genizah, and before long it was identified, though not without disclaimers, as the original text from which the Church's translations were made. Of particular interest was an extra chapter that had appeared in no previous translation and had never before been seen. That chapter contained a litany with noticeable similarities to the central daily petitionary prayer of the synagogue service. In 1924 the claim was made that Jewish liturgy ought to be dated to Ben Sira's time, that is, well before any literary evidence from the rabbinic corpus itself.[10] Before long, but especially in the work of Joseph Heinemann, claims for other early "proto-rabbinisms" became the rage, as scholars once again competed to find earlier and earlier "originals." Heinemann lists them, and summarizes:

> It is not our task here thoroughly to examine each of these supposed
> parallels [to the final Tefillah text]. . . . Even if we were to reject some
> of them, the ones that remain would still sufficiently testify to the exis-
> tence of various "series" of benedictions and petitions similar to those
> in the Eighteen Benedictions [the Tefillah] a full century or two before
> the destruction of the Temple; hence we are justified in accepting the

opinion of the majority of scholars that the first beginning of the Amidah [= the Tefillah] preceded this event by hundreds of years.[11]

At the outset, then, we face the question whether the discontinuity with biblical culture I have posited is not due only to a hiatus of literary evidence for the period in question. Perhaps Ben Sira is a lone but very important sign of a liturgical tradition stretching back beyond the tannaitic era, in which case a rabbinic conception of circumcision complete with a liturgical rite expressing it goes back farther than I claim.

In large part, the question depends on the status of Ben Sira's extra Hebrew chapter. Chapter 36 also contains some putative anticipations of the Tefillah in terms of vague topical allusions, but Heinemann himself admits that "as for their wording, they contain absolutely no similarity to the formulations of the *Amidah* as we know it."[12] Since the extra chapter of Ben Sira is exactly that, extra, and therefore unknown in any translations that have come down to us, our question divides into two distinct parts. First, is chapter 51 authentically Ben Sira, or is it only a late Hebrew addition to the early text? Second, even if it is part of the original work by Ben Sira, is the prayer material in it sufficiently like our Tefillah to warrant the verdict that it is a genuine early form of the Tefillah?

I am not ready to concede that the so-called early prayer parallel in the extra chapter of Ben Sira is in fact authentically Ben Sira's. It occurs in only one manuscript of the many to contain the extra chapter, and the similarity between the lines as we have them in Ben Sira and the actual Tefillah as it emerges in later texts is tenuous, to say the least. The Ben Sira poem is a psalmlike construction organized into two-line strophes, the first of which begins with a normative psalmic world for praise, *Hodu,* "Praise," and the second of which simply repeats the equally well-known psalmic response, *Ki le'olam chasdo,* "For His mercy is everlasting."

The five lines in question follow. I number them consecutively for easy reference as B[en] S[ira] 1–5.

BS1 Praise the Redeemer of Israel [*go'el yisra'el*]
  For His mercy is everlasting.
BS2 Praise the One who gathers Israel's dispersed [*mekabetz nidchei yisra'el*]
  For His mercy is everlasting.

BS3 Praise the One who builds His city and sanctifies it [*boneh iro umekaddesho*]

For His mercy is everlasting.

BS4 Praise the One who causes light to blossom for the house of David [*matsmi'ach keren leveit david*]

For His mercy is everlasting.

BS5 Praise the shield of Abraham [*magen avraham*]

For His mercy is everlasting.[13]

To be sure, some of these phrases also occur in later Tefillah texts. The Palestinian version unearthed by Solomon Schechter, for instance, gives us the following:

Blessed art Thou, Lord, *magen avraham* (blessing # 1 = BS5)

Blessed art Thou, Lord, *go'el yisra'el* (blessing # 7 = BS1)

Blessed art Thou, Lord, *mekabetz nidchei amo yisra'el* (blessing # 10 = BS2)[14]

The two remaining Ben Sira phrases, BS3 and BS4 (*boneh iro umekaddesho* and *matsmi'ach keren leveit david*), on the other hand, do not appear in standard Tefillah texts, although their themes at least (rebuilding Jerusalem and establishing the Davidic monarchy) are commonly present, and in some versions of the Tefillah (for example, in the standard Babylonian version) there is at least some verbal tally—*matsmi'ach keren yeshu'a* ("causes the light of redemption to blossom"), for instance.[15]

But these few minor similarities between a putative Bible-like psalm uttered by Ben Sira in the second or third century B.C.E. and some prayer texts otherwise attested to in eighth- or ninth-century written sources, but referred to obliquely by rabbinic authors of the first or second century C.E., can hardly be the basis for predating the latter practice to the time of the former. That is to say, the occurrence of a litany using biblical language inserted into a manuscript of Ben Sira, and another litany only roughly and partly of the same type used much later as synagogue liturgy, does not imply that the institution giving rise to the first was an earlier form of an institution giving rise to the second.

What we know about oral cultures elsewhere should be applied here. Ritual performers in oral cultures generally master a large repertoire of stock phrases that can then be fitted into appropriate contexts. Walter Ong thus summarizes Homeric scholarship by saying, "The oral poet has an abundant repertoire of epithets diversified enough to provide an epithet for any metrical emergency."[16] We should imagine Ben Sira as such a poet, able to draw upon a variety of epithets describing God's praiseworthy activity. These and other praise epithets were retained in the Jewish ritual lexicon and drawn on again, but this time for a new institution, rabbinic liturgy. The old *Hodu* formula was replaced with a new one, *Barukh atah adonai.*[17] But a psalm exclaimed on one occasion by a gentleman farmer and prescribed liturgy repeated daily by a congregation at worship are two different things.

I see no reason to date rabbinic liturgy in general earlier than the Rabbis and rabbinic institutions, for which we have no independent evidence at all until at least the second century B.C.E., and then only in nascent form.[18] A liturgical circumcision rite, to which I am about to point, should therefore not be presumed to have existed before that time, and it may even be quite a bit later, not until the first century C.E. or so.

By the first century, after all, a great deal had changed. The priestly cult still commanded authority, since in the surrounding Hellenistic milieu it was *de rigeur* for every self-respecting religion to feature sacrifice to the gods. We tend to forget how long and how successfully sacrifice held its own as the obvious centerpiece of religious ceremonial. As late as the fourth century, the emperor Julian still imagined he could restore Paganism to its old glory and rebuild a Jewish sacrificial system along the way.[19] Even Christianity, which had no temple, and therefore no sacrificial system either, built a theology of sacrifice instead, as well as a ritual in which sacrificial imagery and motifs were everywhere. Nevertheless, Christians still found themselves on the defensive against pagan critics, who couldn't comprehend how a religion could be theistic without offering the gods anything.[20] The end of paganism should not be taken for granted, warns Peter Brown.[21] But neither should the new order of synagogal and home worship; it was certainly appearing, but not necessarily as rapidly and as successfully as we usually imagine.

By the first century, however, two novel institutions, the synagogue and the *chavurah,* had made their appearance on the scene. Jews still sacrificed at the Temple, but increasing numbers of them engaged in synagogue and *chavurah* worship as well. The synagogue as an institution is well known, the *chavurah* less so. Yet the circumcision ritual emerged not in the synagogue but in the *chavurah.*

The *chavurah* (pl. *chavurot*) has not received its due as a formative institution. Only our own scholarly myopia can be at fault here, since it is mentioned far more frequently in early rabbinic sources than the synagogue. Yet the synagogue survived while the *chavurah* did not; hence the numerous histories of the former and the paucity of treatments of the latter.[22]

The *chavurah* emerged as a Jewish parallel to the Greco-Roman eating club. It was a fellowship group that met around the table to share meals in common. From the *chavurah* we get the nonsynagogal center for Jewish religious life: the home or, more precisely, the table, which is likened to an altar, around which the sacred gathering meets to consume food with appropriate ritualized behavior.[23] Much of Jewish worship is thus not synagogue prayer at all, but home prayer—Grace after Meals, blessings for various foods, and the Passover seder, which is nothing if not a full-scale remnant of *chavurah* spirituality.

There were several types of *chavurot*. The Pharisees developed ad hoc groups of people who shared a given Sabbath or festival meal, or who attended each other's life-cycle celebrations. By the second century C.E., however, we hear of ongoing *chavurot* (I will call them tableship groups) in which membership is controlled by regulations and to which people belong for an extended period of time. Both cases, however, are alike in that they are governed by particular rules of sanctity with regard to the food that may be eaten. It has been argued that *chavurah* members regularly applied to themselves the rules of extra sanctity that characterized the Temple cult.[24] Food consumed had to be properly tithed, for instance. A distinction was made between *chavurah* members, who could be trusted to have separated the necessary tithes, and the class of people known as *am ha'aretz,* people who could not be so trusted. The former would not eat with the latter.

Since one of the social functions of the *chavurah* was to provide the opportunity for members to celebrate life-cycle events together, we should imagine that the circumcision rite began in the *chavurah*. Evidence from the rite itself supports this assumption, since to this day a festive meal follows the actual liturgy. The same is true of weddings and even funerals, all of which are established life-cycle occasions that go back to Pharisaic times. There is no reason to believe, however, that the liturgy as we have it is that early. The circumcision meal and its accompanying ritual did not necessarily come into being simultaneously. Nor was a later (and purely secular, or at least nonreligious and therefore secondary) meal tacked on to an earlier (and primary) religious ritual, as is apt to be assumed today by pietists who distrust banqueting as the epitome of religious expression far more than our ancestors did. The Rabbis of late antiquity were less puritanical. Far from secular, their banquets associated with rites of passage were known as *se'udot mitzvah* ("religiously obligatory feasts"). These feasts were part and parcel of a larger cultural phenomenon in antiquity: pagans celebrated sacrificial spirituality while Christians feasted at the graves of saints. Many of the instances of first-century feasting mentioned by Ramsay MacMullen are primary expressions of pagan ritual: hundreds of invitations to the effect that "Dionysius asks you to dine" at such and such a shrine; banquet facilities for overflow crowds who made their way to festive occasions; ceremonies known as *lectisternia* in which an icon was produced to share in the festive banquets, though the human invitees often ate freely to the point where "religious meaning was all but forgotten."[25] MacMullen notes graveside feasts among pagans also, but these reach a zenith in Christian society only in the fourth century, when a newly wealthy Church took over the private feasts at tombs of the dead and converted them into public events.[26] In chapter 7 we shall look at a report of a circumcision during the second century, halfway between MacMullen's early data and the late developments chronicled by Brown. A liturgy of the word is clearly presupposed by that time, but even then, what is remembered is not an elaborate liturgy so much as a fabulous feast.

Therefore, circumcision ritual may not have been an original liturgy to which a feast was tacked on, but a festive banquet that eventually attracted liturgical trappings. *Chavurah* ceremony was meal-centered from the outset. By analogy, consider the development of the Passover seder, another *chavurah* event. Evangelists portraying the Last Supper as a seder have little to say about an elaborated ritual beyond the consumption of special foods and some short benedictions. They may have been silent on ritual detail because they had no interest in recording more information. But rabbinic sources prior to the tannaitic period are just as sparse regarding discussion of seder liturgy. The names associated with seder debates tend to come from the time of Gamaliel II or even later still, that is, from the end of the first century to the close of the second.

It was only then, moreover, that synagogue liturgy began to take its final shape. Although synagogues existed in Jesus' and Paul's day—indeed, they preach at them—it is far from clear what kind of liturgy, if any, they participated in at that early period. In all probability, prior to the Tannaim, we have at best the *beginnings* of the elaborate Jewish liturgy of today. Too many people date synagogue and rabbinism too early; then, compounding that initial error with another, they collapse what it took centuries to build into a brief and early era said to be formative. Formative it may have eventually become, but only eventually.

By the second century, however, rabbinic liturgy had taken shape, again largely under the guidance of authorities at the time of and after Rabban Gamaliel. Take, for example, the Rabbis' most typical liturgical genre, the benediction, which is unknown in the Bible but ubiquitous in rabbinic liturgy throughout the tannaitic (70–200 C.E.) and the amoraic (c. 200–550 C.E.) periods.[27] Pharisees may have used their preferred benedictory formula for prayer as early as the time of Hillel and Jesus, but it is not 100 percent certain that they did, since, among other things: (1) the New Testament does not display it as a favored liturgical genre, and (2) many of the pre-70 traditions in rabbinic literature, which do use benedictions, might be later anachronisms, true for the time of their authors but not for the period of which they speak. However, some form of benediction seems to be presupposed by public liturgies held in town squares while the Temple still stood, when the dominant prayer institution was not yet the synagogue but the *ma'amad,* a sort of local democratic representational group that met to worship at specified times dependent on the cultic schedule and on natural disasters like droughts.[28] So I consider the benediction prototypical of rabbinic liturgy, an excellent index of the stages of that liturgy's growth. The most important series of benedictions we have—I call them benediction strings—and the Rabbis' prayer par excellence as a result, is the Tefillah, which was not canonized in any way at all until Gamaliel's day. As late as the generation of Akiba, who died in 135, there was debate on what the Tefillah should be. The rules governing benedictions in general were still under discussion in the third century.

With regard to circumcision, then, if the usual pattern for Jewish liturgy is followed, we might expect to find some liturgical ritual with benedictions at its center by the year 200. The origins of the rite may well go back to the beginnings of the tannaitic era, but probably not much before that, and its evolution ought to include considerable adaptation to later times and places, stretching through the amoraic period, at least, and probably into the Middle Ages and even beyond.

In sum, were there important prayers being said along with the act of circumcision in the first half of the first century, while the Temple still stood and before the tannaitic age had been inaugurated at Yavneh? Possibly, but I doubt it. The story in Luke of John's circumcision mentions no such prayers.

For that matter, however, even the Mishnah is remarkably silent as of the year 200. Our earliest references to a circumcision prayer rite are carried in the Tosefta and the Talmud, along with stories about actual circumcisions embedded in various midrash collections. Some of these references make no claim to being any earlier than the book in which they are found; others are cast in rhetorical form normally said to be earlier. Rabbinic legal writings after 200 retained the distinction in type between what Rabbis before 200 had said (the Tannaim) and what tannaitic successors after 200 (the Amoraim) were saying. There are thus reputed tannaitic teachings regarding a prayer ritual carried in post-tannaitic material. If they are correctly attributable to authorities of the Mishnah, they constitute our first window on the public meanings of circumcision within the rabbinic framework. Even if they are not tannaitic, they nonetheless are consistent with the rest of the material carried in the Talmud, so at worst we would be describing the rabbinic mindset shortly after 200 rather than shortly before it.

But in all probability our sources attest to a tannaitic circumcision liturgy (c. 70–200) that was added to what had hitherto been a physical operation followed by a feast. The cultural mindset explored in the pages that follow are assumed to reflect the inner spiritual life of the *chavurah*-based rabbinic community from that era as well as its rabbinic equivalent shortly thereafter. We want to know what the circumcision liturgy can tell us about rabbinic culture during the formative years following the first-century destruction of the second Temple, but stretching into the second, the third, and perhaps the fourth centuries as well.

That being said, we can move to the rite as we have it and attempt the task of dating the various elements in it. Our goal will be to pare away the post-talmudic accretions, so as to be left with only that body of liturgy that expresses the rabbinic meaning system of the tannaitic and amoraic ages.

Reconstructing the Rite

It is easier to see the trees if we look at the forest. So before isolating this or that element of the circumcision rite for immediate discussion, we require an overview of what the rite eventually became, that is, the way that the rite is practiced today. I shall label its constituent paragraphs alphabetically, and then indicate which sections can be dated relatively early—as tannaitic or amoraic, that is. Our focus remains the tannaitic-amoraic culture of Palestine (and, to some extent, Babylonia as well) that crystallized in the first several centuries of the common era and that left its stamp on rabbinic Judaism ever after.

Since it is such a break with the standard and generally accepted method of studying rabbinic texts, I note again the controversy implicit in my inclusion of both tannaitic and amoraic strata as a single cultural whole. Similarly controversial in liturgical scholarship is my combining these two terms into a single adjective, "tannaitic-amoraic," that modifies the noun "culture."

Normative liturgical research has hitherto seen itself as studying texts, not culture, and therefore has been careful to differentiate its evidence according to the date at which a given text was promulgated. The whole point of the textual exercise was to discriminate stages of development in a rite—or, more precisely, in the set of texts that constituted the ritual script. Such chronological discrimination was possible only if textual strata were kept rigidly separate from one another and then compared to see what textual development was evident from an earlier stratum to a later one. Under those ground rules, mixing tannaitic and amoraic strata constituted a grievous methodical error. Before continuing, therefore, it is crucial that I expand what I have already said regarding the way that my own focus differs from that of my historicist predecessors.

Everything depends on being clear about what will count as a successful finding. The first fault with which I charge the historicist method, therefore, is that its findings (which are dependent on philology) are not "successful"— that is, they do not demonstrate what its finders want them to establish. In its classical format, liturgical philology/historicism seeks to identify a single set of original prayer texts that rabbinic Jews used when the institution called the synagogue service began. But the form-critical critique has made it impossible to imagine that the Tannaim ever had single canonical prayer texts with accompanying paradigmatic liturgical performances. There simply was no universally acknowledged "original" service for us to find. Sophisticated historicist research has managed, however, to stake out a proper domain for its inquiries, with more humble expectations regarding what it may rightfully stipulate about original ritual performances and texts.[1] If we cannot say that a specific set of words was universally recited in antiquity, we can at least identify which words were later accretions, and we can date certain ritual elements as *options* that were in force and therefore can be used to exemplify tannaitic liturgy. Thus my first objection is largely moot, even though popularizers still overstate the significance of philological findings by passing off old research into "original" rites and wording as if scholars still believe in them.

It is therefore my second objection that matters more here. Books are indeed datable, so that data from books ought theoretically to be easily arrayed chronologically according to the book in which they occur. This principle is both undeniable and invaluable. Medieval exegetes served theological ends by lumping together a thousand years and more of textual evidence into a single putative synchronic whole called "Tradition," thus bequeathing to us a picture of a monolithic, unchanged, and unchangeable reality perfected for all time—as befit their notion of a monotheistic, unchanging, and unchangeable God who gave it. Historicism successfully denied this monolithic model, inviting us to differentiate (1) discrete biblical passages with their own specific meaning within the context of the ancient Near Eastern milieu where they were penned; (2) secondary but equally important rabbinic interpretations for which people in late antiquity were prepared to live and die; and (3) yet a third stratum of exegesis forged in the wake of European realities like the Crusades. For instance, it was Julius Wellhausen's breakthrough in 1878 to see Genesis 1:1 as a postexilic invention understandable only when placed in the context of the author's age.[2] The Rabbis, on the other hand, use Genesis 1:1 to demonstrate the compatibility of their creation myth with Neoplatonic philosophy; the very first entry in the largest midrashic compilation to Genesis explains that God used Torah as a supernal template for the details of the physical universe that followed.[3] For the eleventh-century French exegete Rashi (who cites earlier midrashic tradition), Genesis 1:1 proves the Jewish right of ownership to the Holy Land over which Muslims and Christians contended. "If the nations of the world say to the People of Israel, 'You are robbers because you stole the land of the seven Canaanite nations,' they [the Jews] should respond, 'The whole earth belongs to the Holy One Blessed be He. He created it, and He gives it to whomever is upright in his eyes.'"[4] True, dogmatic emphasis on origins has privileged "original" meaning as "real," but again, sophisticated scholarship has lately questioned the arbitrary preference for authorial intent over any given reading in this or that specific historically conditioned community of faith.[5]

What goes for biblical canon goes doubly for ritual, which is nothing if not acted out by successive communities of believers. At least the Bible is a book, which we may indeed read in an attempt, vain or not, to recapture what its author had in mind. A rite, however, is a performance. One need only picture some modern presentations of Shakespearian histories in which the protagonists come alive as contemporary rulers, or even board chairmen, to see how original scripts come newly alive in the hands of creative directors and actors. So, too, the ritual script of circumcision has remained open to new interpretations with which successive generations of Jewish participants have imbued it. The question, therefore, is not when circumcision texts were recorded in books, but what meanings those texts took on for people at circumcision ceremonies. Despite the literary distinctiveness of tannaitic works on the one hand and amoraic works on the other, or even the institutional and social uniqueness of, say, the Palestinian academies in the second and the third centuries, there is remarkable cultural coherence between the public meaning system established at first-century Yavneh and its successors in second- and third-century Galilee, where late tannaitic and early amoraic leadership developed. As I said in chapter 1, what I am after, therefore, is a rabbinic meaning system that did not dissolve or mutate suddenly at the end of the second century just because the Mishnah was promulgated then.

My second objection, then, amounts to the fact that we are after whole systems of thought: first the priestly system evident in Pentateuch, priestly writings, a patrilineal priesthood, and an agricultural economy of planting and reaping; then a rabbinic system dependent on the world of the middle to late Roman Empire, both before and after the year 200 when the Mishnah was promulgated. We can proceed through the ritual, dating what is datable, but only with the prior understanding that we are after ritual, not text. We must engage in what I call going "beyond the text."[6]

We can best proceed in three stages. First I will record the entire rite with a minimum of internal analysis, just enough to allow the reader to get an overall view of what happens and what is said from beginning to end. Then I shall summarize what the reader will just have read, isolating the elements and themes that constitute the rabbinic system. Finally, I will return in chapter 5 to specific questions and concerns that deserve greater attention.

Every discipline has its tedious bits of evidence: dreams for psychoanalysis, kinship systems for cultural anthropologists, and for liturgists, prayers and rites. I wish there were some way to move directly to the chapters on public meanings in rabbinic times and beyond, but there isn't—not a responsible way, that is. The careful stratification of textual evidence into different eras is necessary, albeit laborious, and I can only offer readers unfamiliar with rabbinic textual analysis the option of treating this chapter as a textual excursus that may be passed over quickly en route to what follows, where the evidence is arrayed systematically with an eye toward revealing the public meaning system that it defines.

The Circumcision Rite as We Have It

I include here both the wording and the accompanying instructions for ritual action provided by the standard guide for Orthodox rabbis known as *Hamadrikh,* a Hebrew word that means "The Guide."[7] *Hamadrikh* was composed in 1939 by Hyman E. Goldin, an authoritative voice of the time, known primarily for his translation of Solomon Ganzfried's *Kitzur Shulchan Arukh,* a practical compendium of Jewish law, reorganized and translated so as to be accessible to newly Americanized Jews, who often served as clergy but lacked the kind of thorough Jewish education that had been typical of Europe. *Hamadrikh* is a similar volume, but limited largely to life-cycle liturgy, which it presents along with a synopsis of practical guidance for "the rabbi or anyone officiating at a Jewish ceremonial or ritual" in America.[8] Virtually a classic today, this work was reprinted in 1956 and again in 1986.

Goldin's *Hamadrikh* is not the only source, of course. Other texts provide ritual alternatives, adding some things that Goldin omits or omitting some elements that he includes, especially when it comes to late European folk customs, about which authors felt free to exercise editorial license. As a check against Goldin, therefore, I have consulted an alternative account from Philip Birnbaum's equally reliable *Daily Prayer Book,* which has been a fixture in American Orthodox synagogues since its initial publication in 1949.[9] Here I have consolidated the two accounts into a single version of the rite so as to facilitate comprehension.

My composite account takes into consideration the fact that, even today, if a traditional *mohel* (ritual circumciser) recites the prayers, circumcision is conducted in Hebrew with largely passive invitees limited to listening and looking on. This ritual format is normative among most Americanized Jews who cannot follow the original language and may even be used to praying in the vernacular when they attend the synagogue, or at least to relying for their comprehension on translations of the prayers in front of them. At a circumcision, however, they are given no prayer books. Having no written text before them in any language, Hebrew or English, they are dependent on the aural performance of the Hebrew. For all but the tiny minority who understand Hebrew or who have otherwise studied Jewish ritual and rabbinic texts at some length, the literal meaning of the Hebrew is irrelevant. They must impute to circumcision meanings that are not immediately derived from the spoken ceremonial text. They would probably be surprised to learn some of the things that are being intoned by the expert charged with performing the rite. Both Goldin and Birnbaum supply translations, but they editorialized with "acceptable" English versions of those Hebrew phrases that either are difficult to comprehend or might prove jarring to modern sensitivities. Their readership was, by and large, composed of the second-generation children of immigrants, who were not anxious to retain what they perceived as embarrassing medievalisms in their religious rites. Recognizing, therefore, that the two translations are not literal, I have alternated freely between them, using the version that I thought best reproduced the Hebrew original at any given time. I have even substituted my own translation at times; but generally, what follows is Goldin's version.[10] Because I have sometimes wished to note a biblical source or to put the reader on guard regarding discussions that follow, I have appended editorial comments as notes to the ritual script itself.

Rites, like plays, make for easy participation but difficult reading. At least the acted-out drama has obvious changes of acts and scenes, a taxonomy I have integrated into the circumcision script here both to facilitate comprehension and to provide a ready way to refer back to the rite in later discussion. In addition, each discrete subsection is labeled with a letter. Finally, as in any good study edition of a dramatic script, the lines are numbered.

ORDER OF CIRCUMCISION
Introduction to the Rite: Setting the Stage

1   A.   Candles are lit in the room where the circumcision is to be performed.

2   B.   A chair is set aside in honor of the prophet Elijah, and the following is said:
3   "This is the chair of Elijah the prophet, remembered for good."

4   C.   When the infant is brought in to be circumcised, all present rise and say aloud:
5   "May he who comes be blessed."

6   D.   All present must remain standing to the end of the ceremony.

7   E.   The mohel takes the infant from the one who brought him in, and joyfully
8   says: "The Holy One, blessed be He, said to Abraham our father, 'Walk before
9   me, and be perfect.'*

10   F.   "I am ready and willing to perform the positive commandment that the Creator,
11   blessed be He, gave us to perform circumcision."

12   G.   If the father himself performs the circumcision, he says, "I am ready and
13   willing to perform the positive commandment which the Creator, blessed be He,
14   commanded: to circumcise my son, as it is written in the Torah: 'At the age of
15   eight days, every male among you shall be circumcised throughout the
16   generations.'"†

17   H.   The mohel places the infant upon the chair set aside for the prophet Elijah,‡
18   and recites: "This is the chair of Elijah, remembered for good. Lord, I have

---

*The Hebrew is *hit-halekh lefanai veheyei tamim* (Gen. 17:1), translated by both the 1962 JPS version and the 1989 NRSV edition of the Bible as "Walk in my ways and be blameless." See above, p. 35.

†Gen. 17:12.

‡Alternatively, the *mohel* places the child on the *sandek's* knee. The *sandek* is a medieval role allotted to the person who holds the child during the operation. Birnbaum seems to assume that the *sandek* sits in the chair holding the child while Goldin has the child being placed in the chair directly.

19   *awaited your salvation.* I have hoped for your salvation, Lord, and I have done*

20   *your commandments.† I have hoped for your salvation, Lord.‡ I rejoiced at your*

21   *word, as one who finds great spoil.§ Those who love your law have great peace;*

22   *they do not stumble.‖ Happy is the one whom you choose to bring near, so that*

23   *he may inhabit your Temple court.** Such a one inhabits your Temple court."††*

24   I.   Those present respond: "May we be satisfied with the goodness of your house,

25   your temple's shrine."‡‡

Act 1: Operation Begun and Introductory Blessings

26   J.   The mohel places the infant upon the lap of the sandek [a technical name

27   for the man who holds the child during the operation], and says the following

28   benediction before performing the operation: "Blessed art Thou Lord our God,

29   King of the universe, who has sanctified us by your commandments and com-

30   manded us concerning circumcision."

31   K.   Technically, the operation here has two parts: the incision which separates the

32   foreskin, and the peeling away of the foreskin, so as to uncover the corona.§§

33   The incision is made, and immediately after, but before the uncovering is per-

34   formed, the father, or the sandek (if there is no father), says: "Blessed art

35   Thou, Lord our God, King of the Universe, who has sanctified us by his com-

36   mandments, and commanded us to admit him [the child] to the covenant of

37   Abraham our father."

---

*Gen. 49:18.

†Ps. 119:116. Goldin inserts the following phrases at this point: "Elijah, angel of the covenant, here is what belongs to you, right in front of you. Stand at my right hand and sustain me." I include it only as a footnoted variation on the rite, since it interrupts the flow of a series of biblical citations and is not universally included.

‡Ps. 119:166.

§Ps. 119:162.

‖Ps. 119:165.

**Alternatively, ". . . whom You offer up as a sacrifice." In the biblical context whence the phrase is drawn, the Hebrew *tekarev* means "you bring near," but it may be used here as a double entendre. The same root means "to sacrifice," and we shall see that the motif of sacrifice is abundantly evident, especially in later medieval additions to the rite. See, for example, section Q below.

††Ps. 64:4.

‡‡Ps. 65:5.

§§Described with illustrative diagram by Thomas Goldenberg, "Medical Issues and *Berit Milah*," in *Berit Milah in the Reform Context*, ed. Lewis M. Barth (New York: Central Conference of American Rabbis, 1990), pp. 195, 199–200.

38   L.   Those present respond: "*As he has entered the covenant, so may he enter Torah,*
39   *marriage,* and good deeds.*"

Act 2: Operation Concluded and Naming

40   M.   *After uncovering the corona and cauterizing the wound,* the mohel takes a
41   cup of wine and says: "Blessed art Thou, Lord our God, King of the universe,
42   who creates fruit of the vine."

43   N.   Then he adds: "Blessed art Thou, Lord our God, King of the universe, who
44   sanctified the beloved one from the womb, and set a statute in his flesh, and
45   stamped his descendants with the sign of the holy covenant. Therefore, as a
46   reward for this, O Living God, our Portion and our Rock, command [or: the
47   living God . . . commanded] that the beloved of our flesh shall be delivered from
48   the pit, for the sake of his covenant which He set in our flesh. Blessed art Thou,
49   Lord, who makes [lit.: cuts] a covenant."†

50   O.   He continues: "Our God and God of our fathers, sustain this child to his father
51   and to his mother, and let his name in Israel be (so-and-so, son of so-and-so,
52   his father). Let the father rejoice in what has come forth from his loins, and let
53   the mother be happy with the fruit of her womb, as it is written: 'Let your
54   father and mother rejoice, and let her that bore you be happy.'‡ And it is said,
55   'I passed by you and saw you wallowing in your blood, and I said to you: In
56   your blood, live; I said to you: In your blood, live.'"§

*The Hebrew *chuppah* is generally translated as "wedding canopy." The use of the canopy as we have it today, however, is a medieval addition to the rite, still relatively recent as late as the sixteenth century. In the early period with which we are concerned here, the term meant simply a transfer of a woman across domains, from her father's domain, that is, to the domain of her husband. For detail, see Lawrence A. Hoffman, "Life-Cycle Ceremony as Status Transformation," in *Eulogema: Studies in Honor of Robert Taft S.J.,* ed. E. Carr et al. (Rome: Centro Studi S. Anselmo, 1993), pp. 161–77. See also Joseph Gutmann, who relates the *chuppah* as canopy to parallel Christian development in Europe (Gutmann, "Jewish Medieval Marriage Customs in Art," in *The Jewish Family: Metaphor and Memory,* ed. David Kraemer [Oxford: Oxford University Press, 1989], pp. 47–62). While a canopy of sorts might have been included on occasion, it was not usually part of the rite.

† The above prayer is not easily translated, as the wording is probably corrupt. I have rendered it as literally as possible, but will later attempt to reconstruct its wording and meaning. In particular, it is unclear whether we have a petition to God, "O God, command that . . . !" or an historical recollection, "God commanded that. . . ."

‡ Prov. 23:25.

§ Ezek. 16:6.

57   P.   The mohel now puts some wine on the child's mouth with his finger, and
58   continues: "And it is said, 'He has remembered his covenant forever, the word
59   He commanded to a thousand generations, the covenant which He made with
60   Abraham, his oath to Isaac, and what he confirmed to Jacob as a statute, to
61   Israel as an everlasting covenant.'* And it is said, 'Abraham circumcised Isaac
62   his son when he was eight days old, just as God had commanded him.'† 'Give
63   thanks to the Lord for He is good; his mercy lasts forever.'‡ May this little
64   child, (so-and-so), grow up. Just as he has entered the covenant, so may he
65   enter Torah, marriage, and good deeds."

Conclusion

66   Q.   After that, the mohel stands up and says: "Master of the universe, may it
67   be your will that this be considered by you—and thus accepted as according
68   to your will—as if I had sacrificed him before your throne of glory.[11] In
69   your great mercy, send forth by means of your holy angels a holy and pure
70   soul to (so-and-so) who was just now circumcised to your great name; and
71   let his heart be open as wide as the opening of the hall leading to the interior
72   of the Temple—open to your holy Torah, to learn and to teach, to observe
73   and to do."
74   R.   A prayer for a child after circumcision: "May the One who blessed Abraham,
75   Isaac, and Jacob bless this tender child who has been circumcised, and bring him
76   complete healing, and may his father be worthy of the merit of raising him to
77   Torah, to marriage, and to good deeds, and let us say 'Amen.'"
78   S.   Then they say Alenu, after which they wash their hands, say the blessing over
        bread, and eat the meal.

Outline of the Rite: Identification of Its Earliest Strata

The whole ritual is easily outlined as moving from an introduction, through two acts, and then to a conclusion.

---

*Ps. 105:8–10. The psalm continues, saying, "Unto you will I give the Land of Canaan." But our rite takes the citation of the establishment of the covenant out of context, so that the covenant as Land reemerges here as a covenant of circumcision.

†Gen. 21:4.

‡Ps. 118:1.

Introduction to the Rite: Setting the Stage

1. A–B: The unveiling of sacred props, including, of course, the *mohel's* instruments, but also (in some rites) the lighting of candles, and (in all rites) a chair set aside for Elijah.
2. C–E: Entry of the sacred actors:
    1. The child himself, who is welcomed in C.
    2. The *mohel,* who orchestrates the rite by first welcoming the child and then taking him from the person who brought him into the room.
    3. The father, who will speak later, is already standing at the *mohel's* side.
    4. The *sandek* takes up his position to hold the child.
3. E–G: Introductory statements of intention:
    1. The *mohel's* justification for the rite in biblical terms (E).
    2. The *mohel's* statement of his own willingness to perform the rite (F).
    3. The father's statement of his willingness to have his child circumcised (G). Technically, it is the father's obligation actually to perform the circumcision himself, just as Abraham did. In many places the *mohel* asks the father, "Do you wish to circumcise your own son?" to which he receives the answer, "I want you to do it for me as my legal agent."
4. H (as far as line 18, ". . . for good"): the introductory Elijah material, in which the child is placed on Elijah's chair.
5. H, line 18 ("Lord, . . .)–I: Extension of Elijah material. I mark off the Elijah material for historical reasons. The connection between the original line invoking Elijah (in 4) and the medieval supplements here is not immediately evident. In order to demonstrate some connection, as the chair is set aside for Elijah Goldin inserts: "Elijah, angel of the covenant, here is what belongs to you, right in front of you. Stand at my right hand and sustain me." The greeting of the child (C) is also late, unattested before the Middle Ages.

In sum, none of the introduction is tannaitic or amoraic. All of it is medieval in origin, and therefore not part of the rabbinic meaning system of late antiquity that interests us here. The *original* Elijah material (B, H to line 18) may be alluded to in a midrashic collection from the ninth century, but it is missing from prayer books of the same era. So even if Elijah was associated with the rite by that time, his presence was not yet invoked universally.[12]

Act 1: Operation Begun and Introductory Blessings

If the introduction to our drama (the setting of the stage, as I have called it) is a medieval accretion, the two main acts that constitute the circumcision rite are not. By and large they derive from the very tannaitic-amoraic society whose culture we are investigating. We begin with the operation (K), accompanied by appropriate blessings by the *mohel* and the father (J–K), the two men who share the ritual responsibility here. The blessings evoke a response by those in attendance (L).

Act 1 thus provides us with the elemental constituents of the rite, almost all of which date to the tannaitic age.[13] I say "almost" because there is one important exception—the addition of the words "and good deeds" (1. 39) in the onlookers' response (L). Actually, that too may be tannaitic, but if so, it is a late tannaitic addition, and in all probability it was not added to the rite until the fourth or fifth century (see chapter 5).

I should also point out that when I say that a given prayer goes back to tannaitic times, I do not mean that each and every word as we have it is equally original. There was a time when liturgists thought that Jewish liturgy had been officially promulgated word for word in all its verbal purity, but that after a period of time in which oral rather than written texts were the norm, those original utterances were necessarily confused: hence, the nineteenth-century search after "the original text" of which I spoke earlier. We now recognize that whereas the themes of any given ritual may have been set as early as the immediate post-70 period, the specific verbal execution of those themes probably varied for many years to come. On the other hand, certain literary genre preferences were already at work, particularly the utilization of the blessing formula, so that variation in wording was tempered by a growing tendency toward formulaic and syntactic fixity.

What we have, then, is the favored blessing format, composed of a fixed introductory clause ("Blessed art thou . . . who") followed by any number of conclusions, all of which, however, would have expressed the same requisite idea: namely, an expression by both *mohel* and father that they were doing their duty according to the terms of the covenant. The father's duty, particularly, will interest us as we proceed.

Act 2: Operation Concluded and Naming

The operation is concluded (M) after which the *mohel* says two blessings (M and N), a short one over wine and a longer one of uncertain meaning that concludes with praise for God who made a covenant (line 49). The *mohel* then continues with O–P, a lengthy prayer that is not formulated in the blessing genre (lines 50–65), but that, among other things, supplies the boy with his name.

Wine is a connecting symbol throughout. The first blessing (M) is over wine, which, however, is not drunk, but is apparently held in abeyance until the final prayer (O–P), which introduces the theme of blood with a citation from Ezekiel ("I saw you wallowing in your blood. . . . In your blood, live"), after which the wine is placed on the child's lips. Wine as a symbol of blood will occupy our attention in chapter 6.

How much of this second act is tannaitic? The blessing over wine (lines 41–42) is definitely attested to as being in existence at that early date, as it is contained in the Mishnah's list of blessings over food.[14] But can we be sure that the blessing was said as part of this rite? Wine was ubiquitous in first-century religious ritual, not only among Jews but in Christian and pagan circles also, so its presence would not surprise us. But there are problems connected with that easy assumption, as we shall see. At the moment, we should be wary of dating the inclusion of this blessing in the rite too early. We should say simply that even though the blessing was available, it was not necessarily used here by the Tannaim who gave the rite its basic shape. It was added sometime later, probably in the amoraic period, or even later still. The reason for its addition as well as the process by which it was appended become important for us later in our analysis.

Unlike the blessing over wine, which was said on many occasions, the second of the two blessings (N) is clearly intended just for circumcision and is included among the earliest reports that we have of the rite. We shall see that it is linked to the rivalry between tannaitic Judaism and early Christianity (see chapter 6).

For the moment, let us posit a tannaitic dating for the second blessing, probably a tannaitic or amoraic use of wine, and the addition of a blessing over that wine at some unknown late amoraic date or even later still.

The really questionable item is the lengthy prayer (O), which is nowhere to be found in either tannaitic or amoraic literature. When should it be dated?

The answer to this question is far from certain, and since it constitutes a lengthy discussion in and of itself, I have postponed it until chapter 5. Suffice it to state my conclusion now, however. On the grounds of content and of textual evidence, I am inclined to see the prayer originating with the introduction of the wine (though before the blessing over wine, which came later), probably during the tannaitic or early amoraic era. It therefore constitutes a part of the fabric of meaning that interests us here.

Conclusion

The *mohel* says a final prayer of intent, introducing a new theme, sacrifice (Q), and then a prayer for the child's health (R), to which is appended the same wish that we found in the public response to the father's benediction in act 1 (lines 38–39). The final unit (S) appends a standard prayer called the Alenu. Composed in the second or third century (usually dated to the former) and intended as an introduction to the shofar liturgy of Rosh Hashanah, the Alenu eventually was adapted as a concluding prayer for all daily services. The latter adaptation occurred in Europe around 1300.[15]

Anthropologists distinguish a rite proper from its surrounding swirl of typical activity. The former is the "game" while the latter is the "spectacle." [16] For example, college or professional football games are often accompanied by what has come to be known as "tailgating"—a ritualized display of picnicking and cooking out adjacent to the tailgates of pickup trucks driven to the stadium parking lot hours before the game begins. Concert premieres often are preceded or followed by lavish cocktail parties for the patrons. Friday night Sabbath services in Reform temples are almost invariably followed by the serving of coffee and desserts (colloquially referred to as the *oneg*), the preparation of which is sometimes assigned as an "honor" to a family celebrating a life-cycle milestone. Fourth- and fifth-century Christian funerals featured lavish graveside feasting,[17] and Moroccan Jews venerate their saints not only by visiting the graveside in a ritual called the Hillula, but by spending the rest of the day in a sort of carnival atmosphere that includes elaborate feasting on meat that is slaughtered and barbecued on the spot.[18] The "central" ritual in each case, that for which people claim to have come in the first place—whether the Giants-Redskins game, the opening concert of the philharmonic season, Sabbath prayers, the death of a neighbor, or the anniversary visit to the grave of a revered rabbi—is the game. The surrounding activity is the spectacle. Not all spectacles include eating, but many do; the rite of circumcision seems to fall into that category. Section Q provides a transition from the game of circumcision to its accompanying spectacle, a ritual meal.

Games derive their official meanings from those charged with giving their official interpretations. Sportswriters churn out thousands of pages on the significance of the Giants-Redskins rivalry while theologians are not reticent to offer explanations of why we accompany the dead to their final resting place, or what the Sabbath liturgy is all about. Music critics avidly review this year's treatment of Beethoven's masterpieces, and North African rabbis know exactly why saints deserve visitations each year. But officials tend to ignore the surrounding spectacle, which exists just as surely as the game, but is considered unofficial, and therefore unimportant, by the experts who are charged with guarding the game in all its purity. In their view, the spectacle may even be threatening in that it encroaches on the centrality of the game. The truth is, many people attend football games as much for the tailgating as for the sport that follows. Theologian Tom O'Meara, for instance, notes that on any given football weekend, thousands of fans travel miles to the University of Notre Dame, even though they know in advance that they have no hope of buying tickets for the game, which has been completely sold out for months.[19] They are there for the spectacle. Similarly, whether or not theologians agree with the people's judgment, Jews who find no refreshments following services are apt to be more upset than if they attended the *oneg* but had to do without a sermon. Spectacles carry public meanings, if not official ones, and we ignore these meanings only at our peril.

As we move to chapter 5, we prepare ourselves for an analysis not only of the game but also of the spectacle: the official lines of the ritual script and the unofficial ways of doing things—whether before, during, or after the rite. We include such things as what gets done with the wine and the circumcised foreskin as well as who presents the baby to the circumciser as the ceremony is about to begin. Chapter 5 reconstructs some elementary cultural assumptions implicit in specific parts of the rabbinic rite as it was practiced in the tannaitic-amoraic era. Subsequent chapters look more globally at the rite, identifying its major symbols and its broad cultural implications.

c h a p t e r *5*

Reconstructing the Rabbinic Meaning System

Important questions remain to be answered before we can determine the outlines of the circumcision ceremony as practiced in the first several centuries C.E. We know that the entire introduction that initiates our current practice had yet to be invented—that is, there was no Elijah's chair, no Elijah ritual, and no *sandek.* Aside from the father and the *mohel,* there were an unknown number of bystanders present, including (as we shall see in chapter 7) the mother, who probably held the child.

The liturgy began with the father and *mohel* saying blessings (K). After the father's blessing, the bystanders responded (L), but the nature of that response deserves attention. Here, as in all discussions that follow, I replicate the text from Chapter 4.

The Response by the Bystanders (L)

As we have it, the rite calls for the following:

K. The father, or the *sandek* (if there is no father) says: "Blessed art Thou, Lord our God, King of the Universe, who has sanctified us by your commandments, and commanded us to admit him [the child] to the covenant of Abraham our father."

L. Those present respond: "As he has entered the covenant, so may he enter Torah, marriage, and good deeds."

These texts are first cited in the Tosefta and the two Talmuds; all three sources agree that they are tannaitic. The Babli has precisely what we say today:

Our Rabbis taught: The person doing the circumcising says . . .
[Blessed art Thou . . .] who has sanctified us by his commandments,
and commanded us concerning circumcision; the father says . . .
[Blessed art Thou . . . who has commanded us] to admit him to the
covenant of Abraham our father; the bystanders say, "As he entered
the covenant, so may he enter Torah, marriage, and good deeds." [1]

By the eighth century, the Abbasid caliphate had established Baghdad
as the center of the Muslim empire, with the result that Jewish authorities (the
Geonim) in the area were able to codify the practices of their own literary
tradition (the Babylonian) as normative. Current practice thus follows the
Babli.

But the Babli text of the bystanders' response does not reflect tannaitic
practice. To begin with, the Babli manuscripts themselves differ from the
printed edition in that instead of "As he has entered . . . so may he enter"—a
third-person construction referring to the child—we get a formula in the second person addressed to the *father,* "As you admitted him to the covenant, so
may you admit him to Torah. . . ." [2] This variant talmudic reading is carried in
most versions of the Tosefta and the Yerushalmi as well. [3]

Moreover, after the completion of the Talmud, we enter a new era in
Jewish history known as geonic. Exactly when it began is hard to say, but from
the middle of the ninth century until early in the eleventh, it was marked by
influential responsa sent to Jewish communities worldwide from celebrated
authorities on Judaism in and around Baghdad known as Geonim (sing.:
Gaon). [4] One Gaon, Rav Amram bar Sheshna, wrote a lengthy responsum to
Jews in Northern Spain in which he recorded a comprehensive description of
Jewish ritual practice in his day. Some fifty years later, another Gaon, Saadiah,
wrote a second prayer book. If we examine both of these books for their version of the response, we see that the only form they know is the variant text in
the second person. [5]

The change from second to third person is not the only variation
introduced. As we have it today (in the third-person form), the burden of the
bystanders' ritualized response is that just as the boy has "entered" the covenant, so may he some day "enter" other states of being. But the alternative
second-person versions in our various manuscripts and printed editions disagree as to the states that the child should be expected to reach. Whereas we

wish (with the Babli) that he find his way to "Torah, marriage, and good deeds," the nearly unanimous opinion of the manuscripts, and even of the printed alternatives, is that the proper wish is just for "Torah and marriage."[6]

The tannaitic onlookers differed also in that they intended more than just a pious wish for the child's future. The Babli records that they "say" their part, but the Babli's use of a present principle [*omrim*] is, here as elsewhere, ambiguous; it can indeed mean only that they "say" it, but it may equally connote that they "*must* say" it.[7] The Yerushalmi makes clear that the latter is intended. It rules explicitly, "Those standing there *must say* [*tserikhim lomar*], 'As you admitted. . . .'"[8] This, then, is no mere report of what bystanders usually did, as if upon witnessing a boy's circumcision they were generally moved to wish him well for other milestones in his life. We will grasp the full force of this rite only if we recognize it as *a ceremonial celebration of the obligation that binds men to each other in rabbinic culture.* This is a fully ritualized event in which a father's required benediction over his mandatory act of circumcising his son is followed by an equally required response by the men in attendance, reminding him that he has other things that he will eventually have to do for his son. In the corrected second-person version, we therefore find the men telling the father, "Just as you [did this for your son], so may you," or, better, "so you *shall*" do the other things that fathers owe their sons under their covenantal obligation.

Circumcision was no life-cycle ceremony for a newborn; it was a ritualization of male status within Judaism. Understanding gender as a social category that defines the set of roles appropriate to each sex, we can say that circumcision's primary meaning was social, not biological. It affirmed (1) the admission of a baby boy into the covenant, (2) at the hands of his male sponsor, preferably his father. Moreover, except for the mother, it is men alone who are featured in all the rabbinic stories about circumcision.[9] The gospel account of John's circumcision is ambiguous regarding who came, but there, too, the only named woman is Elizabeth, John's mother (Luke 1:39–56). So, (3) the event was duly witnessed by other males.

In sum: Circumcision was a rite of masculine status bestowal in which one man, the father, initiates a man-to-be, his son, into the covenant with God (conceived of as a man). Other men who witness the event acknowledge that the father has done his duty while at the same time reminding him that his covenantal mentor relationship with his son is not yet over. Twice more will the father do his covenantal duty vis-à-vis his son: introducing him to Torah (the sacred content of the covenant) and marrying him off (so that he can have his own male children and extend the covenant one more generation).

I have here only begun my discussion of what I shall refer to as a "male lifeline." Later evidence for it is overwhelming. For the time being, however, I want to indicate that the third-person construction of our present rite, coupled with its additional words, "and good deeds," might erroneously be taken as simply the pious hope that this child enjoy a good and happy life. We might mistakenly jump to the conclusion that circumcision is just the first life-cycle ceremony for a Jewish child who just happens in this instance to be a boy, and that he will later grow up and enjoy other ceremonies that (unlike this one) he will share with girls. We would be guilty of misreading this rite as the first of many that celebrate the life cycle of an "individual," whereas, in fact, my very point is that it was not the generic life of a universal "individual" but the covenantal life of a man that was being celebrated. Again, the evidence is not all in for this claim, but I will say more, especially in chapter 6.

Rites proclaim social facts that are beyond empirical definition. They erect states of being that define a priori what empirical reality is taken as being. Rites of initiation thus posit social states into which the initiants are inducted. The classical construction of states through which people pass in traditional rabbinic culture, however, has little to do with "individuals" and everything to do with individual "men." The rabbinic rites that celebrate human life do not constitute a story of individuals who are born, grow up, and die; they proclaim instead an eternal covenant carried by males from father to son throughout the generations. Circumcision in the rabbinic system of meanings is the first ritualized display of what matters—not individual people, but the corporate covenant of Torah that transcends them all, and thus, secondarily, the men who carry its sign stamped upon their flesh.

The father's covenantal obligations are not succinctly defined in tannaitic literature, but the Talmud turns to them, citing them in the names of tannaitic predecessors and seeking scriptural bases for the various opinions of what it is that fathers owe their children. But is it "their children" or "their sons"? The Hebrew word *banim* can mean either, but the singular *ben* or its variants—*beno,* for example—can only be "son," "his son," and the like. And that is what we get here. We hear, for example:

A man deserves a son who is (1) well formed (2) strong (3) wealthy (4) wise and (5) long lived. . . . And just as he deserves a son with five qualities, so too he owes him five things: he must (1) give him food and (2) drink; (3) give him clothes and (4) shoes; (5) and guide him.[10]

Nor is this just a convenient use of the male antecedent to mean both male and female children. The various descriptions of the ideal parental relationship as well as the biblical citations used to buttress them demonstrate that it is fathers, not parents, and sons, not children, who are the issue. Discussion of a "wise" son, for example, elicits a reference to educating one's son in Torah, a privilege that is, in general, expressly allotted to boys, not girls. I do not mean to say that tannaitic fathers had no duties toward their daughters and wives. But the responsibilities owed by a man to his children are gender specific, at best asymmetric; and considered in terms of covenantal continuity, it is the father-son nexus that matters.

A well-known mishnaic ruling summarizes the Rabbis' conception of the obligations linking covenanted males: "All commandments that devolve upon the father with respect to the son are incumbent upon men, but women are exempt from them."[11] In other words, covenantal obligations go from father to son, not from mother to son or even parent to son, and certainly not from parent to daughter, not even from mother to daughter, a relationship that does not officially exist for the Rabbis the way the father-son relationship does. Not for nothing does the Passover seder, the covenantal celebration par excellence, feature the ritualized instruction of sons by fathers, and even (eventually, though not at first) the inclusion of some tannaitic lore on the four kinds of son a man may have.[12]

The Mishnah on paternal obligation prompts an amoraic discussion of responsibilities that is summarized neatly in a later commentary by the Italian authority Obadiah Bertinoro (c. 1450–before 1516). It is an accurate and therefore useful synopsis of early rabbinic opinion.

> "All commandments that devolve upon the father with respect to the son": these are commandments that devolve upon a father, things he must do to his son, and they are six in number: circumcise him, redeem him (if he is a firstborn), teach him Torah, teach him a trade, marry him off, and teach him how to swim.[13]

What interests us here are the specifically covenantal duties on the list: the religious obligations that have nothing to do with keeping a child in good health, say, or caring for minors until they grow up and can care for themselves. We have three obvious ones: circumcision, redemption, and Torah study—to which we should add marriage, which the Rabbis define as a covenantal responsibility (see chapter 7). Not so teaching your son a trade, or instructing him how to swim, or feeding him, clothing him, and so on. Redemption, however, is relevant only for firstborn sons, so if we include only *the chain of things covenantally required of all fathers for all sons,* we get circumcision, Torah study, and marriage.

Now we see the full impact of what transpires at a circumcision as the men looking on address the father. The father has performed his first obligatory act: circumcising his son. The men thus charge him with the others: "Just as you admitted him to the covenant, so admit him to Torah study and the marriage canopy." As long as we imagine that "good deeds" was originally included in the list, we will not recognize the class of activities of which these acts are members. But if "good deeds" was added only later on, the original class (without "good deeds") becomes unmistakable. It is the class of covenantal duties (Torah and marriage) remaining after this first duty (circumcision) has been completed.

The Blessing over Wine (M) in Act 2

We normally assume that the use of wine accompanied by a blessing in Jewish ritual is an old tradition, probably from the tannaitic era. As we saw above, wine turns up everywhere in second-century rites, whether Jewish, Christian, or pagan. The Jewish blessing over wine is attested to in the Mishnah. But there is reason to wonder whether that commonsense presumptive dating is warranted here.

To begin with, none of our early circumcision texts include the blessing: not the Tosefta nor either of the Talmuds. If we want to imagine that the blessing was in force nonetheless, but not necessarily cited because its use was taken for granted, or because it was not germane to circumcision (or something like that), we may be right, but we may be wrong also. Arguments from silence are hardly probative.

Buttressing our suspicion that the blessing over wine is not cited because it was not yet being said is the existence of two anomalies with regard to the recitation of the blessing in the context of the rite as it had developed by the Middle Ages. We noted above that by the third century rules about the blessing genre began to proliferate. One such rule required that the blessing formula include God's name. But rules have unintended consequences, and the determination that blessings would henceforth mention the name of God raised the specter that people might say the blessing on an occasion where it was not required, with the unhappy result that, technically speaking, God's name would have been invoked needlessly, which is to say, God's name would have been taken in vain. In order to avoid saying a blessing in vain over a particular food or act, late third- and early fourth-century discussions prescribe that people should make sure to eat the food or perform the act on account of which the blessing is said, and to do so immediately after the blessing in question has been recited. For simplicity's sake, let us label the rule in question as the *Rule of Proper Use,* by which we mean the talmudic rule regarding blessings that is intended specifically to prevent their being said in vain, and that achieves its aim by insisting that people who recite blessings over things must make proper use of those things immediately after the blessings are recited.[14]

Thus, for example, even today in Orthodox Jewish circles where the Rule of Proper Use is still studiously applied, it is common to begin a meal by saying a blessing over bread, and then immediately afterward, without any intervening conversation whatever, to taste a piece of bread. Similarly, on such occasions as the recurrence of an annual holy day, or upon eating the first fruits of one's harvest, or even donning new clothes, rabbinic tradition specifies a blessing to thank God "for keeping us alive, sustaining us, and bringing us to this season." Modern rabbis consider the possibility of extending the use of this blessing also for birthdays, events that premodern Jewish culture rarely noted at all, and which in any event have merely secular significance even for those who do observe them. But again to avoid the possibility of saying a blessing in vain, Orthodox authorities encourage Jews who do use this blessing for birthdays to eat some fresh fruit or put on new clothes immediately afterward, just in case birthdays should not have been included in the contemporary list of events for which the blessing ought to be said. The blessing that otherwise would have been mistakenly said over birthdays would thus still "count" in that it is followed by the proper use of an item for which the blessing is appropriate.[15]

Given the care with which the Rabbis mandated that food blessings anticipate enjoyment of the food in question (that is, its proper use), it is surprising to find in our ritual the pouring of a glass of wine along with a benediction over it, without, however, anyone drinking the wine!

Since the logical consistency of Jewish law implies that blessing regulations ought to hold universally, authorities through the centuries have sought some legal fiction to explain why the Rule of Proper Use is not followed here. Their efforts were hampered because they had no evolutionary conception of how Jewish law unfolded. The problem actually is that as Jewish law changed, late rules conflicted with early precedent, so that absolute consistency, though in theory necessary, was in practice impossible. Thus the Rule of Proper Use was not introduced until the talmudic era (third–fourth centuries), by which time the circumcision rite (which is tannaitic) was largely in place. Had the blessing over wine already been there, we should have expected a talmudic attempt to explain away the fact that the Rule of Proper Use does not apply to circumcision wine. But we get no such discussions until the geonic age and later. Suppose, however, that the wine blessing was added to the circumcision ceremony only *after* the rule had been imposed—after the editing of most talmudic strata but before the end of the geonic period. That would explain why the apparent breach of the Rule of Proper Use is questioned only by Geonim and their successors, and also why geonic manuals cite the blessing in this context whereas talmudic discussion does not.

We might well wonder why the blessing was added at all, given the assumption that the Rabbis would not lightly have mandated a blessing where none is called for. True, they held strongly to the belief that "one should consume nothing before saying a blessing over it,"[16] but, as we have seen, the wine went unconsumed. It functioned symbolically in a way that we have yet to identify.

In sum, we cannot know for sure exactly when the blessing over wine was introduced into the circumcision rite, but it could not have been there yet during the tannaitic or amoraic periods, even though the blessing was known and used in other contexts by that time. The *use* of wine in our rite—albeit unaccompanied by a blessing and in a manner that we have yet to describe—*does* go back to the tannaitic era. Several centuries thereafter the benediction was added, leading post-talmudic authorities to address the oddity of its being there given the fact that no one actually *drank* the wine. I suspect that it was added not by rabbinic enactment at all, but by the folk, who said the blessing elsewhere when they handled wine and did not differentiate here.

We can only estimate when the popular addition of the blessing occurred, but as late as the twelfth century we find the following very interesting testimony by Abraham ben Isaac of Narbonne (d. 1179).

[My teacher] Isaac ben Merwan Halevi was asked what to do about the blessing over wine when the circumcision is held in the synagogue [and, presumably, no wine is at hand]. He answered that [in the circumcision rite] we never say a blessing over wine under any circumstances. This is no different from the case of a blessing over wine [in other circumstances] where there is no wine on hand. We know of the view which likens this to having wine, but after saying the blessing, putting the wine aside until evening, and drinking it then [thus avoiding saying a blessing without drinking the substance, invoking a legal fiction that no time has elapsed between the blessing and the drinking], but we disagree, since it is established to us that once you say the benediction, the wine must immediately be tasted. . . . Therefore we circumcise without a cup of wine.[17]

In other words, people without wine on hand asked the rabbi if they should include a blessing over wine during the circumcision rite anyway. They were informed that circumcision wine is like wine on any other occasion in that a blessing is required only if wine is on hand and drunk (the Rule of Proper Use). But some people who had wine on hand apparently said the blessing and then put the wine aside until the evening meal, at which time they drank it so as to make proper use of it, albeit some hours after the blessing had been recited. Our author rejects this practice. The Rule of Proper Use explicitly demands that the wine be drunk immediately following the blessing. Knowing that circumcision wine is never drunk, he cautions his correspondent that it is better to use no wine at all than to breach the Rule of Proper Use.

The respondent's own words testify inadvertently to the fact that his usage is not the norm. Other people *always* use wine, even though no one drinks it at the circumcision rite, with the result that a legal fiction is customarily applied: wine consumed later in the day is deemed proper use with regard to the circumcision blessing over wine recited earlier. So despite Rabbi Isaac's demurrer, his questioner quite naturally assumed the presence of wine and the blessing at the circumcision rite, as did everyone else in his day. It is probable, therefore, that:

1. The *use* of wine at circumcision goes back to the first several centuries C.E., even though the wine in question was not consumed;

2. only much later, the blessing over wine was appended to the rite, with the result that

3. a conflict now existed with regard to the Rule of Proper Use, so that legal authorities either had to

4. adopt legal fictions to explain away the halakhic infelicity inherent in saying a blessing over wine without drinking from the cup, or

5. (as in Rabbi Isaac's case) do away with the wine—and therefore, with the blessing—altogether.

Let us temporarily move on now to another anomaly that stands out with regard to the wine benediction here. The fourth-century talmudic elaboration of laws pertinent to blessings gave us a second rule as well, which we can call the *Rule of Blessing Strings.* This rule is invoked for a series (or string) of blessings recited in succession.

The issue here is that some blessings exist in what is known as a "long form": that is, rather than simple one-line formulas, they are more like theological "mini-essays" that conclude with a synoptic line called a *chatimah,* or eulogy. The eulogy always begins with a fixed formula, "Blessed art Thou" and then continues with a summary of the act of God for which the blessing is intended, for example, "who brings on evening," the conclusion of the blessing said at sunset. Long blessings may elaborate on the theme for as much as a page before actually summing up the blessing's intent in the eulogy. Some long blessings also start with "Blessed art Thou" before introducing the discussion of the theme that constitutes the blessing's content. But for no apparent reason, other long blessings do not begin that way; they simply launch their discussion without any formulaic introduction at all, reserving "Blessed art Thou" for the first few words of the final eulogy at the end of the blessing.

The Rule of Blessing Strings is a talmudic attempt to regulate the appearance of "Blessed art Thou" at the beginning of long blessings. It mandates that when a series of discrete blessings is combined into a blessing string, only the first blessing should carry the introductory phrase. Despite the rule, however, the liturgy features a number of exceptions, one of the most famous being the wedding benedictions that the Babli ascribes to the Tannaim. The problem there is that the first blessing (over wine, as it happens) is followed by another that also begins with "Blessed art Thou." [18] Similarly, the first blessing of the circumcision rite is a blessing over wine, followed by another blessing that ought not begin with "Blessed art Thou," but does.

We have a simple and probable solution to the anomaly in the marriage rite. The list of blessings as we find it in the Babylonian Talmud is a textual creation designed by the editor for literary purposes. They are examples of alternative wedding blessings originally used singly and interchangeably. It is we, not the Talmud, who refer to them as the "Seven Blessings" (Sheva Berakhot), with the implication that they go together as a unit. The Talmud itself uses the singular, "Bridegroom's Blessing" (Birkat Chatanim). Given what we know about tannaitic liturgy in general, it seems probable that originally a single blessing, known as the bridegroom's blessing, was recited at the groom's home at the time that the bride moved there.[19] But the wording of that blessing, as of all others in use at the time, was not fixed. Various alternatives coexisted or were freely composed on the spot. The editor of the Babli listed several of them, one after the other, inadvertently implying that all of them were said consecutively. No wonder this list does not follow the Rule of Blessing Strings. Except as a literary conceit, it was never a string in the first place.

By contrast, and in support of our reconstruction here, the parallel text in the Palestinian Talmud contains no such list at all. True, the blessings are said as a string today, as they were by geonic times, but that is because their literary appearance in the Babylonian Talmud influenced the geonic authorities to say them all exactly as they appeared in their venerated text.[20]

The same solution can hardly be true of the string of blessings in the circumcision rite, however, for the simple reason that the case of the circumcision texts is precisely the reverse of the case of the wedding text. For weddings, we have a *literary* text that includes a blessing for wine but was not intended as a summary of what people actually did, whereas our circumcision texts are primarily *oral* recollections of the actual rite as observed. In all probability, the tannaitic practice did not include a blessing for wine at all; there was thus no series of blessings to conflict with the Rule of Blessing Strings. Wine was *used,* however, and eventually, as we saw above, the blessing over wine was added. But by then, what had become the second blessing (the one that now followed the blessing over wine) was already fixed with "Blessed art Thou" at its beginning. It could not be altered. Nor could the blessing over wine be placed later in the ceremony where it would not have caused a problem with the Rule of Blessing Strings, since the whole point of adding the blessing was to anticipate pouring the cup of wine, the normal placement of a blessing according to the Rule of Proper Use.

Daniel Sperber confirms the conclusion reached here. He notes that in our current rite, wine is put on the child's lips to drink, yet nowhere in the early literature is that usage called for. He cites various medieval authorities who know the custom, and who read it back to an amoraic Palestinian source whence they claim to have borrowed it.[21] As Sperber sees the development, wine was first used for the mouth of the child, and afterward given also to the mother to effect her recuperation from labor and delivery. Only in the geonic age was a blessing added.[22]

Testimony for the addition comes first from a Gaon, probably, says Sperber (on the basis of an attribution in the geonic collection where this particular communication is found), a Gaon by the name of Tzemach. Unfortunately, we have extant responsa from no fewer than four Geonim by that name: Tzemach bar Paltoi (872–90), Tzemach bar Chaim (879–85), Tzemach bar Kafnai (936–38), and Tzemach bar Isaac (988–97). The editor who collected the geonic texts in question said only that the author is "Rav Tzemach Gaon," without specifying which Tzemach he means.[23] The responsa in the collection are organized according to author, so that clusters of texts are assigned to Rav Tzemachs. But there is no chronological system at work; rather, an editor copied several separate manuscripts, each one carrying responsa attributed to a Gaon named Tzemach, and then arbitrarily combined them into one larger book without differentiating one Tzemach from another. It is therefore difficult to know which Tzemach wrote the responsum in question.

Amram (858–71), too, has the mother drinking the wine for her recovery, and he includes the blessing.[24] All the candidates for our Tzemach lived within a century after Amram died. Moreover, whoever Tzemach was, he takes the use of the blessing for granted; in fact, he is probably the first authority to raise the issue of the Rule of Proper Use, explaining away the blessing by the fact that the mother does in fact drink the wine.[25] So both Tzemach and Amram include a blessing over wine that they consider authoritative. We are probably secure in assuming that the addition of a blessing, probably as a folk custom, was known to most if not to all of the Geonim, some of whom, like Paltoi (842–57) and Amram had occasion to write about it.

In any event, the inclusion of a blessing as part of the official ritual is not original, even though the use of wine within the ceremony was. By the Middle Ages, however, the original function of the wine had been forgotten. Neither European authorities nor their geonic predecessors recognize the original function of the wine, a matter that will loom large as we turn to a final textual conundrum.

The Naming Prayer (O)

We saw above that the naming prayer is not contained in the Mishnah and is cited nowhere in the Tosefta or either Talmud. The normal conclusion would be that it is an addition to the rite, presumably as late as the first source that knows it. If it were added later, however, whoever added it certainly sewed it deftly in place.

The naming prayer symbolically equates blood with wine, an identification that dominates all of act 2, beginning with the fact that the act follows immediately upon that part of the ceremonial action known as *metsitsah,* cauterizing the wound. Blood begins to flow from the time the incision is made, naturally, but only after the foreskin is removed does it appear in abundance, so immediately before act 2, the *mohel* stops it up. That flow of blood is what calls forth the use of wine! I have already referred to wine as a dominant rabbinic symbol, and I shall have a lot more to say about it in the next chapter. For now, I want to lay the groundwork for that discussion.

In chapter 1 I introduced the term "icon" to describe a symbolic item that points to its referent not only because we decide arbitrarily that it should, but by virtue of some inherent characteristic. Our examples were things that the Bible designates as *ot:* the rainbow as an icon of God's promise never to flood the earth again; circumcision as an icon of male fertility. We turn now to wine, an obvious icon for blood.

Jews have usually disliked conceding the iconic property of wine for too reasons. The first is because Christianity depends upon it.

> After supper, [says Paul, speaking of Jesus,] he took the cup, saying, "This cup is the new covenant in my blood. Do this, as often as you drink it, in remembrance of me." For as often as you eat this bread and drink the cup, you proclaim the Lord's death until he comes. Whoever, therefore, eats the bread or drinks the cup of the Lord in an unworthy manner will be answerable for the body and blood of the Lord.[26]

The inherent connection between the Eucharistic wine and the blood of the crucified Christ is well known even to Jews who have never set foot in a church, so that even to entertain the possibility that Christianity shared its symbolism of "wine as blood" with rabbinic Judaism is to court strong denial, usually in the form of the now dubious hypothesis that Christianity developed its symbolism out of its pagan milieu, not from its parental Jewish past. I call this the Radical Disjuncture Hypothesis—the idea that Christianity took aim at all things Jewish and drew its sustenance only from without, never from within. Given the state of current scholarship, which has clearly and abundantly demonstrated the reverse, it should hardly be necessary to point out again that Judaism and Christianity were exceptionally close in their symbolic structure. That is exactly what we will see in chapter 6. Still, there are modern-day Marcions who will find that point difficult to grasp, especially with regard to the icon of wine.

The second reason many Jews find the iconicity of wine as blood so difficult to accept is their knowledge that even though for Christians the symbolic equation *wine = blood* has functioned positively, for Jews it has been catastrophic. Historically speaking, some medieval and even modern authorities have accused Jews of such things as stabbing the Host to make it bleed, or even kidnapping and killing Christian children so as to acquire their blood to bake unleavened bread for the Passover. Ever since 1171, when the blood accusation first was leveled at the Jews of Blois, Jews have understandably reacted strongly against the notion that in the rabbinic tradition, wine actually commemorates blood. To be sure, it was not usually Passover wine but unleavened bread on which accusers fastened their attention. But theological niceties have little impact on visceral responses, and my point is that Jews have acted swiftly to deny that any food, including wine, suggests blood. Needless to say (but I will say it anyway for the sake of emphasis), my claim that Jews and Christians both utilized wine as an icon for blood does not imply that the blood libel has even the remotest shred of plausibility in any of its formulations.

We should not pass lightly over the contiguity between the *mohel*'s act of drawing blood and cauterizing it, and then immediately pouring wine to apply to the child's lips. Now we see why no blessing anticipated this cup. It was not meant to be consumed *as wine* at all, but was instead reserved as an oral transfusion of wine *as blood* for the child. In a nutshell, blood escapes the system; wine as blood enters it.

Moreover, it is at least of interest that the cauterizing method strongly favored by medieval tradition calls on the *mohel* to suck the blood from the wound with his mouth. The Hebrew term, used already in the Mishnah, for this stage of the operation is *metsitsah,* which means "sucking." [27] Recognizing that, technically speaking, the actual circumcision ends prior to the wound being cared for, and wondering, therefore, why *metsitsah* is permitted on the Sabbath, the Talmud ruled that sucking the wound dry protects the child from injury and thus takes precedence over Sabbath prohibitions. [28] This explanation recurs throughout the medieval codes.[29] But it does not explain the necessity of sucking *by the mouth,* a practice preserved staunchly even as late as modern times, when attempts to replace it with more antiseptic means were vigorously rejected by traditionalists. They continued to follow the normal tannaitic cauterizing procedure of sucking the wound orally, which is to say, emulating the act of drinking wine.

When we see, then, the wine being reserved for the infant to drink—a mirror image, so to speak, of the blood being sucked from him at the very same time—and when we observe also the content of the extended prayer that adds Ezekiel's words (lines 55–56): "'I passed by you and saw you wallowing in your blood; and I said to you: 'In your blood, live'; I said to you: 'In your blood, live'" (Ezek. 16:6), we cannot help but notice a certain ritual integrity centering on the symbol of blood. In short: (1) The child's blood flows from the wound, and the *mohel* sucks it out. (2) He pours wine, reserving it briefly for use in the naming prayer. (3) He says a naming prayer that includes the words from Ezekiel, "'In your blood, live,'" after which he puts the wine (as blood) on the baby's lips.

The naming prayer is also a healing prayer, for it says, "sustain this child to his father and mother"—that is, let the newly circumcised child regain his health. We shall see more clearly in chapter 6 that it presents the Ezekiel reference as a double entendre, taking the "blood" from verse 16:6 as denoting the blood of circumcision, to which the Rabbis imputed salvific power. In addition, as we have seen already, one cannot escape the parallelism between the blood of Ezekiel and the wine that the child is given precisely after the verse is cited. The wine, in other words, is treated as if it is about to become blood in the child's system. By it he will be healed, or, quoting Ezekiel, "By your blood, [you will] live."[30]

This sequence certainly seems like a discrete liturgical unit built upon the common icon of wine as blood, even if the naming prayer that cites Ezekiel is unrecorded in the early strata. Still, an anthropological approach that reads connections between actions and words ought ideally to have at least some textual indication that the necessary words were spoken during the historical era when the meaning that the words are said to support was in existence. In the field, the anthropologist can observe the immediate "text" of people's lives: what they do and say in a given ritual performance is assumed to have some inherent connection. If we want to argue that things from two *written* texts belong together, it is desirable at least to know that what they report actually occurred contiguously in the time in question. Thus, the fact that section O (the naming prayer and its reference to Ezekiel) is absent from our extant texts is at least somewhat troubling.

There are, however, several independent *textual* reasons for believing that O was once part of the textual corpus in the amoraic era, if not earlier. First, it is obvious that the Mishnah gives us no complete listing of everything people did. Were we to depend completely on its own witness for the time, we would have no idea about a number of things—for example, the growth of synagogues and the way they were built, a matter known to us only from archaeological evidence. From the texts alone, we would know only that synagogues existed, but we would be sadly misled as to their shape, function, and symbolism. We would be unable to predict the art of Dura, the mosaic floor of Bet Alpha, and the variations in exposure, sometimes toward Jerusalem, but not always so.[31] The case of circumcision is similar: we know that people practiced circumcision, but the only reason we know about some of the details—the act of *metsitsah,* for example—is the coincidence that circumcision was carried out on the Sabbath, so that the Mishnah had to include it in its discussion of Sabbath work limitations. We thus get a partial discussion of the circumcision regulations that were in effect, but only accidentally, as an adjunct to a debate on the rules of work relative to Sabbath observance.[32]

The act of *metsitsah* is not the only detail that the Mishnah does not record as part of a larger discussion of circumcision. Even the basic prayer texts cannot be found there! As we have seen, the texts of the rite come from the Tosefta and the Talmuds. Obviously, the Mishnah had little interest in recording the prayers said at the time, but that omission did not prevent our accepting the testimony of the Tosefta and the Talmuds to the effect that a ritual occurred.

However, we are similarly hampered by the selective rules of inclusion that governed even the Tosefta and the Talmuds. They, too, were not put together by an editor intent on giving moderns a comprehensive description of rites. Clearly, we cannot assume that every text we now have in a rite goes back to the time when some version of the rite was in effect, but when we find a text that fits as well as this one does, and when we know on separate grounds that the other texts with which it fits belong to a particular era, we are entitled to posit the possibility, at least, that this text belongs there too—especially if we have an independent textual history that suggests the same thing.

Neither Amram's text (c. 850) nor Saadiah's (c. 920) includes our prayer, but in its place they carry two fascinating prayers of their own, the petition for the mother's healing that I mentioned above and a prayer for the welfare of the child, in conjunction with which the child is named.[33] Now the omission of a naming prayer in the pregeonic corpus is an oddity in and of itself. That boys were named at their circumcisions in tannaitic times is evident from many sources, including the pericope about John (Luke 1:59, 2:1).[34] Moreover, Amram's prayer is not phrased in the normal Hebrew but in Aramaic, and not even in the Babylonian dialect that Amram otherwise used. It is unmistakably Palestinian. Yet it was characteristic of Amram to polemicize against Palestinian customs that ran counter to Babylonian precedent. The purpose of his celebrated responsum on prayer was to urge new Jewish communities, especially in Europe, to eschew Palestinian teaching and to follow instead the Judaism preached by the Babylonian gaonate.[35] The only exceptions to this rule were customs that may have originated in Palestine but had spread to Babylonia so long ago that their origin had been forgotten. Amram's circumcision prayers in Palestinian Aramaic must be among them. They, too, must have originated in tannaitic or early amoraic Palestine, even though the authoritative texts of the Land of Israel did not preserve them for us.

I said above, in connection with the bridegroom's blessing, that tannaitic liturgy was characterized by alternative expositions of identical prayer rubrics. The themes were set, even though the ways in which those themes were carried out were not. The presence of one prayer on a given theme, therefore, does not vitiate the possibility of there being others that circulated simultaneously; on the contrary, it raises the expectation that there had to be others around. But to be characterized as such, they would have to have some similarity in theme and occur in the same place in the liturgical flow of prayers.

Saadiah's prayer book is somewhat vague on the details of the ritual action; his concern was primarily to provide us with an authoritative text.[36] But Amram describes how things were done.

1. The blessings of the *mohel* and father (J–L) were recited.
2. A cup of wine was poured (M).
3. The benediction over wine and the blessing that praises God for making the covenant (M–N) were said.
4. A healing and naming prayer (carried also in Saadiah and known to Tzemach) was recited (in the same place as our prayer labeled O).
5. The wine was tasted by the mother.[37]

Why the mother drank the wine was an anomaly to Amram and to Tzemach, both of whom felt constrained to explain it. Tzemach was even able to use the fact that she drank it as an excuse for the blessing over wine that had crept into the rite by his day. We will see (in chapter 9) that by the Middle Ages, all women, even the child's mother, were forbidden to attend a circumcision; hence the current rite does not recognize the mother at all. But other than the absence of the mother as a ritual actor, our rite is structured exactly as Amram's was, except that instead of Amram's prayer for naming we have our own.

We should conclude, therefore, that Amram's prayer and our own, being on the same theme and in the same liturgical place, are probably equally early alternatives on the theme of naming and healing.[38] Our prayer begins, "Sustain this child . . . and let his name in Israel be," exactly what Amram's prayer accomplishes, sustaining the child in his time of recovery and giving him a name.

Independent testimony confirms that our prayer goes back to an early age. The twelfth-century authority, Eliezer ben Joel Halevi tells us explicitly that he saw a copy of our prayer in the Palestinian Talmud.[39] It will be recalled that Avigdor Aptowitzer cites other European rabbis who concur as to the existence of old Palestinian material that we do not find in our version of the Palestinian Talmud.[40] Thus, there is every reason to grant the possibility that the prayer under discussion is an authentically tannaitic fragment that did not make it into the official texts that were bequeathed to us.

Why does it matter? Because I will claim in the next chapter that the dominant symbol for the Rabbis was blood, by which they claimed to be saved. The public meanings expressed by that hope are nowhere as evident as in this prayer. Therefore, we must ask when this prayer came into being. I say again that I have no necessary bias in favor of antiquity; it really does not matter to me when we date the piece. But the evidence at this point suggests that we have a coherent tannaitic conviction that blood is salvific, and that the Rabbis' concern for the topic led to the inclusion of the prayer as we have it.

chapter 6

Wine, Blood, and Salvation
in Rabbinic Judaism

The practice of circumcision is not the sole instance of the Rabbis' radical reconstruction of Judaism well beyond its biblical roots. But it is typical. They retained the biblical precedent of circumcision as a covenant rite for males, just as the priestly editor of the Bible would have hoped, but then outfitted it with a liturgy of the word that no biblical Jew could remotely have predicted. They thereby adumbrated a new conception of the Jewish compact with God. Gone is the agricultural imagery; gone, too, is the fertility concern that had so motivated earlier generations. Instead, we get the rabbinic notion of salvation, symbolized by the blood of circumcision, which saves.

If we want to know what matters most in a rite, ask the people who do it what must be done for it to count. In the case of Judaism, that is relatively easy since the legalities are spelled out in some detail. Even a cursory look at the legal corpus demonstrates clearly that the essential event was not the cutting and removing of the foreskin—though that was necessary, of course—so much as it was the shedding of blood. According to Jewish law, if boys are born circumcised they must still have a token drop of blood drawn ritually from their already circumcised penis. Similarly, we have the case of male converts to Judaism, who become social beings in the Jewish community by being circumcised; if they are already circumcised from childhood, they, too, must undergo the drawing of blood.[1]

This symbolic centrality of blood should surprise us, since a cross-cultural survey of the many groups who practice circumcision reveals that, in general, it is not the drawing of blood that matters.[2] To be sure, blood does serve as one of many symbols, even an important symbol in some cases, such as the Ndembu rite as interpreted by Turner. He associates the red blood with what he calls the "dominant symbol" in the immediate postcircumcision phase of his Ndembu ritual, the red mukula tree under which the novices sit until their wounds stop bleeding.[3] But the blood and its mukula tree referent are not central. A great many other things figure far more prominently: the white milk tree, for instance, under which the operation is performed, or the chikoli tree under which the novices' parents assemble. If anything, it is the ritualized movement from tree to tree that matters most. But the rabbinic case is altogether different. It is virtually impossible to read very far in the set of rabbinic texts where circumcision is described without encountering repeated references to the blood of circumcision, the sine qua non of this classic Jewish rite.

We have already seen the centrality of blood in the ritual script. There are explicit references to blood, such as the citation from Ezekiel, "In your blood, live." There are implicit references as well, as in the use of wine to suggest a transfusion for the boy who has just lost blood in the circumcision procedure. We now need to go farther in our analysis of blood as the central symbol of circumcision. We need, in other words, to do the sort of thing anthropologists do when they ask people to describe in an open-ended way what they think they are about. Jewish legal material is distinctly unsuitable for that task, as legal rulings are frequently apodictic; they often withhold the very interpretive explanations that we require. It may be that as legal systems go, Jewish jurisprudence was more exegetical than most,[4] but even so, insofar as we limit ourselves to its legal dictates, we will miss the introspective analysis of cultural meaning that we seek. Hence we turn to that part of rabbinic literature that is not strictly legal, the sources known as midrash or *aggadah*. Our midrash collections span the centuries from the period of the Mishnah until roughly the turn of the millennium 800 years later. Comments of an aggadic character are included also within the Talmuds, where they sometimes play a legal role (a story used as a legal precedent, for instance), even though the literary form in which they appear is not legal but exegetical or narrative in nature.

Our use of rabbinic *aggadah* on circumcision parallels exactly the sort of native judgment on cultural symbols that is commonplace in anthropological descriptions. For example, take Turner's testimony, "I asked Ndembu specialists as well as laymen to interpret the symbols of their ritual" and, as a result, "obtained much exegetical material."[5] As a commentary on the Bible, midrash may seem far removed from direct native explication of a rite that the anthropologist observes in the field. But Jewish ritual is saturated with biblical allusion, and what the Rabbis have to say about what the Bible means frequently sheds light on their ritual practice as well. *Students of rabbinic culture thus have rabbinic exegesis of sacred writ just as Turner and his students had oral exegesis of sacred acts.*

Rabbinic attention to biblical text parallels a culture's concern for its ritual acts in more ways than one. In both instances, for example, it is precise detail that counts. With ritual, even the smallest word or gesture is ripe with significance for ritual actors who are in the know. Who does what and when matters greatly, as, for instance, under what tree the novice sits as the Ndembu rite proceeds. Ritual thus tends toward invariance with regard to the semiotic web of little details in which the ritual meanings are encoded.[6] So, too, in sacred writ, a text that tends toward the invariability of canon, the Rabbis assume that even the tiniest grammatical point has extractable meaning that must be mined.

Then, too, Turner speaks of *symbolic condensation* whereby a given symbol means many things at the same time: the chikoli tree, for instance, "represents among other things, an erect phallus, adult masculinity, strength, hunting prowess, and health continuing into old age."[7] More than any other genre of rabbinic literature, midrash, too, offers instances in which a single sacred word is endowed with multiple meanings. The word of Scripture no less than the word or act of a rite is both multivocal and symbolic; both are examples of symbolic condensation. The Rabbis begin by elucidating a problem in the text. What does a given biblical word mean? Why could Adam and Eve eat from this tree but not from that one? Who spoke to Moses? What was Aaron wearing, and why? These are the verbal signifiers at work in rabbinic language games. Each question generates a set of alternative solutions that from a purely logical point of view are mutually exclusive of each other, but they are allowed to coexist in the religious imagination of the midrashist, who sees many different meanings at work all at the same time. Without apology, the rabbinic editors of our midrashic texts state one meaning, and then say "Another meaning is . . ." (*davar acher*) to introduce another equally valid interpretation of the term in question. In the exegesis of ritual as of text, experts may hold diverse but equally correct interpretations of what little things mean.

In providing his examples of the different meanings inherent in the milk tree, Turner uses two classificatory oppositions that will prove helpful here:

1. Symbols may be classified first of all as leaning either toward an *ideo-*

logical or a *sensory* pole. If sap from a tree symbolizes breast milk, it is sensory; if it signifies the idea of a life force in the cosmos, it is ideological.

2. Symbolic values may further be understood as either *instrumental* or *dominant*. Instrumental symbols are simply means toward ends, albeit with their own exegetical richness so they are by no means unimportant. Dominant symbols, however, are relatively fixed points in culture; their meanings "refer to values that are regarded as ends in themselves, that is, to axiomatic values."[8]

Both oppositions are relative, especially the latter, which seeks to measure the extent to which a symbol serves as a magnetic focus for much that a culture offers. Turner speaks of trees and medicine as these are used in the circumcision rite. But similar conclusions about other things might just as easily have been drawn from any rabbinic work of midrash. There, too, the constitutive parts of the text are equated with a variety of significata, which are easily placed on either the *ideological* or the *sensory* poles and may be viewed as either *dominant* or *instrumental*. Wine and blood as symbols of circumcision are what interest us here. They occur in the rite and in the rabbinic exegesis on the Bible as well. To the extent that red wine symbolizes blood, it is obviously sensory, but it is also instrumental in that it functions as a pointer in a chain of symbolic reasoning that eventuates in the dominant symbol of blood. Ultimately I mean to explore blood as a dominant symbol in rabbinic Judaism—not just men's blood, but women's blood as well. We shall see in chapter 9 that *blood is a dominant and ideological symbol* for the Rabbis, elucidating by its very nature the gender dichotomy that undergirds their system.

Let us begin with the naming prayer (o) of act 2, which I reproduce here for ready reference.

> Our God and God of our fathers, sustain this child to his father and to his mother, and let his name in Israel be (so-and-so, son of so-and-so, his father). Let the father rejoice in what has come forth from his loins, and let the mother be happy with the fruit of her womb, as it is written: "Let your father and mother rejoice, and let her that bore you be happy" (Prov. 23:25). And it is said, "I passed by you and saw you wallowing in your blood, and I said to you: In your blood, live; I said to you: 'In your blood, live" (Ezek. 16:6).

The *mohel* now puts some wine on the child's mouth with his finger, and continues:

And it is said, "He has remembered his covenant forever, the word He commanded to a thousand generations, the covenant which He made with Abraham, his oath to Isaac, and what He confirmed to Jacob as a statute, to Israel as an everlasting covenant" (Ps. 105:8–10). And it is said, "Abraham circumcised Isaac his son when he was eight days old, just as God had commanded him" (Gen. 21:4). "Give thanks to the Lord for He is good; His mercy lasts forever" (Ps. 118:1). May this little child, (so-and-so), grow up. Just as he has entered the covenant, so may he enter Torah, marriage, and good deeds.

Our interest, obviously, is in the verse from Ezekiel. I have already noted the legal requirement to draw blood even from the penis of a child born circumcised and from converts to Judaism who have already undergone circumcision as non-Jews. If we are still not convinced of the symbolic centrality of blood in this rite of the covenant, the inclusion of this apparently irrelevant verse from Ezekiel should put us on guard as to its importance. For what has Ezekiel to do with circumcision? Why include his reference to "wallowing in . . . blood"? Since the context of Ezekiel 16 is not circumcision at all, what then is the connection with circumcision, if not the presumed link between blood and salvation—"In your blood, live!"—which the Rabbis take as emphasizing the salvific symbolism of covenantal blood? Salvation, I grant, is a concept I have not introduced here. We therefore need to demonstrate how kinds of blood—circumcision blood especially, but (as we shall see) distinctly *not* menstrual blood—were symbols of salvation.

Our best source of rabbinic exegesis on this point is a midrashic compendium known as *Pirkei deRabbi Eliezer,* which we can date not later than the ninth century but which has earlier material within it. The common motif of blood that saves runs from beginning to end of this lengthy excursus, drawing together blood of circumcision, blood of the sacrificial system, and blood of the paschal lamb, all of which are designated as vehicles of salvation. The very form of the report recalls Turner's Ndembu exegetical material, for blood here is a condensed symbol to which many equally valid meanings may be said to apply. Because the text as given in the original source is long and rambling, in the interests of facilitating reading I will break it up into six constituent parts corresponding to the various instances in which blood is interpreted.[9] In each case, I have italicized the relevant wording and provided a running commentary elucidating the text.

1. On Yom Kippur, Abraham was circumcised. Every year [on the Day of Atonement] God looks at the *blood* of Abraham our forefather's circumcision, which atones for our sins.

Atonement is effected on Yom Kippur because God looks at the blood of Abraham's circumcision. That is to say, the paradigmatic circumcision blood of Abraham, the first male to be circumcised, saves us from imminent death on account of our sins.

2. Jacob's sons circumcised themselves, and then they circumcised their children. They passed the custom down as an eternally binding precept, until Pharaoh ordained stringent measures, forbidding the covenant of circumcision. But the day they left Egypt, all of them, from the old to the young, were circumcised, as it says, "All the people who left Egypt were circumcised" (Josh. 5). *They took the blood of their circumcision and the blood of the paschal lamb and put it on the doorposts of their homes.* When God passed by to smite the Egyptians, He saw *the circumcision blood and the paschal lamb's blood,* and was filled with compassion for Israel, as it is written, "By your blood, live, by your blood, live" (Ezek. 16).

Here we find the exegesis of the very passage from Ezekiel that we looked at above. Clearly, it was borrowed from the Bible, "read" out of its original context, and inserted into the rite because of its reference to blood. But the command "By your blood, live" is given twice. Believing there to be no redundancy in Scripture, the exegete has to account for this double occurrence. He therefore is reminded of two sources of blood that saves: circumcision and the paschal lamb, both of which, it is assumed, must have been on the doorposts when God "passed by" and saw Israel "wallowing" in all the blood that had been placed there.

The original reading of "*In* your blood, live" has become "*By* your blood, live. This exegesis has been accomplished by reading the Hebrew letter *bet,* meaning "in," as "by", that is, as a *bet,* or ablative, of means. The Rabbis thus read Ezekiel as guaranteeing that Israel lives *by virtue of its blood that is shed in covenant.*

3. "I passed by you [in Egypt] and saw you wallowing in your blood, and said to you, 'By your blood, live; by your blood, live.' " Rabbi Elie-

zer asked, What could Scripture have intended when it wrote, "By your blood, live" two times? It must be that God said, "By the merit of the *blood of covenantal circumcision and the blood of the paschal lamb* I will redeem you from Egypt. On account of their merit you will be saved at the end of days." [10] That is why it says "By your blood, live" twice.

Eliezer emphasizes not only the two types of salvific blood—circumcision and paschal lamb—but also the twin events that constitute God's acts of deliverance: freedom from Egyptian bondage and the ultimate salvation that will occur only at the end of time. Thus the apparent redundancy is explained as having a double meaning: two kinds of saving blood and two occasions when God saves by virtue of such blood. Living after the exodus, the Rabbis generalized from the first act of God's deliverance (deliverance past) to their own future, the deliverance that was yet to come, again because of blood.

4.   Rabbi Ishmael said that Abraham shrank from nothing that God commanded him, so when Isaac was only eight days old, he hurried to circumcise him, as it says, "Abraham circumcised Isaac his son when he was eight days old." *And he offered him as a sacrifice on the altar.*

Our fourth text does not mention blood explicitly, but it does associate Isaac with a sacrificial offering. The motif of Isaac's sacrificial character has attracted a great deal of modern commentary, particularly in connection with Christian doctrine by which Isaac prefigures the sacrificed Christ.[11] Our interest here is the implicit symbolic connection between sacrifice and blood. The editor of the text may have been drawn to include this text at just this place because of his prior comparison of circumcision and the paschal lamb. With the introduction of the lamb, he has embarked on the theme of sacrifice. Just as it is the blood of the lamb that saved, so, too, in sacrifice generally, it is sacrificial blood that effects the end of the sacrifice. I shall return below to the role of blood as the element in sacrifice that saves.

5.   When Joshua entered the Land of Israel, God said to him, "Don't you know that Israel is not circumcised correctly? Circumcise them a second time. . . ." He collected all the foreskins until he had enough to make a mountain of them. . . . Israel took the foreskins *and the blood,* and buried them in the desert sand. When Balaam the sorcerer came along, he observed the desert filled with Israel's foreskins, and said,

"Who can withstand the merit of *the covenant of circumcision blood
[zechut brit dam milah]?*"

There are two references to blood here, both of them interesting. First,
we discover one more time that circumcision blood saved: Balaam is rendered
unable to curse Israel. Again, of course, the notion that blood was the delivering agent is pure rabbinic fabrication, since blood occurs nowhere in the
biblical account of Balaam on which the Rabbis draw.

But the exclamation that the Rabbis put into Balaam's mouth, the second citation of blood, is especially telling. The normal expression for covenant
would have been *brit milah,* "the covenant of circumcision." Had the Rabbis
merely wanted to tell us that circumcision saves, they could have done so without taking the trouble to add the unusual word *dam,* "blood." Their decision
to add that word leaves us with a very unusual syntactic construction: *brit dam
milah,* literally, "a covenant *of the blood* of circumcision." The covenant, then,
is not a covenant of circumcision so much as of the *blood* of circumcision; that
is why it is the blood that saves. Therefore, in the context of discussing salvation, the text must expand the usual term for covenant by specifying "a covenant of blood."

6.   Hence the sages ordained the law that one should bury the *foreskin of blood* in the dust of the earth.

Again "blood" is expressly stipulated, obviously for its symbolic importance, not because we would not know what a foreskin is without the descrip-
tive word "blood." By itself, the foreskin is useless, but covered with circumcision blood, it saves.

We can summarize the entire passage from *Pirkei deRabbi Eliezer* by
saying that the text is filled with references to blood, blood being the organizing term around which the diverse interpretations are gathered. The blood
under discussion is self-evidently circumcision blood, but other blood saves,
too: the blood of the paschal lamb, the blood of sacrifices in general, and the
blood of Isaac as a sacrifice in particular. At this point in the analysis we may
say that the covenant from Abraham on saves; it did so in Egypt and will do
so again at the end of days. But *the covenant is a covenant of blood.*

We have just seen that the foreskin was to be buried in sand, but a most
remarkable alternative custom comes to us from the ninth-century prayer
book of *Seder Rav Amram.*

> Tzadok Gaon said the following. They bring water containing myrtle
> and various very sweet-smelling spices, and they circumcise the child
> so that the blood of the circumcision falls into the water. Then all the
> designated people [*kol hano'adim*] wash their hands in it, as if to say,
> "This is the blood of circumcision that mediates between God and
> Abraham our father [*kelomar zeh dam habrit sheben hamakom le'avra-*
> *ham avinu*]." [12]

The Gaon could not have been clearer about what matters: it is the blood,
which mediates between Abraham (and by extension his male progeny)
and God.

But Amram's custom is even more revealing than it appears. As it
stands, there are at least two questionable points to it, one that is highly significant, the other less so. First the more minor matter for our purposes. Our
source is given in the name of Tzadok Gaon, an attribution that is suspect,
since the only Gaon by that name, who preceded Amram by several years as
the official leader in the academy at Sura (816–18), is not otherwise known
for leaving us responsa, certainly not on ritual matters anyway. Of the many
responsa that are relevant to the study of the canonization of the synagogue
service, I found not one from Tzadok.[13] Moreover, Amram never cites Tzadok
elsewhere. The manuscripts even vary in reporting exactly who the source for
the custom was; but the Oxford manuscript's alternative of "Yitzchak" is
equally improbable, for similar reasons.

Before returning to a consideration of authorship, we should identify
the second and more significant enigma: the identity of the *no'adim,* the "designated people." The term cannot refer to everyone in attendance, for that
meaning would have been conveyed by the more usual term *hakeru'im,* "those
who were invited," or even just *ha'omdim,* "the bystanders," which is the term
that the Tosefta and the Talmuds employ to refer to the onlookers at the rite.
Who was it, then, who was specifically designated to participate in the ritual
washing of the hands using the blood-water mixture?

Fortunately, we have alternative recensions of the Amram responsum in
other sources, including the collection of geonic responsa known as *Sha'arei*
Tzedek.[14] There we find an almost word-for-word rendition of the communication that Amram must have had in front of him, but containing two important alternative words. First, instead of the elusive Tzadok, we find Kohen

Tzedek, the well-documented Gaon in Sura from 838 to 848 and a regular source for Amram elsewhere in his prayer book. But more important: *no'adim* there reads *ne'arim,* meaning "youths," or more technically, "adolescent boys." Both words would have been written without vowels, so that נערים was confused with נעדים the *resh* (ר) and *dalet* (ד) being practically identical in old cursive script.

It is hard to know exactly how the Geonim used the term *ne'arim,* whether for boys just prior to puberty or those just beyond it, but in any case, we now get a good idea of how the rite worked. It featured not just adult men but adolescent boys as well, possibly those about to become *bar mitzvah* in the sense of coming of age as a legally liable Jewish male. As a sort of commemoration of their own circumcision, they washed their hands in the blood mixture of the newly circumcised boy who was just being inducted into their fellowship, as if to say (to cite Kohen Tzedek and Amram), "This is the blood of circumcision that mediates between God and Abraham our father."

But there is even more. The practice reported by Kohen Tzedek turns up again in a medieval work that lists differences in custom between Jews in Babylonia and Jews in the Land of Israel. There we see that using a blood-water mixture was known to be a typically Babylonian practice. We get further information as well: "In Babylonia, they circumcise over water, *and put it on their faces.* In the Land of Israel, they circumcise over earth." [15] And where on their faces did these young men apply the blood? Parallel texts in other medieval collections of geonic responsa tell us precisely—"on their mouths." [16] Just as the newly circumcised child had wine representing blood put on his mouth, so the older boys applied that child's actual blood (mixed with water) to theirs.

At this stage in the argument, it could be objected that both major texts, the midrash from *Pirkei deRabbi Eliezer* and the series of reports on the geonic washing custom, are very late, too far beyond the completion of both Talmuds to qualify as evidence of dominant blood symbolism in the rabbinic system as we have defined it. Blurring the line between Tannaim and Amoraim is one thing; reading geonic texts back some five hundred years into a Palestinian milieu is another. I want to posit a coherent cultural system that takes shape roughly a few hundred years on both sides of the completion of the Mishnah, particularly in Palestine. Its accent on blood could then be associatively linked to the cultural backdrop of late antiquity, with its pagan cults and claims to salvation. Yet *Pirkei deRabbi Eliezer* is a ninth- or tenth-century source, and

Kohen Tzedek was a Gaon from 838 to 848. One might object, therefore, that the blood symbolism in these sources may be only a late innovation of post-talmudic Judaism.

In fact, that is not the case. The symbolism can easily be traced back to the second century by means of the biblical proof texts associated with the twin customs of circumcising over earth or over water. The geonic evidence turns out to be the end of a lengthy exegetical tradition that took shape precisely in the classical Palestinian culture of Tannaim and Amoraim. The Palestinian tradition of circumcising over earth is justified by Zechariah 9:1, "As for you also, because of the blood of your covenant, I send your prisoners forth from the pit where there is no water." Babylonian exegetes, who used water, cited Ezekiel 16:9, "I washed you with water, I cleaned up your blood." [17] The latter verse is actually an extension of Ezekiel 16:6 ("In your blood, live"). The custom it supported may therefore be purely Babylonian in provenance, but the scriptural tradition that supported it was Palestinian through and through, since Ezekiel 16:6 is the subject of exegesis in the *Pirkei deRabbi Eliezer* passage and *Pirkei deRabbi Eliezer* is Palestinian. Also, the naming prayer containing the exegesis in question was known to the medievals as a prayer from the Palestinian Talmud. Finally, a statement of our interpretation from Ezekiel is already fully worked out in an early collection of midrash, the *Mekhilta*. [18]

> Rabbi Matia ben Heresh used to say, "Behold it says, 'I passed by you and looked at you and saw it was a time of love' (Ezek. 16:8). This means the time had arrived for God's vow to Abraham to be fulfilled, namely, that He would save his children. But as yet they had no commandments to perform, by virtue of which they might merit redemption, as it says, 'Your breasts were fashioned and your hair had grown, but you were naked' (Ezek. 16:8)—meaning that they were naked of all commandments. God therefore assigned them two commandments: the sacrifice of the paschal lamb, and circumcision, which they were to perform so as to merit being saved, as it says: 'I passed by you and saw you wallowing in your blood, and I said, "By your blood, live . . . By your blood, live"' (Ezek. 16:6). It says also, 'As for you also, because of the blood of your covenant, I send your prisoners forth from the pit where there is no water' (Zech. 9:11). . . . One cannot obtain reward except by deeds." [19]

Obviously, the emphasis on blood in the lengthy *Pirkei deRabbi Eliezer* text is no late innovation. It is in the *Mekhilta* as well as in *Targum Yonatan,* which renders Exodus 12:13, "Let this blood be a sign to you"—a reference, in context, to the blood of the lamb put on the doorposts—as "*blood of the covenant and blood of the paschal lamb.*" Obviously the redundancy in Ezekiel had been noted by tannaitic teachers, who had already explained it away by observing that both the blood of the lamb and the blood of circumcision can be counted on to save. Indeed, they were given to Israel together precisely so that Israel would be saved by them both.

Then, too, in connection with ritual, we have a tannaitic attribution commenting on the custom of drawing circumcision blood from converts: "Were it not for *the blood of the covenant,* heaven and earth would not stand." The same source cites the benediction for the circumcision of male converts as "Blessed art Thou . . . for commanding up to circumcise converts, by drawing *their covenantal blood* [*lamul et hagerim ulehatif mehem dam brit*]."[20] Exodus Rabbah affirms the understanding that God said, "Fix, therefore, this month [of Nisan] for Me and for you, because I will see in it the *blood of the paschal lamb* and will make atonement for you. . . . I will have pity on you. *Through the blood of the paschal lamb and the blood of circumcision, I will forgive you.*"[21] The *Targum Yerushalmi* glosses the "Bridegroom of Blood" passage (Ex. 4:24–26) by explaining, "How precious is *the blood of this circumcision, which saved* the bridegroom from the hands of the angel of death."

In short, wherever one looks in rabbinic exegesis, the covenant of circumcision is symbolized by the circumcision blood that is extracted, and that blood in turn is explained as a symbol of salvation. This interpretive scheme is tannaitic in origin, but is retained throughout the rabbinic era, all the way into the geonic period.

This is not the place to delve deeply into the connection between the paschal lamb and circumcision; we will return to that theme later. But we should note here that the parallel drawn between the two sources of blood is abundantly evident even in the few texts cited above. Everywhere we look, it is specifically the blood of circumcision and the blood of the lamb that save. In fact, a variant benediction over matzah at the Passover seder, known to us from the Genizah fragments, closely parallels the eulogy of the *mohel*'s blessing following circumcision, "Blessed art Thou who makes a covenant [*koret habrit*]." The Genizah blessing reads, "Blessed art Thou who remembers the covenant [*zokher habrit*]."[22] It is the wine used in the seder, more than the matzah, that symbolizes the blood of the lamb, however. We already saw how, in circumcision, wine is put on the child's mouth when the *mohel* mentions Ezekiel's reference to wallowing in blood. The seder features four cups of wine as well as a sweet pastelike dip called *charoset,* which is made with wine. The Palestinian Talmud associates each cup of wine with an act of salvation, a meaning that is fully in keeping with the salvific symbolism of the two blood instances in question (circumcision and the lamb); but, more than that, it also describes *charoset* as "in memory of the *blood* [of the lamb] [*zekher ladam*]." [23]

The word *zekher* means more than "in memory of." Legally, it is used in the sense of pointing to, as in the common talmudic phrase *Im ein re'aya ladavar, yesh zekher ladavar,* that is, "Though there is no absolute proof for a thing, there is at least something that points toward it." To translate *zekher* in this legal phrase as "memory" makes no sense whatever. We need to discover how *zekher* in the sense of time is similar to *zekher* in the sense of legal evidence. Only then will we understand the full impact of that word as it functions in the statement about memory. We saw that, legally, *zekher* implies a connection between one thing and another, in the sense of pointing toward, so that the mind is moved logically from point A to point B. A suggests B across the divide of logical space, as it were, so that one cannot think of A without considering B simultaneously. The same is true of *zekher* in terms of memory, by which we mean the movement of the mind across the divide of time. Here, too, *zekher* denotes a sense of "pointing toward," but now across time rather than space, such that symbol A automatically invokes the memory of an event B. Here, too, there is something about A that necessarily connects the mind to B, so that to consider symbol A is to have in mind also event B. [24] This symbolic sense of memory is made somewhat clearer by reference to the Christian concept of anamnesis:

> *Anamnesis* is all but untranslatable into English. Memorial, commemoration, remembrance—all these suggest that the person or deed commemorated is past and absent, whereas *anamnesis* suggests the very opposite: it is an objective act, in and by which the person commemorated is actually made present, is brought into the here and now. [25]

Now Judaism has many liturgical instances of *zekher* also, sometimes rendered by the alternative nominal form *zikaron.* Perhaps the most obvious are the Rosh Hashanah prayers known as *zikhronot,* where God "remembers" us. [26] Since liturgically Rosh Hashanah commemorates "the conception of the world,"[27] it is partly the primeval act of creation that is "remembered." But what God remembers most here is the covenant with Israel, a theme developed in detail by the biblical verses that form the centerpiece of the *zikhronot,* telling us over and over how God remembers the covenant with Abraham, Isaac, and Jacob (Ex. 2:24, Lev. 26:42, Ps. 111:5, Ps. 106:45, Ezek. 16:60). "Remember us" and "Remember the covenant," we say. The eulogy of the concluding benediction concurs, "Blessed art Thou who remembers the covenant."[28] Sacred times are thus evoked in the rabbinic system as particularly propitious for God's remembering or, better, for God's "making present" the covenant. These are known technically as *mikra'ei kodesh,* time of solemn assembly, and literally defined in the Kiddush that inaugurates them as *zekher litsiyat mitsrayim,* a "memorial" of the exodus from Egypt. And how is a *mikra kodesh* begun? Over wine, of course, which is itself a means of making present the covenantal reality stretching from Abraham to the present.

Wine thus recollects the covenant. In that capacity, it is also a symbol for blood, *zekher ladam,* and not just the blood of the paschal lamb, but that other blood of the covenant also associated with deliverance, the blood drawn from every Jewish male on the eighth day of his life.

For both rabbinic Judaism and early Christianity, therefore, wine as anamnesis ushered in propitious moments of covenantal memory. Jews emphasized the blood of the lamb and of circumcision. Christians rejected the latter and reinterpreted the former, so that Christ became the second lamb: also slaughtered, also the means to salvation, also on account of his blood. Early Christian exegesis thus borrowed its symbolism from Judaism. As the new lamb of the new covenant, it was the blood of Jesus that symbolized salvation, which was also "remembered" by a cup of wine.[29]

To summarize: The Rabbis replaced the fertility symbolism of the Bible with blood as a symbol of salvation. In this blood symbolism, they merged the two biblical concepts of covenant—sacrifice (from Genesis 15) and circumcision (from Genesis 17).[30] Blood now became the dominant symbol of covenant, both sacrificially (as the lamb) and through circumcision. One form of blood recalls the other; the blood of the paschal lamb and the blood of circumcision become merged because both are items given by God specifically to effect salvation. Both the Passover seder and the circumcision ritual use wine to recollect the blood. Their similar blessings point to the celebrative theme they have in common, the covenant with Israel: "Blessed is God who makes a covenant."

Both covenantal events—circumcision and seder—are male domi-
nated: obviously in the case of circumcision; only slightly less so in the case of
the seder. Women were probably physically present at the seder, but to judge
by the stories told of Rabbis who attend a Passover seder overnight, the feast
was largely for men, who were the sole ritual actors.[31] The seder, too, was then,
at least in part, a male covenantal ceremony, featuring questions asked by a
son of his father, the ritualized passing down of the covenantal story from
father to son, and tales of the different kinds of sons one might have.[32] Both
events feature the common symbol of blood: blood of a male lamb on the one
hand; blood of male Jews on the other. At the induction ceremony, for that is
what circumcision is, the adolescent boys in attendance celebrate their own
covenantal community, even washing their hands in the blood-water mixture
and applying the blood that saves to their mouths; at the same time, wine is
applied to the mouth of the baby boy whose blood is taken, and he is given
his patrilineal name: the son of his father, who was the son of his father, and
so on, all the way back to the first father, Abraham.

In chapter 9 we shall return to blood as a symbol and to the role of
women in the rabbinic symbol system. But first we must linger briefly on a
secondary theme introduced here: the parallelism as well as the rivalry between early Judaism and Christianity.

c h a p t e r 7

Blood, Salvation, Works, and Faith: Circumcision in Early Judaism and Christianity

As a case study in mutual religious ambivalence, the course of Jewish-Christian relations in the first several centuries C.E. has proved innately interesting. Attracted and yet repelled by each other, Jews and Christians established an historical trajectory much like the fabled DNA spiral: swirling around each other in mutual orbit, never coming quite close enough to coalesce, but at the same time, neither one managing to extricate itself from the pull exercised by the other.

Though less well known, the relationship between the rituals of these two faiths may be more interesting still. At least since the turn of the century, for instance, when David de Sola Pool published his influential work on the Kaddish, it has been evident that this Jewish prayer (which had yet to be associated with mourning) is closely related to the Lord's Prayer.[1] Similarly, classic studies have sought roots for the Eucharist in the Passover seder ritual or in normative Jewish feasting practices.[2] Certainly the Christian calendar year derived in large part from the Jewish equivalent, the Pasche, for instance, replacing Pesach (Pischa in Aramaic).[3] But the parallels do not stop at the obvious. The period of Lent as a preparatory period to Easter, for example, probably developed out of a similar time of Jewish preparation for Passover.[4] The foundations of Christian music have also been linked, though only tenuously and indirectly, at least in part to Jewish prototypes.[5] I suggested above, moreover, that the Christian anamnesis parallels the rabbinic conception of liturgical *zikaron* or *zecher*. So even the liturgical spirituality of Jews and that of Christians were once not as far apart as one might imagine today, now that Christian worship has been reformulated by successive waves of influence from monasticism to the Reformation, and Judaism altered similarly by nearly two thousand years of history.

As would be expected, ritual matters display the ambivalence that characterized early Jewish-Christian relations in general. Ceremonial parallels are thus offset by noticeable contrasts as well as by outright polemic between rabbinic Judaism and nascent Christianity. Perhaps the most infamous such polemic is the Jewish *Birkat Minim*, or "Benediction of [actually, a malediction against] Heretics," which is generally dated to the first century and is often thought to be directed at Jewish Christians.[6] For their part, Christians transformed the Jewish Sabbath into a weekly Lord's Day,[7] and read Jewish Scripture typologically to prefigure the Christian Good News. They also instituted baptism in place of circumcision, with the result that early Jewish circumcision liturgy was composed to polemicize against what the Rabbis saw as Jewish defection from the covenant. Christians were not reticent about their own position, so the rite of circumcision and the textual evidence bequeathed about it by both sides provides an excellent index of the extent to which both Judaism and Christianity were anxiously engaged in staking out ideological turf in city after city of the Roman Empire.

The debate on the continuing validity of circumcision best explains the *mohel*'s blessing (N) in act 2. Recall that after the operation and the introductory blessing by father and circumciser, the latter recites the following:

> Blessed art Thou, Lord our God, King of the universe, who sanctified
> the beloved one in the womb, and set a statute in his flesh, and
> stamped his descendants with the sign of the holy covenant. Therefore,
> as a reward for this, O Living God, our Portion and our Rock, com-
> mand [or: the living God . . . commanded] that the beloved of our
> flesh shall be delivered from the pit, for the sake of His covenant
> which He set in our flesh. Blessed art Thou, Lord, who makes a
> covenant.

The autonomy of the Christian community from its Jewish parent was nowhere more evident than in its decision to abandon circumcision. The decisive break is portrayed in Acts 15, recollected by Paul in Galatians 2, and explicated again in Romans 4. Galatians differentiates Paul's mission to the uncircumcised from Peter's mission to the circumcised, but concludes in favor of the former:

We have believed in Christ Jesus, in order to be justified by faith in Christ, and not by works of the law, because by works of the law shall no one be justified. . . . If justification were by works of the law, then Christ died to no purpose. (Gal. 2:16, 21)

Salvation is obtained by faith, then, not by works—or, as the Rabbis would have put it, by keeping the commandments. Now we understand the conclusion to the *Mekhilta*'s exegesis on Ezekiel 16. We first encountered this remarkable claim in chapter 6 in connection with the early association of circumcision blood and paschal lamb blood as blood that saves. Now we examine it again, this time for its emphasis on justification by works, not by faith. I have italicized the relevant conclusion.

> Rabbi Matia ben Heresh used to say, "Behold it says, 'I passed by you and looked at you and saw it was a time of love' (Ezek. 16:8). This means the time had arrived for God's vow to Abraham to be fulfilled, namely, that He would save his children. But as yet they had no commandments to perform, by virtue of which they might merit redemption, as it says, 'Your breasts were fashioned and your hair had grown, but you were naked' (Ezek. 16:8)—meaning that they were naked of all commandments. God therefore assigned them two commandments: the sacrifice of the paschal lamb, and circumcision, which they were to perform so as to merit being saved, as it says: 'I passed by you and saw you wallowing in your blood, and I said, "By your blood, live . . . By your blood, live"' (Ezek. 16:6). It says also, 'As for you also, because of the blood of your covenant, I send your prisoners forth from the pit where there is no water' (Zech. 9:11). . . . *One cannot obtain reward except by deeds.*" [8]

God had promised to save Israel; Israel was innocent enough—indeed, the proper time had come. But "as yet they had no commandments to perform, by virtue of which they might merit redemption. . . . God therefore assigned them two commandments: the sacrifice of the paschal lamb, and circumcision, which they were to perform so as to merit being saved. . . . One cannot obtain reward except by deeds." Here is the classic doctrine of justification by works.

In Romans, Paul applies his doctrine of justification by faith directly to the case of Abraham, who, the Rabbis claimed, merited salvation precisely because he had initiated circumcision (the paradigmatic example of works).

> What then shall we say was gained by Abraham, our ancestor accord-ing to the flesh? For if Abraham was justified by works, he has some-thing to boast about, but not before God. For what does Scripture say? "Abraham believed God, and it was reckoned to him as righteous-ness. . . ." Now to one who works, wages are not reckoned as a gift but as something due. But to one who without works trusts Him who justi-fies the ungodly, such faith is reckoned as righteousness. . . . We say, "Faith was reckoned to Abraham as righteousness. How then was it reckoned to him? Was it before or after he had been circumcised? It was not after but before he was circumcised. He received the sign of circumcision as a seal of the righteousness that he had by faith, while he was still uncircumcised. The purpose was to make him the ancestor of all who believe without being circumcised, and who thus have righ-teousness reckoned to them, and likewise, the ancestor of the circum-cised who are not only circumcised, but who also follow the example of the faith that our ancestor Abraham had before he was circumcised. For the promise that he would inherit the world did not come to Abra-ham or to his descendants through the law, but through the righteous-ness of faith" (Rom. 4:1–3, 9–13)

Thus the general argument over justification by faith or by works found particular expression in the debate over the merit of circumcision, the biblical origin of which was merely a secondary event for Paul, who preferred to ac-cent Abraham's prior *faith* as that which saved him; Abraham's faith, not his circumcision (his works), was the reason he was chosen. The sign of circum-cision was merely, "a seal of the righteousness that he [already] had by faith, while he was still uncircumcised."

The Rabbis responded to Paul's claim by saying:[9]

> [Why did God divide the Red Sea?] Rabbi Bannah said, "Because of the merit of the deed which Abraham their father did. . . ." Simon of Teman said, "Because of the merit of circumcision. . . . For it is said, 'Thus says the Lord: if not for my covenant of day and night, I would not have appointed the ordinances of heaven and earth' (Jer. 33:25). Go and see which covenant obtains day and night. You can find none but the commandment of circumcision."[10]

To be sure, the Rabbis were not averse to faith, just as Paul was not opposed to deeds. They therefore admitted that there was a proper role for faith, but only insofar as faith is what prompts the acceptance of God's commandments. Thereafter, one demonstrates faith precisely by keeping the acts that God mandates. Thus, they claimed:

> Great indeed is faith before Him who spoke and the world came into being. . . . Whoever accepts one single commandment with true faith is deserving of having the holy spirit rest on him. We find this to have been the case with our forefathers. . . . Abraham inherited both this world and the world to come as a reward for the faith with which he believed.[11]

The issue did not go away. Rabbis issued one polemic after another in favor of circumcision while the Church Fathers never tired of reiterating their agreement with Paul, for the very physicality of circumcision made it an appropriate sign of a deeper distinction between rabbinism—its exegesis and its religious anthropology—and the rival Hellenistic approach that sought to displace it. Daniel Boyarin thus claims that the Pauline spiritualization of "circumcision of the flesh" is an apt discursive parallel to its anthropological asceticism.[12] Paul's preference for inner faith over outward works, the former being spiritual and latter necessarily being bodily, is a further elaboration of what Boyarin sees as rabbinic Judaism's essential acceptance of embodiment and its Christian opponents' insistence on transforming bodily Judaism into an affair of the spirit.

For Christians, then, circumcision of the flesh was replaced by circumcision of the heart—the promise given first in Deuteronomy 10:16 and then reiterated by Jeremiah 4:4: "Circumcise yourselves to the Lord; remove the foreskins of your hearts." Clement of Alexandria, for instance, explains that Paul had Timothy circumcised only because, as a man born to a Jewish mother, he might better "accommodate himself to the Jews" and convince them more readily of the truth of the new covenant. Titus, by contrast, born to a Gentile mother, needed no such outward sign on his body, because "circumcision made by the hands profits nothing." Tertullian quotes Jeremiah expressly to prove that circumcision of the flesh is merely temporary, a sign of a "contumacious" people, whereas spiritual circumcision of the heart "has been given for salvation to an obedient people."[13] Each Church Father therefore repeats the charge that with Jesus and the new covenant, the law is null and void; justification comes through faith alone while circumcision is forbidden.

It has long been recognized that the *mohel's* second blessing (N) must be seen against the background of this Jewish-Christian debate on the continuing efficacy of circumcision as a vehicle for salvation. Scholars have offered various hypotheses for exactly why that is the case. For instance, the beginning of the blessing presents us with an unidentified "beloved one" who is said to have been sanctified from the womb.

> Blessed art Thou, Lord our God, King of the universe, who sanctified the beloved one from the womb, and set a statute in his flesh, and stamped his descendants with the sign of the holy covenant.

But who is this "beloved one," and what could sanctification "from the womb" denote?

Already in 1962, Sidney Hoenig suggested that sanctification in the womb had to be seen as a polemic against nascent Christian doctrine. He refers us to the announcement of Jesus' birth in Luke 1:35. Mary questions whether, as a virgin, she can bear a son, and receives the following reply: "The holy spirit will come upon you, and the power of the Most High will overshadow you. Therefore the child to be born will be holy; he will be called Son of God." Hoenig now cites the Christian insistence on the unique sanctity of Jesus, a doctrine that Celsus felt obliged to address. He countered Christian claims to the special sanctity of those who live in Christ by saying that everyone is a child of God. Likewise, says Hoenig, Jews constructed a doctrine of Jewish sanctity going back to the fact that Abraham, too, was uniquely sanctified, not just at birth but already "from the womb."[14]

Hoenig may be right, but before passing judgment on his claim, we first ought to look at another benediction, this one carried by Genizah fragments and geonic responsa as well.[15] It was once part of the ceremony of Pidyon Haben (Redemption of the Firstborn, to which I will return in another context). Though no longer the case, it was once common for the priest to address the child and to recite a lengthy benediction expressing the rabbinic view of embryology. Made up largely of biblical snippets that describe how a fetus takes shape in the womb, it began, "Blessed art Thou who sanctified the fetus in its mother's womb." The Hebrew word rendered here as "womb" is not identical in our two sources: the *mohel's* blessing uses *beten,* literally, "belly," but used regularly elsewhere for "womb"; in the parallel Redemption rite, we get *me'ei imo,* "the mother's innards," but again, a term already found in the Bible (e.g., Isa. 49:1, Ps. 71:6) to mean (among other things) the womb. Either way, we have two benedictions that ascribe sanctity to someone and hold that he assumed that status while still a fetus.

It may be, therefore, as Hoenig would have it, that the doctrine of uterine sanctification was in general adopted by the Rabbis as a response to Christian theology. If so, the priest's blessing in the Redemption of the Firstborn means more than anyone has yet imagined. But it is sometimes a mistake to read too much into liturgical language. At the very least we would prefer to find express discussion of such an important claim somewhere in the midrash; to the best of my knowledge, evidence confirming Hoenig's hypothesis is lacking there. For that matter, we do not even know for sure that the circumcision benediction is about Abraham, though I think (as we shall see) that Abraham is the most likely candidate for the elusive "beloved one." Nevertheless, even if Abraham was seen as having been sanctified from the womb, we can at best speculate that the rabbinic authors had Luke 1:35 (or at least the Christian doctrine of which Luke is said to be speaking) in front of them, or that they intended their claim as a means of demonstrating the parallel sanctity of all Jews in the face of the church's claim regarding the sanctity of all Christians.

What we can learn, however, is that the Rabbis took an essentialist view of holiness, which they regarded as an actual quality that inhered in some people, just as much as blue eyes or dark hair (in chapter 9, I shall return to this very important point). In the case of the firstborn male, it was patently clear that the child was sacred: he belonged to God. That was the whole point of the redemption—to release him from his sacred status so that he could lead a normal life thereafter as a nonpriestly *yisra'el,* that is, as a man who is neither a priest (a *kohen*) nor a Levite (a *levi*) but just an ordinary Jew. The blessing explains how the child received all his characteristics, his flesh and bones, his soul, and his sanctity, which the Rabbis posited as an endowment from the womb along with everything else that was his. In the circumcision blessing, too, we have someone described as innately holy, probably Abraham. The blessing therefore posits the quality of holiness, and in keeping with rabbinic embryology tells us at what point he was so endowed. There may be nothing more to it than that.

But is the "beloved one" Abraham? Medieval exegetes were divided on this question, some thinking it was Abraham, others Isaac, and still others Jacob.[16] These are late reports, of course; they may not even reflect ancient

exegetical traditions, much less the original intent of the framers of the benediction. The "beloved one" in question may simply have been identified eventually with the three possible patriarchal candidates from Jewish liturgy, any
one of whom might have been "sanctified from the womb."

But tannaitic liturgy was not formulated in a cultural vacuum. Especially
noteworthy is the pervasive influence of Gnosticism, especially its categorizing
of experience into warring realms of light and darkness, good and evil,[17] with
the corollary belief in an independent kingdom of evil, which could prove
damaging in two ways. First, it was the abode of the angel of death, and the
source, therefore, for all mishap including early death. Second, it was the place
whence evil in general arises, and the cause, therefore, of human temptation.
The evil side of human beings is attracted to the evil side of the cosmos. Left
to its own devices, it will overwhelm us, leading us on to evil deeds ourselves.

Assuming this binary cosmology, David Flusser and Shmuel Safrai have
posited circumcision as a rabbinic prophylactic against the attraction of this
kingdom of evil.[18] Jews could hope for righteousness because circumcision
protected them from temptation.[19] But what about people who were born
before Abraham accepted circumcision? It became logically necessary for the
Rabbis to explain how there could be righteous men at all in that earlier era, a
problem they solved by holding that worthies like Adam, Seth, Noah, and
Shem were *born* circumcised. But they could hardly adopt the same exegetical
strategy for Abraham, since the Bible says expressly that Abraham circumcised himself at the ripe old age of ninety-nine. Flusser and Safrai thus conclude that the Rabbis awarded Abraham the unique status of sanctity from the
womb, an outstanding act of divine grace open to no one else thereafter. Abraham's unique righteousness, despite his uncircumcised status and in the face
of evil all about him, was a gift from God, an act of pure grace.

On the one hand, this is nothing but an echo of Paul's claim that Abraham "received the sign of circumcision as a seal of the righteousness that he
had by faith while he was still uncircumcised" (Rom. 4:11). Paul emphasizes
Abraham's justification by faith whereas the Rabbis consider Abraham's righteousness as a gift from the period before he was even born, thus preferring
to see it as an act of pure divine grace without any prior faith to justify it.[20] We
might say that, for Paul, because Abraham believed, he was saved; for the
Rabbis, because Abraham was saved (by sanctification in utero), he believed—that is, he remained untempted, by virtue of a birthright unknown to
other mortals. On the other hand, even though Abraham lived ninety-nine

years in that state of grace, the Rabbis are perfectly clear that eventually he had to adopt circumcision if his righteousness before God was to continue. This claim was in keeping with their overall insistence on circumcision of the flesh as an everlasting requirement of God's covenanted People, a claim we see echoed in the blessing's further statement that "God stamped his [Abraham's] descendants with the sign of the holy covenant."[21]

Most puzzling of all is the fact that the current wording of the blessing is confusing; more likely, it is in error.[22] Three early sources—the Tosefta, the Babli, and the Yerushalmi—cite it, but somewhat differently, and even the Geonim do not agree on how it should be read. The problem is that almost nothing seems right about the second half of the blessing (N2).

1 (N1) Blessed art Thou, Lord our God, King of the universe, who sanc-
2 tified the beloved one in the womb, and set a statute in his flesh, and
3 stamped his descendants with the sign of the holy covenant. (N2)
4 Therefore, as a reward for this, O Living God, our Portion and our
5 Rock, command [or: the living God . . . commanded] that the beloved
6 of our flesh shall be delivered from the pit, for the sake of his cove-
7 nant which He set in our flesh. Blessed art Thou, Lord, who makes a
8 covenant.

1. To what does "therefore" (line 4) refer? Presumably, it is in apposition to "as a reward for this," but that identification is of no help whatever, since we still wonder about the identification of "this." Whatever "this" means, it must be a human act that warrants a reward; but there seems to be no human actor in N. It is God who "sanctified the beloved one," "set a statute in his flesh," and "stamped his descendants" ever after with the sign of circumcision.

2. In lines 6–7, we get "for the sake of his covenant which He set in our flesh," which is, at best, redundant with "as a reward for this" (line 4) and at worst directly contradictory, in that salvation can either be a reward for what we do, or it can be something that is entailed by the covenant and therefore intended for God's sake, but not both.

3. As my parenthetical translation indicates, we have a controversy over the word "command" (line 5). Since the Hebrew original צוה (*ts.v.h*) is unvocalized, it can be taken either as the imperative, "command!" = צַוֵּה (*TSaVeH,* as I have rendered it in line 5), or as a third-person singular perfect, "commanded" = צִוָּה (*TSiVaH,* as in the bracketed alternative in line 5). The

larger sentence in which it is embedded thus means either "As a reward . . . God commanded that the beloved be delivered," or "As a reward, God, [please] command that the beloved be delivered." Either way, the subject of the blessing is salvation, since "the pit" is used rabbinically as a euphemism for the biblical She'ol.[23]

Part of the solution to these interwoven textual difficulties lies in the long-recognized fact that many variant versions lack the apparently redundant claim "for the sake of his covenant which He set in our flesh." We can omit it then, thus obviating the theological opposition between circumcision as a means of deliverance and deliverance for the sake of circumcision (the second issue before us). But the key to a proper understanding of the passage as a whole, I believe, is the correct reading of the subject of the various verbal clauses in the first sentence. Word order will become important in my suggested reconstruction, so for the moment, I will ignore preferred English syntax, and render the English in a word-for-word equivalent to the Hebrew text.

> Blessed art Thou, Lord our God, King of the universe, who (A) sanctified the beloved one from the womb, (B) a statute in his flesh he set, and (C) his descendants he stamped with the sign of the holy covenant.

As my statement of the first textual problem indicates, every translation assumes that the subject for all three verbs ("sanctified," "set," and "stamped") is God. That is how I have been rendering it until now. But a closer reading reveals the possibility that we may have more than one subject here. First of all, it is evident that the claim in A has nothing immediately to do with circumcision at all; it tells us only that prior to circumcision Abraham was sanctified from the womb (and hence was able to be righteous, if we understand the claim the way Flusser and Safrai suggest). There is actually no need to imagine that A was even originally connected to B and C. As my word-for-word translation indicates, there is no *vav* ("and") before clause B. By contrast, B and C are connected by the conjunctive "and"; they stand alone, without A, as a pair of self-sufficient claims about circumcision. We might even rename them B1 and B2, thus indicating the complementary set that they are.

In other words, B1 and B2 go together as two related statements about circumcision. B1 says, "He [God] set a statute in his [Abraham's] flesh"; B2 adds, "He stamped his descendants with the sign of the holy covenant." "His descendants" must be Abraham's descendants. But the subject of B2, "He," need not be God. It might be Abraham. Recalling the fact that A is not inherently connected to B (1 and 2), and remembering again that the Hebrew original is unpunctuated, we might try inserting a period after A. We should then read B as presenting two statements about circumcision, the first (B1) having to do with God's circumcision of Abraham and the second (B2) dealing with Abraham's continuation of circumcision on his own descendants.

If we revert to preferable English word order, and if we omit the redundant "for the sake of" clause, our new reading would thus be:

> Blessed art Thou, Lord our God, King of the universe, who sanctified the beloved one [Abraham] from the womb. He [God] set a statute in his [Abraham's] flesh, and he [Abraham] stamped his descendants with the sign of the holy covenant. Therefore, as a reward for this, O Living God, our Portion and our Rock, command [or: the living God . . . commanded] that the beloved of our flesh shall be delivered from the pit. Blessed art Thou, Lord, who makes a covenant.

"Therefore, as a reward for this" now makes perfect sense. "This" refers back to the prior sentence. It is Abraham's act of circumcising his descendants, precisely the covenantal act that was at issue for Jews in the first and second century. Abraham becomes the model for all Jewish fathers in that he insisted on circumcising his son. His action, as the saving deed par excellence, led to the reward that the next sentence appropriately introduces by "therefore"—that is, Abraham circumcised his descendants, and "therefore, as a reward for this [act]," God granted salvation.

We turn again, then, to the final textual difficulty, the two alternative translations of the Hebrew צוה (ts.v.h) as "command" צַוֵּה (the imperative) or "commanded" צִוָּה (third-person perfect). Either would be acceptable; at one time, based upon a variant geonic reading, I thought that the former was probable.[24] But now this closer analysis suggests to me that the latter is preferable. The blessing thus provides three events in sequence. First, God consecrated Abraham in the womb, thus granting him righteousness even before he adopted circumcision. But second, Abraham's righteousness led him to accept God's commandments, including, above all, male circumcision which he performed on himself and on Isaac, so that third, God promised salvation to his progeny ever after—assuming, of course, that later fathers circumcise their children too. Circumcision is thus the most exemplary of the "good works," the saving power of which Christian attacks denied.

Now we understand the addition of "and good deeds" to the bystanders' response. The English phrase "good deeds" is our own colloquial equivalent of the more theological "good works"—in Hebrew, *ma'asim tovim.* As we saw above, the original formula was more than a pious wish for the child's future welfare; it was a covenantal charge directed at the father: "As you admitted him to the covenant, so shall you admit him to Torah and to marriage." This is the variant carried in most versions of the Tosefta, both Talmuds, *Siddur Saadiah* and *Seder Rav Amram.* Its status as the original formulaic response cannot be in doubt.

We need to inquire, therefore, as to what connection there is between (a) circumcision, Torah instruction, and marriage (all of which are the father's covenantal obligations to his son), and (b) *ma'asim tovim* ("good deeds" or "good works"), which are not and cannot be the father's responsibility, since whether or not the child ultimately performs good deeds is up to him alone. The performance of good deeds thus seems to fall into a different category entirely. How it got added to the circumcision rite will tell us a great deal more about the public meaning that the rite had for the Rabbis who participated in it.

We have seen that, in the first few centuries, a raging debate occurred between Jewish and Christian exegetes over the relative merit of Abraham. Both took for granted that he was worthy of God's selection as forefather. But Christians insisted on his justification through faith alone, whereas Jews asserted that his faith first had to be demonstrated by deeds, circumcision being first among them. Circumcision was thus a singular example of such deeds and also, given its privileged status as the unique act by which covenantal continuity was guaranteed, a grand metonym for saving works in general. Recall the *Mekhilta* to Ezekiel 16: "One cannot obtain reward except by deeds" (*ma'asim*).[25] "Deeds" (*ma'asim*), of course, is just another way of saying "good deeds" (*ma'asim tovim*).

But not all *ma'asim tovim* are equal. Chief among them are those involving blood that saves, of which there are three varieties. First, there is sacrificial blood in general, the point of the sacrificial system being the remission of sin and the reestablishment of a right relationship with God. Second, there is the paschal lamb, the paradigmatic sacrifice that saved Israel in Egypt, which was replicated annually as long as the cult lasted and then recollected symbolically through wine and *charoset* at the seder even when the cult was gone and actual sacrifice ended. Last, we have circumcision blood. According to the midrash in *Pirkei deRabbi Eliezer,* it, too, was sacrificial blood that saves; it, too, had therefore been applied to the lintels in Egypt; and it had duly delivered Israel from Balaam's curse in the desert. As the naming prayer (O) made clear, it continues ever after also to deliver "the beloved from the pit," since God had promised Ezekiel, "By your blood, live."

But even as the *Mekhilta* was being composed, even, that is, as it trumpeted the good news of salvation by deeds not faith, the Temple had been destroyed, and sacrifice ended, since Deuteronomy had long ago prohibited offerings anywhere but in the Temple precinct.[26] Thus of the three specially salvific acts involving blood, only circumcision was left.

It could be argued that *ma'asim tovim* was added to the circumcision ceremony simply because circumcision was the means of admission to a covenant that demands good deeds just as it does Torah study and marriage. That is, insofar as circumcision is a father's obligation to his son, it is part of a set that includes Torah and marriage. Insofar as it is also part of the set of things that save (*ma'asim tovim*), it is connected with sacrifice and the paschal lamb, both of which ceased functioning with the demise of the Temple. We might assume, then, that Torah study and marriage (from set 1) would be associated more or less naturally with good deeds (the totality of set 2) via circumcision, a major exemplar of one set and the sole remaining exemplar of the other.

This argument is a specific application of a more general point, namely, that cultural constructs are arrayed in sets of related entities; if sets overlap such that a member of one set is also a member of another set, their entities may be related to each other through their connection to the set member that they have in common. Further, two entire sets may be linked by virtue of an item that exemplifies the two sets in question.

More formally, the argument would look like this:

Set 1 (Father-Son Obligations):
> Set Members: Circumcision
> > Torah education
> > Marriage
>
> Logical Entailments: Circumcision (one such obligation) implies Torah education and marriage (two other such obligations).

Set 2 (*Ma'asim tovim* = Acts that Save):
> Set Members: Sacrifice
> > Paschal lamb
> > Circumcision

Logical Entailments: Circumcision (one act that saves) implies the paschal lamb and sacrifice (other acts that save). But of the three, only circumcision remains. In the following chart, we therefore bracket sacrifice and paschal lamb as defunct.

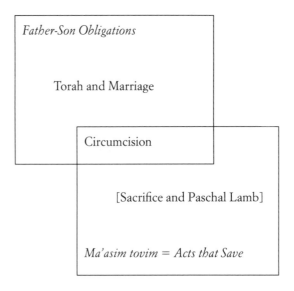

Father-Son Obligations

Torah and Marriage

Circumcision

[Sacrifice and Paschal Lamb]

Ma'asim tovim = Acts that Save

From the perspective of the father-son tradition, then, circumcision evokes related moments in the boy's covenantal lifeline with which the father is charged: his education in Torah and his eventual marriage. From the perspective of acts that save, called *ma'asim tovim,* circumcision is reminiscent of sacrifice in general and the paschal lamb in particular, both of which are now defunct. With circumcision now the only remaining instance of *ma'asim tovim,* the set of good deeds became merged with the set of father-son obligations because they share the common term "circumcision." "Good deeds" was thus added to the bystanders' response in the circumcision rite, which now suggested not only father-son obligation but salvation as well.

Naturally, after "good deeds" was added, the second-person address to the father charging him with the fulfillment of his obligations to his son had to be altered so as to include the new term which was beyond the father's power to effect. He could be asked to teach his son Torah and to find him a wife, but not to bring him into "good deeds," which the son alone could accomplish. So instead of the second-person charge to the father ("just as you brought him . . . so shall you bring him"), the third-person wording ("just as he entered . . . so may he enter") now emerged as preferable.

That, at least, would be a purely formal explanation for the addition of *ma'asim tovim* to the ritualized bystanders' response. It is equally possible, however, that the addition of "good deeds" was not only formal but substantive—a direct polemic against the emerging Christian community, which insisted on faith, not works, as the vehicle to salvation. The tannaitic midrashic lessons that stress justification by works can probably be explained that way. The textual corpus we call midrash functioned as oral preaching after all, and scholars have routinely traced the presence of midrashic lessons to the theological debates that the preacher sought consciously to address. It is therefore tempting to imagine the bystanders' response in the circumcision rite as reacting to the same forces.

Yet there is absolutely no evidence that ritual necessarily evolves in the same way that sermons do. Preachers then as now may address the issues of their day. The whole idea behind a sermon is to make a point, often a point that might be challenged because rival ideologies deny it, and in the second century Christianity denied the saving grace of circumcision and good works. But, even so, the question remains as to whether formulaic ritual responses are affected by ideological trends in the same way that open-ended sermonic content is—especially in an oral society where what people say at a rite is dependent on what they have always said rather than (as in modern times) on what a newly revised prayer book or an ideological watchdog committee tells them to say. Ritualized speech acts are notoriously slow to change. Relative invariability is their hallmark. So while it is possible that ideological concern with the efficacy of good works is what led the Rabbis to mandate a change in the bystanders' response at the circumcision rite, it is, I think, unlikely. Even if they had wanted to alter the response for theological reasons, it is not at all clear that they could have done so.

A third possible explanation emerges from a curious midrashic tale about a wonder-working Rabbi in late second-century Galilee, Simeon bar Chalafta. We have two recensions, one in Ecclesiastes Rabbah (ER) and the other in Deuteronomy Rabbah (DR), both being compilations of uncertain date. The DR passage may be as late as the eighth century, but the story in its ER form is much older. It is reproduced there in the original Palestinian Aramaic, the folk language in which it must have circulated originally. ER is actually two tales sewn together by an editor, but the editor's redaction is relatively transparent so that the seams of the two stories are still evident. In the DR account, however, an editor has worked hard at harmonizing the tales, even translating them into Hebrew to match the language of the midrashic collection in which they have been embedded. In both cases, they are evoked in the context of a consideration of human mortality. DR discusses the approaching demise of Moses while ER takes up the theme from Ecclesiastes 3:1–2, "To everything there is a season . . . a time to be born and a time to die."

I reproduce below the earlier and more complete version from Ecclesiastes Rabbah, dividing it into its constituent parts. A running commentary compares it to its companion recension in Deuteronomy Rabbah. As we shall see, the theme that unites the tales in both accounts is the saving effect of good works against the power of evil.

Editorial Preamble

> 1. There is a story about one of the great men of Sepphoris who happened to have the opportunity to celebrate a circumcision, so the men of Ein Te'enah went up to pay him honor. Among those who went up was Simeon bar Chalafta.

Thus far we have an editorial introduction that has been tacked onto an older story, which is about to be told. Its language is standard midrashic Hebrew, whereas the story that follows will be passed on in the original Palestinian Aramaic, the language in which the editor received it.

DR says simply, "It happened once in the days of R. Simeon ben Chalafta, that he went to a circumcision where the father of the child threw a feast." The DR version then moves directly to Story 2, omitting Story 1 entirely.

Story 1

> 2. When they arrived at the gateway, they heard the sound of some children playing in front of one of the houses.

The setting of the story at the gateway may be more than fortuitous. The word *polon* for gateway appears elsewhere not just as an ordinary city gate but as the gate to everlasting life.[27] In addition, the Rabbis viewed the gate as a place of judgment: it was there that they thought the ancient Sanhedrin had met to pass judgments in criminal cases. It was also a symbol of ultimate judgment for each of us, "the closing of the gates" being an image used to describe the final service on fast days, most notably, Yom Kippur. In this story, some children and their father are about to be judged.

> 3. They looked at Simeon bar Chalafta, and saw that he was handsome.[28] They said to him, "You may not move from here until you do a little dance for us."
>
> He responded, "I can't do that for you, since I am an old man." He rebuked them but they were unafraid. He looked up and saw that the house was about to cave in, so he said to them, "Pay attention to[29] what I say to you. Go and tell the owner of this house [the children's father, as we shall see] that if he is asleep, he should wake up, since the beginning of sin is sweet, but its end is bitter."
>
> The sound of their voices awakened the owner of the house, who came out and crouched at the Rabbi's feet. He said, "Rabbi, I beg of you not to pay attention to the words of young and foolish children."
>
> "But what can I do," replied the Rabbi, "seeing that the decree [of punishment] has already been made? However, I can suspend the decree long enough for you to bring out whatever you own from the house."
>
> As soon as he [the owner] brought out whatever he owned from the house, the house reared up and collapsed.

Story 1 ends here. Were it not for the editor's preamble, we would never even know that the purpose of Simeon's visit was to attend a circumcision. Indeed, it probably wasn't in the original version, which DR omits altogether. Story 1 features Simeon bar Chalafta as a latter-day Elisha (from 2 Kings 2: 23–24). When children mocked Elisha, he invoked wild animals to kill them. Here children mock the Rabbi, who casts an evil eye on their father's home. The difference here is that it is the father, not the children, who is held responsible. He awakened in time to avoid dying in the ruins of his house, and he even manages to save his possessions, but he loses his home as punishment for his children's offense. The theme of Story 1 is: "The beginning of sin is sweet, but its end is bitter." That is, it may be tempting to avoid the responsibility of educating one's children (the beginning of sin), but paying for their sinful behavior is a bitter consequence. Fathers must teach their children Torah so that they know better than to sin.

Story 2

> 4.   They went to fulfill the commandment of circumcision.

This is the original beginning of the story, retained despite its redundancy with the general preamble that the editor supplied to begin story 1. As part of the text that the editor already had before him, it appears in the original Aramaic. Its content, however, is the equivalent of DR's short introduction. "It happened once in the days of R. Simeon ben Chalafta, that he went to a circumcision."

> 5.   The father of the child fed them old wine, saying, "Drink this good wine, for I petition[30] the Master of heaven that I may feed it to you at his [the son's] wedding feast."
>   They answered, "As you admitted him to the covenant, so may you admit him to Torah and to marriage."

Of great interest is the fact that the bystanders' response is consistent with our reconstruction in that it lacks "and good works." It stands out from the Aramaic of the tale as a whole because it is in Hebrew, the normal language for prayer. It must have been the standard ritualized response for the occasion. The story's authors simply embedded it in their account the way people would have said it. Since, as we saw, the response probably dates to tannaitic times, successive tellers of the tale would have known it and cited it in its authentic original.[31]

We now understand better the context in which the bystanders' response occurred. Permeating the rite is the public understanding that circumcision is the beginning of the male lifeline of which marriage is the end. No official prayer announces this connection, but the father here expresses hope that the men who have come for the circumcision will return for the wedding. Appropriately, the guests shout back, "Just as you circumcised him, so may you bring him to Torah and to marriage."

Story 2 is a mirror image of Story 1. The first father was derelict in his covenantal duties and was punished. This father is obedient to the covenant. His son will outwit the angel of death.

> 6.   At the sound of their words, Rabbi Simeon bar Chalafta went out into the darkness where he met the angel of death,[32] who said to him, "You trust in the power of your good works,[33] else you would not go out at an unpropitious time."

DR omits this opening remark of the angel of death, summarizing instead from his own editorial third-person vantage point, "Certain of his own strength, he [Rabbi Chalafta] went out at midnight to go home." But the ER original provides a significant element that DR has lost. The Aramaic that I translate variously as "petition" or "trust in the power of" (depending on the context) is *rachets.* Above the father "petitions" God (*ana rachets bemareih dishemaya*) that he may see his son married; here the Rabbi "trusts in the power of his good works." Only because of his good deed of circumcision does he dare ask for (or trust that he will receive) protection against evil, exactly as the angel of death says of the Rabbi: "You trust in the power of your good works." The evident moral is that good works save: the good deed of the father who takes care to circumcise his son, and the good works of the Rabbi, though it is not clear exactly what good works we are talking about in the latter case—whether his rabbinic record of good deeds in general or his attending the circumcision in particular.

> 7. He [the Rabbi] said to him [the angel of death], "Who are you?"
> "I am the angel of death," he replied.
> "Why are you upset?" he asked further.
> "I am upset by the hard things I hear from people every day."
> "What are those?" the Rabbi asked.
> He responded, "This child whom you circumcised today is fated to
> have me carry him away from here when he turns thirty days old. But
> the boy's father gave you wine to drink, and said, 'Drink this good
> wine, for I petition the Master of heaven that I may feed it to you at his
> wedding feast.' I heard that and was saddened, for their prayer [*tselot-hon*] has annulled the decree."

What prayer could he mean? The third-person masculine plural, "their," is telling. It must be some prayer that "they," meaning the guests at the circumcision, said. But the only prayer mentioned there is the bystanders' response. We know already that the response reinforced the father's role in furthering the male lifeline in that it acknowledged his first covenantal act toward his son while looking ahead to the other two acts (Torah and marriage) that would complete his responsibility. But the response is also a good deed in and of itself; it, too, is part of the liturgy with prophylactic potential to annul a decree of death. These two meanings, affirmation of the father's male responsibility toward his son and a protective device against the angel of death, are both present in the earliest stratum of the tale—from the time, that is, before "good deeds" was added to the bystanders' response.

But as it ultimately develops, the response does even more. Its inclusion of the additional phrase *ma'asim tovim* also makes it a prayer to the effect that the child will complete his male lifeline rather than die young on account of insufficient good deeds to protect him. In the paradigmatic case represented by our midrash, we have Rabbi Simeon and his colleagues actually present; since they possess their own good deeds, their response is sufficient in and of itself to annual the decree of death. But typical little boys can hardly expect the presence of Rabbis with good deeds enough to save them. So the normal ritual response is outfitted with a petition that circumcised boys ever after grow in their own good deeds and become independently protected against evil mishap.

> 8. "As you live," said the Rabbi, "Show me my fate!"
>
> He [the angel of death] replied, "I have no power over you or over your colleagues, because every day you work at Torah and the commandments and doing righteous acts, so that God augments your lives."
>
> "May it be God's will," said the Rabbi "that just as you do not control our fate, so may you have no power to annul our words."[34]
>
> They petitioned for God's grace and the child lived.

The final line is difficult. Again, we have an unknown "they" who pray, but this time removed in time and place from the onlookers at the circumcision rite. As the form is participial, *ba'ein*, it may just summarize "people petition and the boy lives." But I have taken the penultimate *yodh* of בעין to be a scribal error for a *vav*, with the original word being בעון *be'on*, the Aramaic third-person plural masculine perfect; thus: "They petitioned." I think, in fact, that most of section 8, everything from "'As you live'" to "They petitioned" is an isolated insertion that should be removed as out of place. Then we would have "Their prayer [*tselot-hon*] has annulled the decree" (the end of 7) followed by "They petitioned . . . and the child lived" (the end of 8). These phrases fit together nicely as a self-contained story about how ritual prayer saves children.

The beginning of section 8, repositioned as a conclusion to the story, then becomes an addendum on the subject of how good works save the Rabbi himself; it also indicates the relative importance of works and prayer. It is the

Rabbi's good works that make his prayer effective. "I have no power over you or over your colleagues," the angel of death explains "because every day you work at Torah and the commandments and doing righteous acts." The Rabbi summarizes, "Just as you do not control our fate, so may you have no power to annul our words."

To be sure, the actual words *ma'asim tovim* are replaced here with "work at Torah and the commandments and doing righteous acts." But the DR parallel leaves no doubt. It sums up by saying, "God takes pleasure in your good deeds [*ma'aseikhem hatovim*] and augments your life."[35]

Our newly combined version would thus read:

He [the Rabbi] said to him [the angel of death], "Who are you?"

"I am the angel of death," he replied.

"Why are you upset?" he asked further.

"I am upset by the hard things I hear from people every day."

"What are those?" the Rabbi asked.

He responded, "This child whom you circumcised today is fated to have me carry him away from here when he turns thirty days old. But the boy's father gave you wine to drink, and said, 'Drink this good wine, for I petition the Master of heaven that I may feed it to you at his wedding feast.' I heard that and was saddened, for their prayer [*tselot-hon*] has annulled the decree. They petitioned and the child lived."

"As you live," said the Rabbi, "Show me my fate!"

He replied, "I have no power over you or over your colleagues, be-cause every day you work at Torah and the commandments and doing righteous acts, so that God augments your lives."

"May it be God's will," said the Rabbi, "that just as you do not con-trol our fate, so may you have no power to annul our words."

It will be recalled that Ecclesiastes Rabbah, though perhaps as late as the eighth-century as it stands, contains much older material as well. Story 1, for example, is probably tannaitic and told in Aramaic. It preserves the origi-nal bystanders' response without "good deeds." Let us assume, however, that by the time ER was compiled "good deeds" had already been added, so that the editor would have noted its absence in the version of the story that reached him. While we cannot know for sure, I am inclined to think that the editor would have corrected the text he received so as to match his own practice, thinking that the final two words of the bystanders' response had simply fallen out accidentally. The fact that the editor of ER included the response without the addition of "good deeds" suggests that at least some people in Palestine were still saying it that way—and, if so, it becomes harder still to identify the addition as a concentrated rabbinic attack on Christianity in some earlier era.

For our purposes here, we need only conclude that, at the very least, there is no reason to believe that the addition of "good deeds" in the circumcision rite represents a direct and conscious polemic against Christianity. I have argued that ritual is not text but performance. Especially in a society that lacked printed prayer books, "fixed" responses by ritual participants would have been hard to alter, even if there had been a concerted rabbinic effort to do so. Moreover, given the amorphous structure of the tannaitic rabbinic class, it is hard to imagine that a well-orchestrated effort by all Rabbis could have been mounted in the first place. At best, we have isolated midrashim by specific rabbinic authorities that constituted exegetical proofs for the rabbinic system, including its insistence on the efficacy of good deeds. On methodological grounds alone, however, it is difficult to argue from midrashic exegesis to standardized liturgical formulae.

And if this methodological caveat were not enough, we have an implicit testimonial by the editor of Ecclesiastes Rabbah, who could have added the extra words to the story he passed along, and probably would have, had his practice been to say them. But he did not, precisely because he saw no problem with the bystanders' response as it stood without the added element.

It is hard to know when the change was made, but we may very well have a Babylonian innovation, either during the amoraic period itself or later still, even as late as the Geonim. As we saw, our standard Babli version has the extra words, as do Amram and Saadiah. Yet the geonic masters do not render the verb in the third person; they maintain the original second-person address to the father. Amram, however, *always* hews closely to his Babli paradigm; proving the validity of the Babli tradition is the very point of his prayer book.[36] There must therefore have been some tampering with the Babli tradition even after the middle of the ninth century. Whether the extra words also were a later "correction" to the Babli text or whether they were authentic to the Babli in the first place seems to me to be unanswerable.

One more issue is raised for us by the circumcision story that we have considered. Granted that both Christians and Jews were committed to the proposition that they would be saved—whether by faith or by works—what did they mean by "salvation"?

Standard wisdom on the subject holds that salvation for both communities meant deliverance to some sort of life beyond the grave. This seems so obvious that one hardly even bothers to supply textual substantiation for the claim. Jesus himself, as well as Paul and the early Church in general, are clear enough on the subject. On the Jewish side, one cannot read very far in rabbinic literature without coming across equally certain testimony to rabbinic visions of a world to come, for which this earthly life is but a mere antechamber. A quick survey of the Mishnah, for instance, reveals such statements as: "This world is like an antechamber before the world to come; get ready in the antechamber, so you can go into the great hall." Similarly: "Those who are born are destined to die, and those who die are [destined] for resurrection."[37] Elsewhere the Mishnah encodes the pietistic advice of Pinchas ben Yair, who teaches that the entire purpose and end of the good life is resurrection of the dead.[38] To deny the cardinal doctrine of resurrection was to give up one's right to a place in the world to come, and instead to be relegated to the ultimate punishment of such evildoers as the generation of the flood (Gen. 6), the Sodomites (Gen. 13), the spies who brought a negative report on the Land of Israel (Num. 14), and the Korahite rebels (Num. 16). For all of these, the Rabbis held that their ultimate punishment was to be denied the one thing that mattered: a share in the afterlife.[39] The Rabbis' faith in a world to come cannot therefore be in doubt.

Scholarly opinion also has assumed that Jews and Christians were not alone in this concern for life eternal; that, on the contrary, they exhibited their own version of a more general societal trend that was in evidence even in earlier Hellenistic times but that became more and more powerful as the Roman Empire entered its later stages. Explanations of the rise of otherworldly consciousness have varied. Nevertheless, it has been taken as axiomatic that the shift in expectation from this life to the next did in fact characterize both rabbinic Judaism and Christianity in the first two centuries C.E., just as it did other forms of Hellenistic religion at the time. Whether people satisfied their need to be saved in the next life by pursuing the cults of Mithra and Sybele or by engaging in Jewish and Christian alternatives, it seemed perfectly evident that their behavior was driven by an overwhelming concern for salvation as life after death. "What seems to emerge in clear outline," says Ramsay MacMullen, comparing the educated views of Plutarch on one hand and Tertullian on the other, "is a considerable clientele . . . in the Greek-speaking world, among whom prevailed some faith in an agreeable afterlife."[40]

But MacMullen sums up the evidence from the philosophical and therefore literary informants only to indicate the grave doubt we ought to have about the ability of the Great Tradition to represent the Little Tradition of the masses—not just the illiterate street people, but also the well-educated citizens of late antiquity who may have harbored little or no need for salvation in terms of life after death.

Equally reliable evidence to the contrary comes from the inscriptions MacMullen collects, which lead him to ask, "What, in fact, did people want from the gods?" What they wanted was, above all, healing. Asclepius is called the savior not because he promises life after death, but because he controls this life, the only one there is.[41] People prayed for a whole assortment of things: health first and foremost, but also beauty, children, freedom from slavery, protection in war, safety from natural disasters, relief from taxes, and even the restoration of hair.[42]

> Among felt wants, the modern observer expects to find none sharper than the need for life, promised for ever. But . . . assurances of immortality prove unexpectedly hard to find in the evidence. Even the longing for it is not much attested. . . .
>
> In all the "oriental" cults in general, whether of Atargatis, Mithra, Isis, or Cybele, the element of resurrection has received emphatic attention in studies old and new. . . . It should really not be taken for granted, as it often is assumed, that people who believe a god might rise from death also believed in such a blessing for themselves as well. The conjecture needs support, and finds none. Moreover, [in the cult of Attis] . . . ritual cleansing in the blood of a bull has been taken as a sign of a belief in the possibility of life after death. What it was actually thought to grant, however, was an extension of one's earthly existence, in a state of ritual purity, and then only for a limited term of years.[43]

MacMullen's insistence that average men and women of antiquity were moved by needs of this world far more than by aspirations for the next finds a ready echo in our circumcision tale. Just as MacMullen was surprised at the absence of a theologically sophisticated salvation theme in his inscriptions, so, too, a practiced reader of rabbinic texts must confess astonishment at the same lacuna in our Rabbah tale.

How is salvation represented there? Not as life after death, which goes unmentioned completely, but as protection from the angel of death, which is to say, staying alive here in this life, the only one anyone seems to recognize if we judge by that account alone. That Jews believed in deliverance by blood symbolism, of which the seder and circumcision were two primary vehicles, I think is plain to see. But what did they mean by deliverance?

We are again in the realm of public, though not official, meanings. As a condensed symbol, blood meant many and different things to people then, no less than prayer does to people now. Without doubt, as my sample citations from the Mishnah demonstrate, the Rabbis encoded the promise of religion in terms of an afterlife, resurrection, and the world to come. The guarantee of a world to come was the *official* meaning of rabbinic rites in general, including circumcision, which was appropriately practiced even on an infant who died before his eighth day in the belief that circumcision might still be required if he was to inherit his proper eschatological reward. For many people, however, circumcision meant *un*officially what we find in the story of Rabbi Simeon, nothing otherworldly at all, but a guarantee of long life even for those already fated to be carried away prematurely by the angel of death.

Circumcision bore other meanings, too, meanings not connected to the highly abstract theology of a world to come or to commonsense prophylactic measures against untimely death. Circumcision symbolized the gender status in rabbinic society where men and women were emerging in binary opposition: men whose very flesh was thought to be marked with the covenantal sign, and women who were covenanted only secondarily, by virtue of their fathers and husbands; men who were charged with knowing God's commandments, teaching them to new generations of men-to-come, and women who were not; men who officially attended covenant meals—the seder and the circumcision feast—and women who did not. The whole system becomes manifest in the duality of male and female blood, the former, as we have seen, being positively viewed as salvific, the latter earning the opprobrium of rabbinic commentators, who continue to treat it as the priests had, as laden with impurity and ringed with taboo. This male/female dichotomy encoded in the blood symbolism of circumcision on the one hand and menstruation on the other is our next example of public meaning in rabbinic culture.

Gender Opposition in Rabbinic Judaism: Free-flowing Blood in a Culture of Control

The liturgical portrait that has emerged so far is of men celebrating ritual circumcision and seeing in it the drawing of male blood that saves. We move now to a consideration of the female side of the picture, the shedding of menstrual blood that is deemed to pollute. Simultaneously, we return implicitly to the theme with which we began: the Rabbis' identification of a human life cycle with a male lifeline. That theme is played out in the public celebration attendant upon circumcision blood as opposed to the absence of all public attention to menstruation, which exists in the rabbinic scheme of things only as an uncontrollable and threatening natural disorder, likened to a river flooding carefully cultivated land. Finally, paralleling the cultural visibility of men but the cultural invisibility of women, we should add the well-known centrality of men in the rabbinic system of liturgy in general as opposed to the absence of women there.

Though not absolutely identical, these three phenomena are closely related:

1. ritualized male circumcision as a "cultural" act that saves, but non-ritualized female menses as a "natural" act that pollutes.

2. the presence of men as socially recognized human agents with their own culturally celebrated lifeline, but the relegation of women to the category of natural object—the object, that is, of the action of men, who act upon the women as they act upon other natural objects in their environment. The status of a woman is then a function of her relationship to a man, who is her *ba'al,* her master.

3. the ubiquity of men in the institutionalized *liturgical* life of rabbinic Judaism in general as opposed to the invisibility of women there.

Far from arcane ritual symbolism, the positive meaning read into circumcision and, its mirror opposite, the negative implications projected upon
menstruation, undergirded the social absence of women in rabbinic religious
institutional life. Before turning to the antithetical symbolism of male and female blood, therefore, I want to summarize what we know about the religious
marginalization of women in the complex of liturgical institutions in rabbinic
society. Only then, in the second half of this chapter, will I return to the theme
of blood as a symbol of the gender dichotomy within rabbinic Judaism. In the
next chapter I will extend the theme of blood as an iconic symbol of the cultural opposition between men and women, and return in the chapter thereafter to the relative role of men and women in the rabbinic life cycle.

We have already seen that the Temple cult, dominated as it was by
priestly concerns, was very much a male domain. But what about the liturgical
but noncultic rabbinic arenas of synagogue and *chavurah?*

When one thinks of the liturgical alternatives to the Temple, it is the
synagogue that first comes to mind, and until recently few things have seemed
as certain as the absence of women there. To judge by the evidence of tannaitic
literature, women had nothing to do with the synagogue: they were not
counted for the purpose of establishing the presence of a prayer quorum, were
not even commanded to worship, and were excluded by Jewish law from leading men in prayer. They did have a certain role in home ceremonial—prepar-
ing for the Sabbath, for example.[1] But rabbinic texts prescribe a version of
synagogue life in which women's activity is proscribed.

The synagogue is not the only extracultic institution with a liturgical life
of its own. We hear also of a fast-day liturgy, held in the public square some
time prior to the Hillelite-Shammaite period (that is, in the first century and
a half B.C.E.), by a group called the *ma'amad.* If women were in attendance,
they are completely overlooked. The account is highly stylized, so that the
event portrayed may not have occurred precisely as our author describes it;
for that matter, it may never have occurred at all. Regardless, we have at the
very least an editorial assumption of who the socially relevant actors must have
been: all men. The situation in question is a drought, which evokes a public
rite wherein a man addresses other men on the need for repentance. He punc-

tuates his remarks with a concluding litany that recalls biblical personalities whose petitions God heard, all of them men: Abraham, Joshua, Samuel, Elijah, Jonah, David, Solomon, and, most significantly, "our fathers at the Red Sea," but not, for example, Miriam, whose biblical predominance is ignored here.[2]

Another early form of liturgical celebration outside the Temple precinct took place in the tableship groups known as *chavurot,* which proliferated in rabbinic society as the Jewish equivalent of Roman eating clubs. There, too, we find no official female presence. The *ma'amad* and the *chavurah,* not the synagogue, are the two most preeminent liturgical rabbinic institutions during the pre-70 (or Pharisaic) period.

Tannaitic legislation for and description of the synagogue in the period immediately following the Pharisaic era appear to be compatible with *chavurah* recollections of festive eating and *ma'amad* traditions of fast-day worship. A reasonably logical reconstruction, therefore, has been that insofar as the synagogue was a religious rather than a civic entity, it was influenced by the ambience already established by these two other ritual arenas: the male-dominated *chavurah* on the one hand and the equally male-oriented *ma'amad* on the other.[3] Though the synagogue may have existed as early as these other ritual loci, it became a place for prayer only relatively late in its evolution, at which time rabbinic gender attitudes already visible in the *ma'amad* and the *chavurah* entered the synagogue as well.

True, this reconstruction has not been universally acclaimed as the "received wisdom" on the subject. Despite all evidence to the contrary, scholars and popular observers alike have preferred viewing the synagogue as a place of prayer from its very inception and, in that regard, as being an early importation from outside of Palestine. As recently as 1988, Joseph Gutmann could report the following:

> That the origins of the synagogue as an institution central to Jewish life
> can be traced to sixth-century B.C.E. Babylonia has so often been re-
> peated in scholarly texts that it has been accepted as an unassailable
> and established fact. Scholarly opinion has simply assumed that, after
> the destruction of the First Temple, the Judean exiles in Babylonia
> would have needed and demanded a substitute for the lost, destroyed,
> Temple of Jerusalem. No archaeological proof of the existence of the
> synagogue in sixth-century Babylonia exists. Neither the Greek word

synagoge, nor its Hebrew and Aramaic equivalents *Bet-hakeneset* and *Bei-khenishta* are mentioned in Ezekiel or anywhere else in the Hebrew Bible. Still, the theory of the Babylonian origin of the synagogue has taken firm root and is quoted as if it were gospel.[4]

Gutmann does not overstate the case. Early literature is veritably filled with descriptions of this presumptive Babylonian spirituality out of which the synagogue is said to have emerged.[5] Even the authoritative *Encyclopedia Judaica* tells us:

> It is to the period of the Babylonian exile that one must look for the origins of the synagogue. Not only has it been *assumed* that the Exiles, deprived of the Temple, in a strange land, feeling the need for consolation in their distress, would meet from time to time, *probably* on Sabbaths, and read the Scriptures, but it is in Ezekiel, the prophet of that exile, that one finds the first *probable* references to it. It has been *suggested* that in the repeated mention of an assembly of the leaders before Ezekiel (8:6, 14:1, 20:1) one can point to the actual beginning of the synagogue. More definite, however, is the "little sanctuary" in 11:16, and *it may have been* a true instinct which made the Talmud (Meg. 29a) apply it to the synagogue.[6]

The words I have italicized hardly confer an aura of certainty. Such phrases as "it has been assumed," "it has been suggested," and "it may have been . . . true," together with "probable references" and "probably on Sabbaths," do not inspire confidence. And for good reason! Other origins of the synagogue have been postulated as well: a *proseuche,* or "prayer house" in Egypt, dated to the reign of Ptolemy III Euergetes (246–221 B.C.E.), for example, or civic gatherings in postexilic Palestine.[7] But the evidence is sparse for any single line of evolution, and in the end we are relegated to uncertainty.

In all probability, the synagogue began as a civic gathering place having little to do with daily liturgies—just what one would expect from the Greek title *synagoge* and the parallel *bet hakeneset,* both of which mean "a place for gathering." How and when rabbinic liturgies find their way there, and how indeed it comes about that Rabbis themselves are associated with these originally nonrabbinic "meeting places" remain mysteries still. Lee Levine sums up the array of functions ascribed to synagogues by voices as diverse as the

Gospels, Pauline epistles, Mishnah and Tosefta, talmudic *baraitot,* midrashic collections, and Josephus:

> What exactly took place in the ancient synagogue? . . . It was . . . a center for the entire community, serving as a place for study . . . for law courts . . . for the collection of local charity funds . . . as a hostel . . . and as a place for social and political gatherings.[8]

With the exception of reading Scripture and expounding upon it—not necessarily liturgical functions tied to a prayer service per se—the rituals we associate with worship and life cycle ceremonial are noticeably absent from this list. Levine is therefore being charitable at best when he reaches the cautious conclusion that "the place of prayer in the ancient synagogue remains in question."[9] After a comprehensive analysis of textual and epigraphic data, Ezra Fleischer has fewer scruples about challenging the presumed central role of the synagogue in the development of rabbinic worship patterns. He mentions such things as: (1) the normal Palestinian word *synagoge* (a meeting place) as opposed to the term found outside the Land of Israel; *proseuche* (a praying place); (2) the structural similarity, nonetheless, of synagogues in and outside the Land, a characteristic that prohibits our assuming that diasporan synagogues may have been overwhelmingly different from Palestinian ones;[10] (3) the evidence from the synoptic gospels and from Paul, as well as from Josephus, who, for example, singles out the Essenes as people who pray in the desert but says nothing about daily prayer in synagogues; (4) the centralized design of synagogue space, apparently planned to allow auditors to hear the reading of Scripture and to take part in a discussion following, but not necessarily orchestrated for the purposes of prayer; and (5) inscriptions such as that of Theodotus, where we hear of a synagogue expressly for Torah and study, but certainly not for prayer.[11] All these things lead Fleischer to observe, "Given the sources in our hands, it is necessary to emphasize that [before 70 C.E.] of the things normally subsumed under the category of Jewish liturgy [*tefillot yisra'el*], the synagogue contained only the reading of Torah and prophets."[12] But it is not only the distinctly rabbinic activity of statutory prayer that is lacking; Rabbis' names are customarily missing from such things as synagogue inscriptions. The names that are included indicate just how distant this early synagogue as civic center was from rabbinic concerns.[13]

The synagogue was therefore very much an institution in process, hardly a monolithic rabbinically controlled structure, perhaps even as late as the end of the second century. To describe it as if it were already the rabbinic ideal that it eventually became in post-200 rabbinic literature is to overstate the influence of the Rabbis of that period. It is to ascribe too much institutional centrality and too much rabbinic control to an era that was still highly diverse and by no means unified behind that single rabbinic model of what society would become.[14]

This more modest understanding of the synagogue as a general civic meeting place without any guaranteed rabbinic domination, even as late as the promulgation of the Mishnah in 200 C.E., is particularly enlightening regarding the role of women in institutional Jewish religion. Their purported absence as spiritual agents, as reported in the official rabbinic accounts of Mishnah and Talmud, should have been suspect long ago, given the contrasting role of prominent women in Hellenistic religions generally and in Christianity in particular.[15] Certainly since the appearance of Bernadette Brooten's *Women Leaders in the Ancient Synagogue* there can be no doubt on that score.[16] Ross Shepard Kraemer sums up recent literature and draws a sharp contrast between the Rabbis' implication that women were absent from Jewish religious life and the fact that they were involved not just in synagogue officeholding but in other things as well (though her evidence within Palestine, as opposed to the Diaspora, is modest and not generally supportive of the notion that men and women freely intermingled at religious events, sharing them equally).[17] Judith Romney Wegner differentiates private from public domains, holding that rabbinic legislation excludes women from the latter but not the former.[18] The synagogue was, of course, public. Yet at least in the Hellenized institutions from which the data confirming women's activity come, women were there playing public roles.[19]

We do *not* know enough about the early synagogue *within Palestine,* where rabbinic legislation could have had an impact. Nevertheless, it is certainly clear by now that even though the rabbinic system *eventually* became coexistent with the synagogue, it was certainly not that way until well into the amoraic period or later. Even our study of circumcision as a rite by which males were initiated into a rabbinic and male-dominated religious system should be seen as a slow evolutionary process that took place over the course of many centuries. To be sure, rabbinic discussion presents the system as already fully complete and universally accepted in tannaitic days. More likely, however, circumcision as the sine qua non outfitted with the public rabbinic meanings that I explore in this book was originally limited to small groups of rabbinic authorities and only eventually came to dominate Jewish thinking generally.

Before resuming our analysis of circumcision blood as a symbol of male/ female structural opposition within the mature rabbinic system, we should look more carefully at the various institutions that have merely been mentioned thus far. The symbolic opposition that I describe does indeed characterize rabbinic literature and ritual, but we want to know the extent to which that literature and ritual dominated society in the early years under discussion here. We therefore need to estimate the degree to which rabbinic culture in general permeated Palestinian institutional life during the tannaitic and early amoraic eras.

First, the Palestinian synagogue: One outstanding characteristic of the Mishnah is not the detail with which the putative rabbinic institution of the synagogue is described but just the reverse, the uncanny extent to which it is ignored. Though rules for synagogue establishment, maintenance, and behavior eventually proliferated,[20] one can read through page after page of mishnaic instruction on prayer without so much as suspecting that a synagogue is even in existence. Of course, it was. Josephus describes it and Jesus attended it. But in the first century, it was still far from a secure bastion of rabbinic Judaism.

Thus the evidence that Brooten marshals to demonstrate the prominence of women in synagogues is not at all inconsistent with the rabbinic approach to women as implied by the symbolism of circumcision that we shall examine, as long as we realize that we have two parallel but independent phenomena here. Brooten finds women acting in a variety of synagogue leadership roles, including that of "Elder," "Mother of the Synagogue," and, above all, *Archisynagogos*, or "Head of the Synagogue," a rule the Rabbis knew as *Rosh Hakeneset* and traceable to the pre-70 period.[21] Regardless of the leadership roles to which women could aspire, however, there was one that remained closed to them: women could not be Rabbis. If women were eventually exiled from their leadership capacity in the synagogue, that can only be a testimony to the Rabbis' success over the years in superimposing their rabbinic system on an institution that was originally not their own—or not exclusively theirs at any rate.

The synagogue was not originally religious but civic; it was therefore not rabbinic and had little to do with rabbinic ritual. Because the synagogue represented the community or the *polis* rather than the rabbinic faction within it, the Rabbis stuck closely to the *chavurah,* where meal liturgies developed, and to their *bet hamidrash,* the academy where they studied and pioneered public liturgy simultaneously, rather than to the *bet hakeneset,* the synagogue. By the year 200, the rabbinic daily prayers may have been transferred from the *bet hamidrash* to the synagogue, but even that is not clear. The Mishnah does know that the synagogue is a sacred place: one does not, for example, take shortcuts through it the way one might through an alley or a store with a front and a back entrance. But mishnaic legislation is otherwise sparse at best when it comes to synagogue rules, precisely because the synagogue was not yet the primary locus for rabbinic liturgy, and certainly not the place the Rabbis preferred for their own prayer. Their public liturgy of the hours, so to speak, the morning, afternoon, and evening worship that we take for granted today as synagogal in its essence, was still pursued in the *bet hamidrash,* where Rabbis studied Torah as their primary occupation but also paused when necessary to worship their God. Not that the *bet hamidrash* was an architecturally discrete building, the way universities are today. But it was a social institution, a disciple circle clustered around the teaching activity of a given rabbinic sage.[22] To apply an idiom from Damon Runyon, it was a floating crap game, but being legal, it moved publicly wherever its rabbinic teacher went; it was not limited to, or even necessarily connected with, a building or a synagogue, which, understandably, both Pharisees and Tannaim rarely mention.[23]

By contrast, the Mishnah supplies abundant details about *chavurot,* both expressly and in rules for table fellowship that take for granted the *chavurah* as an institution paralleling the *bet hamidrash* in importance. Here, too, we have to exercise care, since even within the Mishnah's pages, we have the same Hebrew term *chavurah* used in three different contexts.[24] First—and of least concern to us—there are references to courtyard meals, which may represent an early institution in which people living side by side in a common courtyard ate together. The determining factor here is accidental geographical propinquity.[25] Second, we find *chavurot* meeting in other locales, largely as ad hoc groups to celebrate festive events, most notably, the Passover. This is a voluntary coming together of people having nothing to do with geography. Occasion, not place, is the determining factor. It would be too much to say that someone actually "belonged" to these *chavurot,* since they existed only as long as the meal in question was being eaten. People joined as many such groups as they had celebratory feasts to eat, either for holy days or for "life cycle" events.[26] Those who joined would become known (for purposes of discussion and description) as *b'nai chavurah,* "members of a chavurah."[27] There is still no indication that these ad hoc *chavurot* were established to keep out the *amei ha'aretz,* that is, the average Jews, who were suspected of being less than punctilious in matters of food tithes and purity. Almost anyone could join them, priests as well as ordinary Jews,[28] but not "women, slaves or minors."[29] It was apparently here, in these ad hoc groupings, that tableship ritual, including the Grace after Meals, was established, so that we eventually get a ruling against "women, slaves and minors" participating in that prayer specifically.[30]

But a third, and later, stratum gives us a very different picture: ongoing *chavurah* groups to which one belonged for extended periods of time. Here we find new members participating in a sort of induction ceremony whereby they take responsibility for the rules of purity that the group considers critical.[31] These are the ongoing *chavurah* groups that Jacob Neusner and others have identified as the sacred gatherings in which ordinary Jews took upon themselves the rules of tithing and ritual purity hitherto associated only with the priestly caste.[32] They, too, seem to have excluded "women, slaves and minors," though with a slight caveat. Since these were ongoing groups that committed whole households to tithing and purity rules over time, even those exempted—a man's wife, children, and servants—had to vow their loyalty to the rules. However, only the men swore loyalty directly to the *chavurah.* They alone were actual members, answerable to the other *chaverim.* Their wives, children, and servants were answerable to them, whether as husbands, fathers, or masters.[33] A *chavurah* was, after all, a public institution, even if it was in someone's home. Women could not eat there as members in their own right because they were excluded from the public domain.

In sum, excluding the Temple and the academy, we have three interlocking institutions here: the synagogue, the *chavurah* as ad hoc table celebration or as ongoing tableship club, and the *ma'amad.*

I have said little about the *ma'amad* since there is little that is even known for sure. Our purposes require only that we recognize that it arose out of the Temple cult. Its public worship had originally paralleled the occasions when sacrifices were offered in Jerusalem. Regions of the country took turns sending bystanders to the daily sacrifices, while back home the *ma'amad* met in the town square at precisely the time that the delegation would have been overseeing the Temple sacrifice. Eventually, the town gathering also met on an ad hoc basis in the event of national distress, particularly droughts.[34] The *ma-*

'amad was thus an extension of the Temple, with, we may presume, all the gender bias taken for granted by the priests. We should not be surprised, therefore, to find that women had no official role there.

The *chavurah,* too, was connected to the Temple, though not directly, in that its ongoing meetings had nothing to do with the rhythm of the sacrificial system. But it owed its existence to the underlying cultural motifs of priestly piety, priestly tithes, and priestly purity in that the *chaverim* sought to emulate the priests' lofty state. Since it was the Rabbis who were the *chaverim,* the *chavurah* was rabbinic through and through. It is therefore constantly mentioned in the Mishnah and Tosefta, and associated with meals that men attended. Since women were often present at meals in late Roman antiquity in general, we ought to picture women in attendance at *chavurot* also, but they are passed over in our sources. They were marginalized, present physically but not socially.[35] Like observers at a scholars' conference today who merely listen while official invitees discuss their papers, whatever women might unofficially have said went unrecorded.

The synagogue, as we have seen, was at first *not* influenced in any serious way by the Rabbis, who mention it only in passing in their writing and who preferred to pray in their study circles rather than in what was essentially a civic meeting place. For some time, then, women seem to have shared power with men in the synagogue. But their role there must have ended whenever it was that the rabbinic system was ultimately adopted as the mandate of the synagogue as well.

We are now in a position to summarize the institutional marginalization of women in early rabbinic Judaism. Both *ma'amad* and *chavurah* were male-dominated from the outset. It is in these two places that rabbinic ritual thrived before moving to the synagogue. Circumcision would at first have been symptomatic of *chavurah* spirituality, that is, the religious celebration that we now consider part of the life cycle, and therefore an event for which the *chavurah* came into being. The male blood drawn during the circumcision rite symbolized the salvation inherent to the role of men, but not women, in the rabbinic system. Eventually, the male/female duality also came to dominate the hitherto more egalitarian synagogue. Meanwhile, rabbinic attitudes toward menstrual blood completed the symbolism of male/female opposition, as female blood was outfitted with a taboo that marginalized its existence within rabbinic culture, just as the women who shed it were marginalized within rabbinic society.

We saw above that blood became the dominant rabbinic symbol of the covenant: blood of the paschal lamb—which had to be a male lamb—to recollect the exodus of God's People Israel; blood of circumcision—again, obviously, male—to symbolize the covenant ceremony for individual males being inducted into the covenant that goes back to Abraham. It is this blood that saves. At the induction ceremony, the men in attendance celebrated their own covenantal community, with the adolescents about to enter puberty even washing their hands in the blood-water mixture, according to geonic testimony. Only at his circumcision did the boy get a name, being known thereafter as the son of his father, who was the son of his father, and so on, all the way back to the first father, Abraham.

In contrast to male blood that saves, however, we find a fear and even loathing of female blood, which the Rabbis surround with remarkable taboo. We shall see presently how the Rabbis creatively expanded the taboo against menstrual blood, but they were not the first to postulate it. Given all we said before, we should not be surprised to find out that their interdictions go back originally to the P author of the Bible.

> When a woman has a discharge, her discharge being bloody from her body, she shall remain in her impurity seven days; whoever touches her shall be unclean until evening. Anything that she lies on during her impurity shall be unclean; and anything that she sits on shall be unclean. Anyone who touches her bedding shall wash his clothes, bathe in water, and remain unclean until evening. Be it bedding, or be it the object on which she has sat, on touching it he shall be unclean until evening. And if a man lies with her, her impurity is communicated to him; he shall be unclean seven days, and any bedding on which he lies shall become unclean. When a woman has had a discharge of blood for many days, not at the time of her impurity, or while she has a discharge beyond her period of impurity, as long as her discharge lasts, she shall be unclean. Any bedding on which she lies while her discharge lasts shall be for her like her bedding during her impurity; and any object on which she sits shall become unclean, as it does during her impurity. Whoever touches them shall be unclean. He shall wash his clothes, bathe in water, and remain unclean until evening. When she becomes clean of her discharge, she shall count off seven days, and after that, she shall be clean. On the eighth day, she shall take two turtledoves or

two pigeons, and bring them to the priest at the entrance of the tent of meeting. The priest shall offer the one as a sin offering, and the other as a burnt offering; and the priest shall make expiation on her behalf for her unclean discharge before the Lord. (Lev. 15:19–30)

Particularly now that women have been admitted to scholarly circles, this passage has begun to attract considerable attention. What is it about menstrual blood that so repulses the biblical author P? A variety of speculative views can be found on the subject,[36] including the possibility that it is "the polluting 'opposite' of purifying sacrificial blood,"[37] or that it opposes circumcision, not sacrifice, since circumcision is a man's birth into his cultural state whereas actual childbirth is "merely" birth into the state of nature, meaning that the signs of this birth—first and foremost the mother's blood connected with it—had to be devalued.[38] Others see it as an innate threat to maleness, or to the P author's conception of the holy as "everything in its place."[39] Then, too, it may that this is ambiguous blood, once intended for life, but flowing now because potential new life did not occur, and thus it becomes blood that is to be avoided.[40] The possibilities seem endless.

My own analysis differs from most others in that I emphasize the context of the P passage and its literary shape. At first glance, we seem to have the entire rabbinic fear of menstrual blood already provided in the biblical stratum preceding rabbinic exegesis. But that is not the case. Leviticus 15 is a carefully constructed essay not on menstrual impurity per se, but on genital impurity, embedded in a larger series of such essays on other forms of impurity that the community should avoid. The two preceding chapters, for example, discuss leprosy and plagues, describing the means by which they are diagnosed and the necessary pollution-avoidance behavior they entail. The chapter prior to that details rules relevant to childbirth. Here we get the final such essay, this one on the subject of sexual emission. What we do not have, in other words, is a separate essay on women as sexual pollutants, so much as we have a treatise on sexual pollution in general, in which both female and male pollution are described with equal concern.

In fact, the structure of the Levitical essay on genital emissions is so arranged that the dichotomy between men and women has been carefully subsumed under another organizational scheme, one in which gender is irrelevant. As Jacob Milgram points out, this chapter is structured chiastically, in an ABC–C'B'A' pattern, equally divided between men and women, where

BB′ stands for "abnormal" discharges and CC′ for "normal" discharges. We can depict the structure as follows:

A. Introduction (verses 1–2a)
  B. Abnormal male discharges (verses 2b–15)
    C. Normal male discharges (verses 16–17)
      D. Sexual intercourse (verse 18)
    C′. Normal female discharges (verses 19–24)
  B′. Abnormal female discharges (verses 25–30) [motive (verse 31)]
A′. Summary (verses 32–33)[41]

The structure is striking both in what it says about genital pollution and in what it omits.

1. Normal pollution (C, C′) is classified as short-term impurity (seven days for menstruants—the time assumed to correspond to an average menstrual flow—and one day for seminal emission).

2. Abnormal pollution (B, B′) for both men and women brings about a whole week of impurity with the need to offer a sacrifice the next day. All in all, however, the cases of men and women are asymmetrical, since the impure state for men increases from one day (normal) to seven days (abnormal), whereas women remain impure for seven days in both instances. Taking men as his standard of normality, P may therefore have seen menstruation itself as abnormal. Still, it is not technically abnormal, as is the case he is dealing with here, a form of gonorrhea, the victim of which he calls a *zav* (masculine) or *zavah* (feminine).[42] Gonorrhea differs from ordinary discharges in that it has secondary consequences regarding contagion: its impurity is presumed to be transmittable from men as from women second- or even third-hand to persons coming into contact with it.[43]

Other details are available as well. Yet what this carefully constructed Levitical essay does *not* provide is a delineation of impurity along male/female lines. Normal/abnormal is the structural key. Both men and women suffer from both possibilities, but other than the seven-day menstrual taboo and the parallel single-day case for a seminal emission, neither men nor women stand out as a more serious case of pollution concern.

The section on the menstruant, therefore, is not set off along with other cases relevant to women. Rather, it comes at the proper place for the female instantiation of "normal" emissions, just as the female *zavah* is not classed as a specifically female problem but as the mirror image of the *zav,* the equivalent male predicament. To be sure, the menstruant is quarantined longer than the male equivalent of "normal pollution," a man who has had a seminal emission, and we may therefore have P's gender bias operating in a relatively minor way within a larger taxonomy that is not gender based. Alternatively, that difference may simply derive from the fact that the seven-day menstrual time span has no parallel for men, in which case there is no gender bias whatever here.

Certainly, if we compare the male and female cases in any given category, we find that the rules of passing on impurity are identical. Take the *zav* and the *zavah,* for instance. The rules of transferring impurity (to bedding or to anything that the impure person sits on, and then to anyone who touches that object) are the same; the remedy (washing one's clothes, bathing in water, and remaining unclean until evening) is also the same; and the ultimate cleansing act (two turtledoves or pigeons as a sin offering and a burnt offering) apply to both cases as well (verses 4–25).

Consider the case of sexual intercourse itself. The chiastic structure dictates that it be dealt with in the middle of the discussion of impurity. We get an address first to the male who emits the polluting element, semen; anything that semen touches must be washed and is unclean until evening. The parallel warning is then given to women. Intercourse renders men and women equally unclean, so that women also have to "bathe in water and remain unclean until evening" (verses 16–18).

In sum, Leviticus 15 is a tightly constructed essay on genital pollution, arranged chiastically but not along gender lines. In what may be an added verse to the otherwise tightly constructed chapter (v. 31), *all* Israelites, men and women, are warned to be on guard against uncleanness. In case we have any doubt about the overall structure of the essay, we find the apt conclusion in vv. 32–33:

> Such is the ritual concerning one who has a discharge, and him who has an emission of semen and becomes unclean thereby, and concerning her who is in her menstrual infirmity: anyone, that is, male or female, who has a discharge, and also the man who lies with an unclean woman.

"Anyone . . . male or female"—that is the key to Leviticus, which establishes impurity rules, but does not discriminate between men and women.

Both are agents of impurity insofar as either emits any bodily substance through the sexual organs. The remarkable thing is how the Rabbis interpret the same rules with an entirely different criterion in mind.

Of the six "orders" (or books) that constitute the Mishnah, one deals almost exclusively with purity rules, providing us with an excellent index of the way the Rabbis reconceptualize the cases of sexual impurity detailed in Leviticus 15. They erase the chiastic scheme in which men and women are equally regarded as potential sexual polluters. Leviticus had set off genital pollution as a case in itself, and then within that category treated men and women equally. By contrast, the Mishnah adopts a hierarchy of pollutants in which sexual sources of impurity do not form a single category. Rather, male and female sexual emissions are arranged separately on the hierarchy such that genital causes of impurity can now be considered from the perspective of whether they are male or female in origin.

Biblical impurities, then, are rearranged mishnaically, so that they constitute a hierarchy.[44] At the top of the scale is the most serious category, *av hatumah* ("father of impurity"), below which is *vlad hatumah* ("offspring of impurity"). Moreover, the category of *av* is not simple but compound, having within it several degrees of impurity. Although the details need not concern us, we should take note of the novel categorization scheme that effectively dismantles the biblical principle of nongendered organization.

In the Mishnah's classification scheme, the place occupied by a pollutant on the hierarchy of pollution sources depends on many factors: the extent to which any given item's contamination extends—to human beings and vessels, but not to foods; the ways in which contamination occurs—by direct contact or by mere proximity under the same roof; or the length of time a victim must spend in the state of impurity before returning to the normal state of ritual purity. The scheme is not altogether independent of the Bible.[45] In the Bible, too, different pollutants have different degrees of contagion, more or less far-reaching consequences, and so forth. But in the Bible, these issues are secondary to the observable features of the pollutants themselves. The rabbinic classification system, on the other hand, is directly tied to nonobservable data. Empirical observation is quite sufficient to discriminate such biblical categories as plagues or sexual emissions after all, and Leviticus is organized into separate essays on each such *observable* disease or condition. But no amount of observation can tell us whether a pollutant transfers its impurity directly or not, or to dishes but not to liquids, or for one day rather than seven.

It is these qualities of the pollutants that matter most in the mishnaic hierarchalization. The Mishnah has thus replaced empirical categorization with a set of organizing principles taken from a system that the Rabbis already assume, and which they then map onto the world of phenomena around them.

The Mishnah's presumptive explanation of why things fall where they do on the pollution scale is not really an explanation at all but a mere restatement of the system. That is why more than one consideration separates one kind of *av* from another. The Mishnah first has recourse to the inherent principle of *extent* of pollution; if that fails, it tries *method* of pollution; when that does not work, it cites *length* of pollution. But none of the three—extent, method, or length—is an explanation so much as it is the Mishnah's internal monologue on some of the system's own patterns. We cannot *see* what pollutes what, for how long, and in what way, so the Mishnah tells us how the rules operate; but it does not tell us how the system arrived at those rules in the first place. If there is a ruling principle here, we shall have to look outside the Mishnah to find it. One could settle for the citation of biblical prooftext, but at some point biblical prototype fails, and we seek some internal logic within the system itself.

In 1986 Howard Eilberg-Schwartz and I met at a symposium organized by Riv-Ellen Prell at the University of Minnesota. We discovered that we had independently arrived at complementary theories regarding the taxonomy of impurity regulations. His work dealt primarily with biblical material while my own concentrated on rabbinic sources, but with a few exceptions (which I note below) we found our work to be in harmony. We both had become convinced that the key to understanding the map of pollution, and therefore the taboo against menstrual blood, was to be found in the concept of self-control.

Eilberg-Schwartz has since published his own findings.[46] In one way or another, several authors had claimed that taboos regarding bodily fluids vary according to the extent to which they are associated with life. Lightly shed, they represent life wasted; hence the taboo against spilling them for non-procreative purposes.[47] The human corpse, the very embodiment of death, represents the highest level of impurity while menstrual blood and spent semen—representing life potential wasted—are also prominent pollutants, albeit on a level lower than an actual corpse.

In *The Savage in Judaism* (1990), Eilberg-Schwartz expressed support for the claim that the life/death hermeneutic explains much of biblical and rabbinic impurity taboo, despite "some anomalies that stubbornly resist this symbolic interpretation."[48] His 1986 paper was less welcoming of the theory, more worried about the anomalies, which are also my concern here. Among other things, semen pollutes even during intercourse, hardly what one would expect if the essential opposition is semen properly expended for procreative ends versus semen spilled in nonprocreative acts. Then, too, why should blood from birth be impure if such blood is only a side effect of successful new life? Above all, in the rabbinic hierarchy of pollutants, a nonseminal discharge (the *zav*) makes a man unclean longer than the ejaculation of semen.[49] The problem is that semen is on the lowest rung of the *av* category while the *zav* is higher up in the seriousness of its implications. Yet the nonseminal discharge of the *zav* has nothing to do with procreation, and therefore ought not count as a pollutant at all.

It is above all the anomaly of the *zav* relative to normal seminal discharge that leads Eilberg-Schwartz to formulate a principle that works not only for emissions from the sexual organs but for all bodily fluids: urine, earwax, semen, and so forth.

> The fluids which are released from the genitals thus comprise a system which expresses various degrees of human control. Urine, at the one end, being the most controllable, can never contaminate the body. Sperm which is ejaculated, and thus subject to human control on certain occasions, makes the body impure only until evening. Menstrual blood, non-menstrual blood, and nonseminal discharge are completely uncontrollable, and consequently make the body impure for seven days. In other words, there is a direct relation between the controllability of a bodily fluid and its power to contaminate the body.[50]

Of course, the discharge of semen is not entirely voluntary. It is sometimes ejaculated while a man is asleep, for example, a fact that Eilberg-Schwartz accounts for by saying that "sperm . . . is . . . subject to human control [only] on certain occasions." But in general Eilberg-Schwartz holds, "it represents a muscular event, and therefore is associated with human control more than the release of non-seminal fluids."[51] I shall return to Eilberg-Schwartz's explanation of seminal discharge in terms of muscular control shortly. In the meantime, it is important to see how completely his proposed etiology of the rabbinic taboos regarding bodily fluids works. The very Hebrew terms themselves "differentiate clearly between one who is a master of his action, and one whose body fluids flow without his consent."[52] Menstrual blood, of course, is completely uncontrollable; it thus shares with nonseminal emissions the status of pollutant. Urine, on the other hand, assumed to be controllable by any socialized adult, is not classified as a pollutant; and "tears, saliva, mucus, milk and ear wax [which also do not pollute] are similar to urine in that a person can exercise a similar amount of control over them."[53]

Finally, let us reconsider the case of semen, where even medieval opinion seems to side with the hypothesis that it is willfulness and self-control that matter most. Leviticus 15:18 says, "When a man has an emission of semen, he shall . . . remain unclean until evening." But what causes the impurity? The medieval exegete Ibn Ezra explains, "This means [only if the emission is] against his will [*shelo virtsono*]."[54] Clearly, the prevailing principle here, too, is the perceived opposition between control and noncontrol, with the Rabbis labeling bodily emissions that flow of their own accord "pollutants."

With this understanding of the hidden hermeneutic at work in the rabbinic classification system for bodily fluids in general, we are almost ready to return to the symbolic role of men's blood and women's blood. First, however, the linguistic image of the *zav* as "one who has—but does not control—a flow," as opposed to the rabbinic assumption that the man who ejaculates is in charge of what he does, deserves further scrutiny. As to the imagery, we should note that the *zav* (and, of course, his female equivalent, the *zavah*) are not the only cases where imagery of free-flowing fluids can be found. The Hebrew word for menstruant may not have that connotation, but the Rabbis apply their own metaphors that leave us in no doubt about what they thought.

> The sages constructed a metaphor with respect to a woman: (1) a room, (2) a front hall, and (3) a room upstairs. Blood in the room is unclean. If it is found in the front hall . . . it is presumed to come from the *fountain* [the uterus].[55]

Similarly,

> Women are like vines. There is a vine whose wine is red, a vine whose wine is black, a vine whose wine is abundant, and a vine whose vine is sparse. Rabbi Judah said, "Every vine has its wine."[56]

With these two metaphors, we return full circle to the circumcision ritual, where we also saw wine functioning to suggest blood; here menstrual blood suggests wine. But above all, in the Rabbis' idiom, the menstrual flow is like a fountain, spurting forth, whereas (to anticipate) the whole point of drawing circumcision blood is that it is controlled, dependent entirely on the *mohel* who takes a single drop if need be, and stops up the wound.

The issue of control is important to the pollution potential of semen too, although the truth is that semen is not as controllable as the Rabbis would have it. I here part company with Eilberg-Schwartz, who, we recall, holds that the emission of semen "represents a muscular event, and therefore is associated with human control more than the release of non-seminal fluids." But surely the vagina, too, is a case of musculature. While it is not a voluntary muscle totally under the woman's control, neither is the muscle in the man's penis. Why should the Rabbis have overlooked the fact that at the moment prior to ejaculation a man has no more control over semen than a woman has over menstrual blood? Or that nocturnal emissions are even more unpredictable than the average woman's period, which at least is expected around a given time? Moreover, why should we believe that tears are controllable? or breast milk? or earwax? or mucus that escapes in a "runny nose"? True, our own culture cleans up the human body in such a way that we like to imagine we have control over all such emissions. We cough involuntarily, and turn our faces away from an observer who pretends not to observe until we finish wiping our noses and mouths with a tissue. We keep our ears well-groomed. We "fight back tears," even though we know of times when "tears well up and overwhelm us," for which we may even dutifully apologize. Adults should not be "cry-babies." But all of that is our own cultural imagination at work, tidying up the untidy facts of bodily substances that defy our will more than they obey it.

Eilberg-Schwartz and I agree that the key to body-fluid pollution should be sought in the issue of control. But I do not think we can treat body control as biological, even when the anatomical facts are clear. What matters here is a social phenomenon, for the Rabbis' decision to see themselves as controlled and women as loose goes beyond the anatomical features of relative musculature. At issue is a deeper perception that the Rabbis have of men on the one hand and women on the other. We shall see in the next chapter that this underlying perception takes us back once again to blood as the Rabbis' primary means of symbolizing gender issues. The binary opposition obtains between men who are in control of their blood, so of themselves, and therefore of society; and women who, lacking control of blood and therefore of self, are thus denied control of society as well.

c h a p t e r **9**

Control and Transformation: "The Raw and the Cooked" in Rabbinic Culture

A common theme that runs throughout the rabbinic literature on circumcision is the fear of losing control. Consider, as an example, the following responsum, dealing with the question of whether the blessing said by the father should precede or follow the operation. Normally blessings introduce the acts they define, but astonishingly enough, our rabbinic authority tells us that the circumcision blessing should follow the surgical procedure. His logic is telling:

> Thus wrote Sar Shalom [a ninth-century Gaon]: The father should say his blessing . . . only after the operation is completed. Our sages taught that blessings over commandments always precede the commandment, but circumcision is different, since we are afraid that it will not work out [*nitkalkel hamilah*]; [and in such a case, if the blessing has already been said,] the blessing will have been said in vain [that is, without the successful completion of the act toward which it points]. Now, if you should object to that line of reasoning, saying that if so, the same logic ought to hold for the blessings said over slaughtering animals and blowing the shofar [both of which are also matters whose success is hard to predict in advance, yet the blessing is not similarly delayed in their case], the response to your objection would be that they are not in the same category as circumcision, since they are in the power of the person saying the blessing, and that person can reasonably expect to do them [*hanakh tartein beyado shelo ve'ika lemeimar dematsei me-kayem leho*], whereas in the case of circumcision, the act is entrusted to someone else [the *mohel* and not the father who says the benedic-

tion], and who is to say that he [the *mohel*] will fulfill it properly [*milah beyad acher hu, mi yeimar demakeyem lah*]?[1]

The fear of a botched job is portrayed as reasonable here. But is it? Why should the expert at this operation be trusted less than other experts elsewhere? We regularly hand complex tasks over to such specialists precisely because they do not fail at them, whereas we, who have little aptitude for the job, probably will. To blame the Gaon's fears on gross superstition, or on heightened anxiety that is "naturally" attendant upon circumcising a child, is merely to beg the question.

The Rabbis' fear of losing control is not unique to circumcision. It is a powerful theme in rabbinic life in general. "Who is mighty?" asks the well-known mishnaic adage. "The one who controls his impulses [*hakovesh et yitsro*]."[2] I want to claim that the entire rabbinic system is based on a cosmology of order in which it is men's role to impose order in human affairs, paralleling a male God's primeval act of ordering the cosmos. The *halakhah* is nothing if not the system of imposing order on creation. Men learn the Torah, which is God's master plan for order on earth, and which they then use as a pattern for their own actions. The Mishnah is their classification scheme providing the possibility of order and clearing up anomalies along the way.

One particular anomaly, it has been argued, is women, to whom the Mishnah allots an entire sixth of its attention, namely, Tractate Nashim.[3] For the Rabbis, women pose a constant threat of disorder, impulsive behavior, a failure of self-control. The texts that illustrate this underlying rabbinic theme are clear and abundant. Before presenting them, however, I must explore the cosmological bases on which the rabbinic gender dichotomy depends.

The rabbinic system presupposes two domains, the sacred (*kodesh*) and the profane (*chol*).[4] Sacred/profane is the standard cultural opposition popularized by Emile Durkheim and successive theorists in the sociology of religion. "Profane," however, has negative connotations in English. At least with regard to Jewish sources, therefore, the word "everyday" is preferable and will generally be used in what follows.

Most recent literature on the concept of the holy has abandoned Durkheim and turned instead to the work of Mary Douglas. This move seems to be part of a broader paradigm shift toward what is very generally called the postmodern. Older literature was essentialist. It believed holiness was inherent in things—one could experience it, know it, write a phenomenology of it. Although Durkheim reduced holiness to its social basis, he, too, could talk about it as something "out there," tangible, albeit manufactured by the group experiencing it. What makes nontheistic religions religious for him is precisely the fact that their adherents also experience rites, things, truths, and practices as sacred rather than as profane. A rite, thing, truth, or practice is by definition one or the other.[5] From Durkheim it is only a short way to other universally cited sources in the older literature, some of them in revolt against Durkheim's reductionism but in agreement regarding the holy as the essence of religion. Rudolf Otto, for example, saw his task as providing a phenomenological survey of sacred experience.[6] Mircea Eliade begins with Otto and then investigates how the sacred breaks in on human consciousness, human space, human time, and so forth.[7]

What Durkheim was for Otto and Eliade, Douglas is for a new generation of scholars. Douglas's interest, however, is the making of meaning in culture generally, and the way in which meaning depends on cultural classification in particular. Locating the sacred within the very system of classification itself is a positive boon to many modern scholarly projects, not the least of which is the feminist concern of explaining why women are so frequently marginalized when it comes to the sacred. If the sacred depends on cultural classification, there is reason to expect that men as cultural classifiers would have excluded women.

It was Jacob Neusner who first applied Douglas's systemic thought in a thorough way to biblical and postbiblical data. His topic was purity and impurity, however, not holiness per se, so he touched upon Douglas's claim that holiness and purity are interrelated in Judaism, but he stopped short of identifying the two as one and the same thing.[8] Other scholars, however, want to go farther. Jerome Neyrey sums up the argument:

> What is meant by "purity"? It is an abstract way of interpreting data.
> Purity is best understood in terms of its binary opposite, "dirt." When
> something is out of place, or when it violates the classification system
> in which it is set, it is "dirt."[9]

So far so good. That is indeed Douglas's claim, and it works remarkably well. If matter out of place is dirt, then matter in place is its opposite, cleanliness (or purity, as Douglas uses the word). We exemplify this opposition whenever we shuffle papers from their random position on our desks into piles that correspond more or less to categories in our heads. A stray note or an old list lying in the middle of the desk is dirt. But call the first a reminder of a book to read and the second a record of student grades, and then assign each to a pile with other papers like themselves, and you have cleanliness.

In actual fact, however, a subtle but important confusion has crept in. We need to keep carefully separate the way we think of the system and the view we have of its parts. The part of the system that is the piece of matter out of place is called "dirt." The adjective "dirty" may describe that piece of matter relative to the unpolluted system, but it may also describe the system into which dirt had been inserted. A system that is not dirty is pure, so that "purity" is a quality of the system but not of any piece of matter that makes it up. For non-dirt, that is, matter in place, we have no word at all. Douglas argues that purity is a quality of systems to which no dirty matter has been added; pollution is a quality born of alien parts, namely, those parts that do not belong within the system because they have no place within it. Matter as dirt thus pollutes systems because it has no place.

Neyrey's failure to differentiate system from part leads him to the error of identifying purity with holiness. In Douglas's scheme purity is a quality of the system—the organization of all its parts as matter in place. Neyrey wants to hold that holiness is the same thing: a system where everything is in place, and he attributes this view to Douglas. By contrast, I claim that rabbinic Judaism sees holiness as a quality of things, not of systems. The ideal toward which rabbinic culture strives is a system called the cosmos in which everything is in place, and where, therefore, purity inheres. As to holy and profane, however, these are diametrically opposite qualities of things, acts, relationships, and so on that make up the cosmos. It is precisely these things that cannot be mixed without compromising the purity of the system. Holiness is not identical with purity. Purity is what we call a system where holiness and its opposite are not comingled. The parts of such a system are either holy or everyday, but they may not be both.

Since Neyrey reads his system out of Douglas, we must return to Douglas again. Her argument seems to be that (A) purity is category integrity; (B) category integrity is a manifestation of what she calls "wholeness"; (C) wholeness is the same as holiness.

I readily assent to A. Purity is a system's capacity for proper order, pollution comes from things that defy systemic categorization, and impurity is a systemic defilement brought about by dirt, which is matter out of place. I agree, too, that category integrity is a form of wholeness (B), as Douglas uses the word. But what of the claim that wholeness is holiness (C)? That does indeed seem to be Douglas's argument; but wholeness of what? Insofar as she has in mind the system, wholeness is synonymous with integrity. Using the word adds nothing to the argument, which stands or falls without it. If we rephrase the argument without this confusing term, we get: (A′) purity is category integrity; (B′) category integrity is holiness.

What is at issue, then, is the validity of B′, which Douglas extracts from her reading of Leviticus. As she puts it, "Since each of the injunctions against impurity is prefaced by the command to be holy, so they must be explained by that command."[10] But she confuses the system with its parts, for purity explained by holiness does not mean that purity *is* holiness. Purity is the desired end of the system; holiness is a quality to be sought by its parts.

The Israelites are God's holy People; they live in holy space, are entrusted with a holy Torah, and charged with keeping a holy calendar. What they are not to do is mix the holy with the unholy—to act unethically, for example, which would amount to a holy People performing unholy acts— because if they do, they will have mixed categories and brought about pollution. The holy, then, is a category of things, the binary opposite of unholy. Impurity occurs when these two categories—the holy and its opposite—are mixed.

This insight leads us back to Jewish cosmology in which the key task is to keep the holy separate from the unholy (the everyday) lest the holy be polluted. Sometimes this requires actions designed to transform things from one category into the other. Popular theology rooted in late Hasidism presumes that the desired transformation is from the category of the everyday to that of the sacred. But for the Rabbis of the classical period, it is the other way around. The universe is holy in its essence, belonging to God who made it. It presents itself to us as sacred, so it must actually be *de*sacralized before we can use it. This view of things runs completely contrary to everything most of us have been trained to think, but an objective reading of the rabbinic sources leaves no doubt about the matter.

Take, for example, the blessing system for food. "The earth is the Lord's and the fullness thereof," says Psalm 24:1. So the Rabbis rule that humans who are not in a state of sanctity, as the raw earth and its produce are, must *release* food from its sacralized state before consuming it. The release of such food into the realm of potential human consumption (the everyday) is what blessings accomplish. That is why (as we saw) blessings are normally said *prior* to the act they denote. "One should eat nothing before saying a blessing . . . for to make enjoyable use of this world without a blessing is to be guilty of sacrilege [*me'ilah*]".[11] Blessings are thus a desacralizing vehicle, for they function to render sacred food "profane," removing it from the earth's inherent delivery system and making it fit for everyday human consumption.[12] Some things cannot be so desacralized: the first fruits of one's produce, for example, or the first three years of a fruit tree's harvest, or the portion of any given produce that must be tithed. All of these are foodstuffs that must be offered back to God; only what is left over after the offering can be eaten.

There are other examples, some more complex than others, that have nothing to do with food. In chapter 7 we referred to the ceremony of Pidyon Haben ("Redemption of the Firstborn), according to which a father must redeem a firstborn son from the priest by paying the latter a token monetary compensation. But why should redemption be demanded at all? The answer is that firstborn males are held to be inherently sacred, just like the universe in its pristine state; they, too, belong to God. Therefore, they must be redeemed from God if they are to live a human, that is, an everyday, life.

The rabbinic system thus establishes a basic dichotomy with regard to the things that constitute the cosmos as system; they are either *kodesh* or *chol*, sacred or profane (everyday). But the system is more complex still, since the times, places, people, and things that are holy are not equally so. Rather, holiness occurs in various degrees: the Holy of Holies, for example, being holier than the Temple courtyard, which in turn is holier than the Land of Israel in general, though all three are holy to some extent, whereas space outside the Land of Israel is not holy at all.[13] Similarly, the Sabbath is holier than Rosh Chodesh (the New Moon), though both are holy to some degree, and therefore different than weekdays that are "everyday" in nature. When a holy day ends, a prayer of *havdalah* (separation) must be said so as to distinguish "between holy and the everyday." That, at least, is the wording used on a Saturday night as the Sabbath is ending. But if the Sabbath is followed by a festival, so that one holy day comes immediately after another, the words are altered to read, "You [God] have made a distinction between the sanctity of Sabbaths and the sanctity of festivals. . . . Blessed art Thou, O Lord, who distinguish [not between holy and profane, but] between holiness [of one degree] and holiness [of another]."[14] The same is true of holy things, those, that is, that belonged to the Temple in antiquity, dedicated to sacred use by the sacred

castes assigned to do God's work there. And finally, there are the sacred castes
themselves: in the realm of people, a priest (a *kohen*) is holier than a Levite (a
levi), who is holier than an average Israelite (a *yisra'el*), but all three belong
to the holy People, as opposed to non-Jews who do not. Non-Jews are to hu-
manity what *chutz la'aretz* ("outside the Land of Israel") is to space and what
sheshet yemei hama'aseh ("the six workdays") are to time. Everywhere, then,
the rabbinic system provides not for a simple dichotomy so much as a graded
scale, going from the very holy to the barely holy and only then to the realm
of the nonholy, the everyday.

	Everyday	Sacred
People:	Non-Jews	"regular" Jews (*yisra'el*); Levites; priests; high priest
Place:	Outside the Land of Israel	the Land entire; Jerusalem; Temple mount; Holy of Holies
Time:	Six workdays	*chol hamo'ed* [everyday part of festive periods]; festivals and Sabbath; Yom Kippur
Things:	Everyday utensils	*hekdesh* (sacred things used only by priests in Temple)

The everyday, too, may have its degrees of "everydayness." This is one
of the ways in which the English word "profane" fails to capture the subtlety
of the rabbinic system. The opposite of *kodesh* ("holy") is *chol*, but not everything that is *chol* is "profane" in the sense of being unclean. Most things that
are *chol* are not unclean at all; they are simply "ordinary," opposed to the
specialness of the holy. But within the class of the ordinary, some things are
positively evil, existing, if you like, at the extreme end of the line leading away
from the *kodesh/chol* divide, just as the most sacred things exist at the extreme
end of the line going the other way. The extremes are intense. Israelites in the
holy sector, but nonetheless near the middle of the line as a whole, must fear
the "satanic" at one extreme (like the angel of death in our story from
chapter 8) and the Holy of Holies at the other extreme, which only high
priests, who are extreme themselves, may enter. In the last chapter, we saw
that potential pollutants exist in various degrees of impurity. Now we see that
holy things are similarly arrayed along a spectrum. In both sets of phenomena—potential pollutants and holy things—the rabbinic mental process
of hierarchical ordering is evident.

If it is the case, then, that things are never merely holy or everyday but
somewhere along a line between the two, it becomes necessary for us to emend

what we said before. First, regarding foodstuffs, it is not absolutely true that blessings completely desacralize food, though it is true that they lower the level of its sacrality to the point where ordinary Jews can eat it. In general, we can conclude that *the goal of the rabbinic system is not always to desacralize the sacred, but to be able to transform human actions to the degree called for by any particular concatenation of time, space, human actors, and circumstance.* True to Douglas's model whereby purity is order, and true also to Israel's essence of being a holy People charged with not profaning (that is, polluting) the holy with the everyday, rabbinic Jews take great care not to mix categories. Time, space, actors, and activity must be of equal holiness. The Temple precinct, for example, was conceived as a hierarchy of holiness, so that the holier one's status, the farther inside it one could go. The holiest class, priests, can enter parts of the Temple that ordinary Israelites cannot, and the holiest priest, the high priest, can even enter the Holy of Holies, but only at the holiest time of the year, Yom Kippur, and only after particularly sacred preparation.[15] Even then, his access is carefully limited: "As to the Holy of Holies, a high priest enters therein once a year for the sacrificial service of the Day of Atonement, four times in the day; if he entered it five times, he is liable to the death penalty."[16] By contrast, women, who cannot go as far inside the Temple as even average men (Israelites), were limited to occupying the "Women's Courtyard," an area of such moderate sanctity that "even though it merited special distinction . . . unclean people who enter it are free of punishment."[17] The whole point of the rabbinic system is to transform unequals within the set of person, place, thing, and time so that all are of equal status on the sacred-everyday spectrum; only then does the desired action occur with felicitous results.

The cosmological scheme behind this system is what we would call astrology. Astrological systems presuppose a finite set of recurrent stellar arrangements through which the earth moves as part of its natural course through the heavens. At one extreme of observation, we have large groupings of arrangements called the four seasons; just below that, we have the twelve constellations. But the constellations change continually, so that each day— indeed, each moment—features its own unique heavenly array that typifies just that day or moment and no other; it will recur only once a year.

The appeal of astrology, however, lies in the assumption that this changing heavenly array is not objectively disposed to everyone equally; hence the importance of knowing the class into which one falls—whether one is a Leo or a Pisces, for example. Only then can one predict whether or not the array in question is auspicious for this or that activity.

The Rabbis knew astronomy well, and they accepted it, albeit with ambivalence.[18] They demurred from attributing divinity to the stars and even labeled idolaters *ovdei kochavim umazalot,* "those who serve the stars and constellations." Some held also that it was forbidden even to consult astrologers, meaning, probably, pagan astrologers who consulted stars as they did the gods.[19] But for most, study of astrological science was mandated, since the stars are not separate divinities but merely God's handiwork.[20] Living under planetary influence was a hallmark of being human as opposed to animal.[21] The heavenly disposition of elements known as *mazalot* do affect people, even Jews. Naturally, the Rabbis hesitated to assign the Jewish People to a star. They argued instead that whereas other peoples may have their own star, Israel's fate is directly controlled by the God who made the stars in the first place. Israel is therefore immune to absolute planetary influence.[22] Nevertheless, God had arranged the solar system with an astrological temporality that even Jews could not ignore.

The astrological roots of rabbinic Judaism go deeper than is generally imagined. Of particular importance to us is the rabbinic term *zeman.* The Jewish calendar is astrological in its essence in that it is predicated on the existence of an annual cycle of time with recurrent periods and moments that make astrological demands on Jews—though not on others, who follow the dictates of their own guiding stars. Each such recurrent "moment" in cosmic time is called a *zeman.* Thus the arrival each year of a moment in which a miracle occurred (as on Chanukah) necessitated a blessing that recalled the past, but only in terms of the *zeman* when it happened, the *zeman,* that is, which was recurring again: "Blessed art Thou . . . who wrought miracles for our ancestors in those days and at this *season (bazeman hazeh].*"[23] Even the common Shehechiyanu blessing, now said over virtually every milestone in the Jewish year, was originally tied to the notion of an astrological cycle. The Talmud employs it for building a new home or coming into possession of new objects. Later its use was standardized for a variety of instances, most notably the first day of a recurrent holiday and the eating of the first of a seasonal crop.[24]

Every *zeman* is thus a singular astrological configuration with its own inherent quality, so that, for example, the fifteenth of Nisan is *zeman cheruteinu,* "the *zeman* of freedom": the exodus occurred on this day, and on this day, too, final redemption will take place, for freedom is its essence. As Rabbi Joshua maintained of Passover eve, "On that night, they were redeemed, and on that night we will be redeemed in the future."[25] Every sacred moment was thus introduced with a prayer called the Kedushat Hayom, the "Sanctification of the Day," in which the type of *zeman* typical of the day in question was noted: *zeman matan torateinu* ("the *zeman* of revelation") for Shavuot (Pentecost); *zeman simchateinu* ("the *zeman* of joy") for Sukkot; and so on.[26]

The point of these introductory prayers was not to *make* the arriving *zeman* sacred, but to *recognize* it. The system thus calls on human beings not to transform each particular *zeman* when it comes—that would be impossible—but to transform themselves and their actions to meet the *zeman* in the same state of sanctity that the *zeman* itself presents. In that way, humans meet cosmos in matching harmony.

The fulcrum for this system of transforming human actions to meet cosmic requirements is that particular set of commandments known as *mitzvot aseh shehazeman gerama,* normally translated as "positive commandments dependent on time." Time dependency here, however, would be more accurately understood astrologically; as a *zeman* occurs, Jews are expected to match their behavior to it so as to bring about a desired effect that the *zeman* auspiciously offers. Taking into account the technical meaning of *zeman* as astrological configuration, a more precise translation of this category of commandment would be "positive commandments entailed by the inherent nature of the *zeman.*" And here we return to our main interest in this chapter, women, for women are exempt from that very class of commandment!

Why should that be? The answer one typically encounters is that women are busy with home and family, so they may not be available to do what the time requires. There are problems with this hypothesis, not the least being that some of the positive *zeman*-dependent commandments find their locus in the home and therefore should be entrusted specifically to women, not denied to them. But education of children, for instance, is *not* given over to women, as it would have been had family matters been assigned to wives and mothers. If the Rabbis wanted to exclude women from duties that conflicted with homemaking and motherhood, they could have said so; they didn't. They did, however, rule emphatically that women are not obliged to keep *zeman*-dependent duties. We have to understand why.

For Wegner, who also noted the insufficiency of the homemaking-motherhood rationale, women were exempted from these commandments so as to discourage their entry into "the public domain of religious practice."[27] This, of course, is her general thesis: that women were granted autonomy in the private sphere, including the bringing of lawsuits and the making of legal deeds and promises, but they were not allowed to be public persons. She is generally correct. But the issue of time-bound commandments goes deeper than that.

Women are not the only class that is so exempt. The deaf, the retarded, and minors constitute a class of three usually cited together as a group of people likewise freed of such responsibility. Interestingly, mishnaic texts usually do not classify women as a fourth member of that group. That is because the exemption from *zeman*-dependent duties applies to women for a different reason than for the others. The deaf, the retarded, and minors are all part of a single set in that the Rabbis presume them to lack the sense necessary to perceive what each *zeman* demands. Misunderstanding the deaf as also "dumb," rabbinic society treated them as unintelligent. The retarded were seen as self-evidently unable to comprehend the sophisticated demands of each arriving *zeman.* Minors, by definition, are not yet mature enough in understanding to be held responsible for their every act. Women, however, were believed to have the sense to understand the system but to lack something else: the self-control to practice it.

In sum, with regard to gender, the rabbinic system presents a cultural diad of in control/out of control. Men are controlled, they learn the system of controls, and they exercise control to transform the environment; women are the opposite: they are out of control; they are nature; they are wild, loose, unable (by temperament) to master the application of those commandments that must be done precisely "on time." Therefore, the system necessarily exempts them from those commandments.

In a word, men are nature transformed by culture; women are nature, dependent on culture, that is, on men. They enter men's domain at times like marriage (thus requiring one-sixth of the Mishnah to tell their men how to deal with them), but they are never fully "culturated." They do not learn Torah and are not obliged to effect culture's—that is, Torah's—transformation of nature. Using Lévi-Strauss's celebrated categorization scheme loosely, we can say that men, as culture, are the cooked while women, as nature, are the raw.[28]

I know that I tread on thin ice by claiming that for the Rabbis women are to men as nature is to culture, and that, consequently, men transform women along with the rest of the God-given cosmos. By making that claim, I enter a debate current in anthropological circles since Sherry Ortner published her article "Is Female to Male as Nature is to Culture?" in 1974. Ortner was convinced that the equation of men with culture and women with nature is universal, rooted biologically, among other things, in women's bodies.[29] Her critics have tried to provide one counterdemonstration after another. To cite but two such essays, we have Maurice and Jean H. Bloch demonstrating that the Lévi-Straussian binary opposition of nature/culture is modeled after a philosophical bias rooted in the romanticism of Rousseau:

> Anthropology is heir to a polemic where the opposition of nature and something else is part of the attempt to understand society and at the same time to criticize it; it is not heir to a set of organized concepts clearly defined. What we find when looking at these notions of eighteenth-century France is the language of challenge. Here we are clearly in the field of ideology in turmoil.[30]

Carol P. MacCormack also warns against the wholesale application of this dichotomy, since, among other things, the concepts of nature and culture are themselves products of culture; that is, they are far from universals. She asks:

> How can we agree that the following set of metaphors represent universal human cognitive structure?
> Nature : culture ::
Wild : tame ::
Female : male[31]

Indeed, we cannot agree. The key word here is "universal." I do not mean to claim that rabbinic Judaism recapitulates universal ontological categories, but only that the empirical evidence for this particular cultural system supports the hypothesis in this particular instance. MacCormack helps us establish the case when she notes that "structuralists using the Lévi-Strauss model . . . define men as actors and women as acted upon." It is, according to Lévi-Strauss, "men who own and women who are owned."[32] She objects to this as a universally true description of the way things are—and rightfully so. But the Jewish case is unambiguously organized exactly this way. In the Mishnah, for example, "a woman is acquired" in marriage whereas "a man *mekadesh*," literally a man "sanctifies."[33] I shall later claim that the verb *mekadesh* here means "to bring into covenantal relationship as a woman belonging to a man," for we are seeing that women have no entry into the covenant of their own and must depend on their father's or husband's covenant connection. For our purposes here, all we need note is the obvious fact that a woman is the passive object of a man's active agency. He "sanctifies" her while she is just "acquired" by him. MacCormack, then, could have been describing Judaism, where indeed it is "men who own and women who are owned." Lest there be any doubt on this score, consider the rabbinic taxonomy that expresses the reason that a man may not have intercourse with a woman married to another man. She is *eshet ish,* literally, "a[nother] man's woman." Her husband, moreover, is her *ba'al,* her "master" or "owner."

I think it is abundantly clear, then, that the husband is the one who transforms nature into culture here. That is to say, women, as nature, are admitted to their husband's access to the covenant, which is culture, by the act of marriage; similarly, they leave it when they are divorced.[34]

Empirically speaking, then, it is clear that in rabbinic Judaism women are indeed "wild nature" while men are "controlled culture." To judge by Lévi-Strauss, in fact, it is the very essence of nature to be "wild," for whereas culture is a system of discrete categories, nature is inherently continuous, without boundaries or limits, except insofar as cultures apply them.[35] Frederick Turner agrees, drawing our attention to the horror with which culture views nature.[36] The long march of urban civilization from the days when hunter/gatherers camped around fires to the medieval walled city and even our own urban metropolis features a great fear that the frontier, the wilderness, the wilds of nature will bring our cultural enterprise crashing down around us. Culture is "cooked"; it is under our control. Nature is "raw"; it is untamed, beyond our ken; it is hurricanes and sandstorms and tidal waves, against which humans erect barrier reefs, artificial walls, and sandbags. The world as it is given is "raw," but the Rabbis meet it and tame it with halakhic prescriptions, blessings, and ritual. Sandbags applied after the storm has passed are useless in containing the flood; blessings applied after the *zeman* has passed are useless in tapping the auspicious destiny that a *zeman* offers. Thus men, but not women, are responsible for *mitzvot aseh shehazeman gerama*—positive commandments that depend on the arrival of a *zeman.*

It is the Rabbis' claim of women's innate wildness as against men's natural self-control that I want to demonstrate here. What interests us is the fact that the dichotomies of nature/culture, women/men, and wild/controlled are symbolized by the archetypical blood of the two sexes. The essence of circumcision is the willful and controlled drawing of blood according to Toraitic command, that is, according to cultural dictate. Women, on the other hand, are characterized by blood that flows naturally, uncontrolled by culture. It is taboo for men to have contact with this blood, for it is a source of ritual impurity—tantamount to a tidal wave overwhelming the cultural breakwater. But if blood were to come out of a man's penis, that blood would not contaminate![37] What remains for us to see now, is the survey of rabbinic material on women as uncontrolled creatures of nature.

The issue of control, polarized by gender, is seen most clearly in issues of sexuality. The Rabbis are positively obsessed with the need to exercise self-control in sexual matters. I can illustrate this obsession with the case of the biblical Joseph, whom the Rabbis call *Hatzaddik,* "the saint," because he withstood the temptation of Potiphar's wife, whom they name (as in Islamic lore) Zuleika. In the series of mythic portraits that follow, I note particularly the imagery of blood that is linked isomorphically to looseness or control. Looseness is always associated with rampant sexuality; it is symbolized by flowing blood and overflowing water; this looseness is projected onto women. Control, on the other hand, is held to be sexual propriety, and is the natural condition of Jewish men who have undergone circumcision.

> Rabbi Judah said, "*It was the day the Nile overflows its banks* and everyone came to watch [the Egyptians, like the Nile, are considered loose], but he [Joseph, who is controlled] stayed home to do his work and figure out the accounts of his master. . . ." R. Shemuel bar Nachman said, "He really stayed home to do his work." [Others doubt that Joseph could have restrained himself and maintain that he stayed home when no one was around so as to carry out a liaison with Potiphar's wife.] R. Hiyya said, "[Even alone with her in the house, he was able to withstand sin because] the image of his father appeared to him and *it cooled his blood* [*tsinen damo*]."[38]

Lévi-Strauss wants us to treat all versions of a myth equally, without regard for relative age or evidence of "authenticity." Even if he is not correct in urging us to do so, there can be no doubt about the centrality of the information presented thus far, for it occurs in virtually every version of this story.[39]

Genesis Rabbah adds the moral comparing sexual temptation to temptation in general:

Joseph thought, "My father was tried and my grandfather was tried. Could it be that I will not be tried?" God said, "I swear to you that I will try you more than them."[40]

Yet another version combines the looseness of the Nile's flow with the image of blood flowing loosely—the blood of women, who lack the control necessary to withstand temptation.

> [On the day that the Nile overflowed, Potiphar's wife, Zuleika] commanded her maid-servants to prepare food for all the women, and she spread a banquet before them in her house. She placed knives upon the table to peel the oranges, and then ordered Joseph to appear, arrayed in costly garments, and wait upon her guests. When Joseph came in, *the women could not take their eyes off him, and they all cut their hands with the knives, and the oranges in their hands were covered with blood.*[41]

By contrast, the midrash portrays Joseph as totally controlled. Finding himself sexually aroused while alone in the home of his temptress, he concentrates on his saintly father to regain self-control. Assuming that the rabbinic tale presupposes scientific knowledge of the relationship between blood and an erect penis, we find the Rabbis telling us, in effect, that Joseph willed himself to lose his erection ("cooled his blood"). His willpower is cited as the paradigm for Rabbi Tzaddok and for Rabbi Akiba. But they are really just examples of "every Rabbi at his best." The former comes to mind because his name, *Tzaddok,* comes from the same root as Joseph's *Hatzaddik;* the latter is selected because his full name, after all, is Akiba ben *Joseph.* The story of the former is particularly instructive:

> [Rabbi Tzaddok was sent as a captive to Rome, just like Joseph,] where a prominent noblewoman [Potiphar's wife updated] purchased him as a slave and sent a beautiful maidservant to tempt him to lie with her. When he saw the maidservant, [unlike the women at Zuleika's party, who "could not take their eyes off" Joseph] he fixed his eyes on the wall and lay silent and motionless all night.[42]

Finally, I add an opaque remark carried in the Rabbah to the effect that Joseph was about to capitulate to Zuleika, but at the last minute, "he examined himself and did not find that he was a man [*badak et atzmo velo matza atzmo ish*]." Translators are convinced that this means he became impotent, an interpretation that has good precedent on its side. To begin with, the Rabbah source says expressly, "The bow was drawn but it relaxed."[43] His blood cooled, as we saw. But whereas the earlier account credited Joseph with successfully willing his own impotence into being, this one cannot imagine that Joseph could have restrained himself. A third version should be cited also. Here Joseph buries his fingers in the sand, allowing the semen building up within him to be ejaculated through his fingernails into the earth rather than into the woman before him![44] So Joseph either willed his blood to cool by conjuring up his father; or he ejaculates through his fingers into the ground rather than capitulate to the wild woman before him; or, to his own surprise, he simply failed to attain an erection in the first place.

Still, we must ask, why did he have to examine himself? Didn't he know without looking? Is examination the way a man discovers he is impotent? It may be that we have a double entendre in the Rabbis' account. One lesson is indeed simply that he was impotent. But when the Rabbis insist that he looked down at himself and discovered he was not a man, they may also be alluding obliquely to his circumcision. On this second reading, Joseph examined himself and saw that he was circumcised—which is to say, not entirely a man. He has been made over from the state of nature where men act out their sexuality with wild abandon; instead, by virtue of his circumcision, he has entered the state of culture, where Joseph, as saint, now practices self-control—the very self-control that women, always in the state of nature, are incapable of showing. His circumcision is a prophylactic here against the evil inclination, as the Rabbis would have put it. This latter reading becomes normative in later rabbinic thought, for by the time of the Zohar, Joseph becomes associated with the *sefirah* called *yesod,* which is the phallus on the primeval man. Only circumcised men are presumed to be able to practice sexual self-control. Not to do so is equivalent to misusing the covenant (the *brit* of *milah*) and thence to abrogating the covenant of the People Israel as well.[45]

A cultural system presents itself as a seamless whole, weaving its connections throughout the universe inhabited by its members. Every step we take in unraveling its rules obliges us to take one more step, to extend the rule we have unearthed until, ideally, the entire system is clearly delineated before us. A certain amount of incongruity is passed over in human system-building, but, by and large, the proof of the pudding lies in its texture, which, in this case, must appear seamless, coherent, and smooth. The categories we posit must satisfy the evidence of the behavior we observe, allowing us to make sense of it. These categories must also demonstrate connections between the behavior under consideration and other behavior of which we are aware. Here we would have to extend our analysis to such things as the sacrificial system, where blood is willfully shed so as to render sacrificial meat edible (by the proper class of consumers, naturally). Sacrifice is the reverse of blessings. Blessings transform sanctified produce of the inherently sacred earth so that unholy people can eat it; shedding animal blood transforms inherently profane animals into sacred offerings for God and God's priests. Similarly, can it be that shedding circumcision blood, which, as we saw, is expressly likened to a sacrifice, is what transforms Jewish men into a sacred People? The Rabbis believed that the sacrificial cult also depended on human control. They held that without the exercise of human will by the agent of the deed, the deed itself, even if perfectly performed up to the last detail, was insufficient.[46] Both the sacrificial system, therefore, and circumcision are (1) the shedding of blood; (2) in accordance with human will, following a carefully delineated set of demands that effects the transformation of raw matter into entities with cultural significance.

There are other loose ends that need attention, too, but at this stage, I am content to claim the following:

1. Blood is the dominant symbol of circumcision.

2. That the entire rabbinic system is expressible in terms of transformations along a graded holy-profane spectrum is, in a sense, not even provable. But it does seem to me to be a cogent approach to understanding rabbinic culture. It goes beyond the usual rhetoric of "repairing the universe," "achieving salvation," or some other such end taken from within the system's own repertoire of explanation, and therefore in need of further explanation before it can tell us anything.

3. That one such transformation is the shedding of blood seems well documented with regard to sacrifice; it remains to be seen if it works as an interpretive metaphor for circumcision, but I think it does.

4. Finally, I am convinced that the culture of the Rabbis is definable in terms of the following equation:

men : women :: cooked : raw :: controlled : uncontrolled :: agents
who transform : agents who do not transform :: "cultured" blood
flow : natural blood flow

This equation is not particularly palatable, but it is accurate, I believe,
as a description of the Rabbis' vision of the world. As Ortner would have
predicted, rabbinic men view themselves as controlled: that is their very
strength; they control their impulses. By contrast, they paint women as inherently uncontrolled. Rabbinic law, in fact, requires women to bind their hair so
that it does not fly loosely in the marketplace. Married women risk divorce if
they yell so loud that their neighbors hear them, if they talk to just anyone on
the street, if they do domestic work like weaving outdoors—if, that is, they
demonstrate their tendency to break out of the self-containment that rabbinic
culture mandates as part of its taming of women who are nature.[47] Similarly,
when discussing which characteristics a child inherits from the father and
which from the mother, the midrash assigns what we might call the Apollonian
traits to the father and the Dionysian traits to the mother. "The father provides
the white substance out of which are formed the child's bones, sinews, nails
and brain as well as the white of the eye." By contrast, "the mother provides
the red substance out of which are formed skin, hair, blood and the back of
the eye."[48] So males here are white, bloodless, hard like sinews and nails, logical like the brain, while females are red. Red is for wildness, for blood, for skin
that bleeds, and hair that flies about wildly. Women then are innately wild like
their blood; they are beyond self-control, not to be trusted with commandments that must be done when and only when the proper time arrives.

What women thought of this system, we do not know. We do not know
the extent to which they followed it or, for that matter, even knew it. They
held positions in the synagogue, let us recall, regardless of what the Rabbis
had to say. Similarly, women had their own religious life, including some involvement in the male ritual of circumcision, to which the Rabbis bear testimony in passing. Recall the presence of Elizabeth at John's circumcision, for
example. Our next step will be to survey the evidence on women's spirituality
as the rabbinic system was taking shape, to find the point at which women
truly disappear from the rabbinic rite of circumcision.

c h a p t e r *10*

Women's Spirituality and the Presence of Mothers in Rabbinic Ritual

In 1981, George Jochnowitz, a scholar in the field of romance languages, knocked on my door to inquire about a custom he had encountered in a fourteenth- or fifteenth-century manuscript, having to do with a blessing that Jewish women said in Provence. It was similar to another blessing that is well known to us. In conjunction with a morning benediction intended for men, which reads "Blessed art Thou . . . who has not made me a woman,"[1] the fourteenth-century Spanish savant David Abudarham describes a blessing for women:

> Instead of ". . . who has not made me a woman," women are accustomed to saying, ". . . who made me according to his will," the way one justifies bad fortune [*kemi shematzdik et hadin al hara'ah haba'ah alav*].[2]

Abudarham's custom may have been widespread, since it became usual not only in Spanish circles but in Ashkenazi environs also, and is still called for by Orthodox prayer books worldwide.[3] Yet Jacob ben Asher, a prominent rabbinic member of the prior generation and possibly Abudarham's teacher, does not record the custom, even though he gives this rubric of the service great attention.[4] So Abudarham may be testifying to a new custom about which Jacob ben Asher knew nothing, or which he ignored as an unimportant fad. By the sixteenth century, however, Joseph Caro considers it obligatory for women to say ". . . who has made me according to his will,"[5] and thereafter, their doing so seems to have been taken for granted. Whether Abudarham's exegetical interpretation of the women's blessing as a justification of bad fortune was widely known is, I think, doubtful; at least, it rarely turns up elsewhere.[6]

In Jochnowitz's manuscript, having nothing to do with the official rabbinic corpus and composed in Shuadit, a language spoken by Jews in southern France until the early nineteenth century, women thanked God altogether differently. They said, "Blessed art Thou . . . for making me a woman."[7]

Here we see the selectivity of rabbinic texts. With remarkable univocality, our rabbinic textual tradition gives us a faulty impression of a singular custom developing universally and without impediment, first in Abudarham's Spain, then in Joseph Caro's *Shulchan Arukh,* and then in published prayer books all over the world. Were it not for Jochnowitz's chance manuscript, which is not even in Hebrew and certainly well outside the rabbinic literary tradition, we never would have known that contemporaneous with Abudarham's Spain, at least some Provençal women were "responding" to the men's prayer, "Blessed is God who has not made me a woman," by saying just the reverse: "Blessed is God who did!"

On a much larger scale, we have a similar case of unofficial women's ritual being passed over: the literature known as *tkhines,* supplicatory devotions written for (and sometimes by) women, usually in the vernacular, whether Yiddish, Italian, French, or English, beginning in the seventeenth century.[8] Because *tkhines* are not part of the rabbinic system, the standard compendia of Jewish literature have almost universally ignored them, an oversight described by Chava Weissler, who notes the complete absence of an entry for *tkhines* in Ben Jacob's *Otsar Hasefarim,* a standard work of Hebrew bibliography, published in 1880. "Prayers for women in Yiddish were not considered worthy of a detailed bibliographic entry," she writes. "They seemed ephemeral compared to the enduring classics of Jewish tradition, such as the Hebrew Bible, the Talmud, and the Midrash."[9]

Officially listed or not, women's devotions were widespread.[10] What passes for official practice, therefore, says nothing of unofficial custom: not in seventeenth-century Europe, where women had their own *tkhines,* and not in fourteenth-century Provence, where women said at least one benediction that was not officially recorded and perhaps others as well. The same is true of the period under discussion here: the first several centuries C.E. when the "rabbinic system" was taking shape. What women did among themselves, or even with public recognition and in full view, may well have escaped the reportage of Rabbis, who noted only what they considered noteworthy. We know, for instance, of a first-century dancing ritual for women, held on Yom Kippur and on the fifteenth of the Hebrew month of Av.[11] An anthropological field-worker would have had no trouble recognizing it as a celebration of women's spirituality, but the Rabbis, who knew it only as unofficial practice, merely mention it in passing. Similarly, the authorities in the Palestinian Talmud knew that women kept a New Moon holiday, but since it was limited to women, they classified it as a custom (*minhag*), not a law, and therefore allotted no attention to it other than declaring it permissible.[12] We even hear of "women who spin yarn by moonlight," hardly a rabbinic category, but very likely a women's ritual of some sort.[13]

I wish to explore these sparsely mentioned women's rituals so as to establish the presence of unrecognized women's ritual in the very early years that concern us, my overall goal being to paint a picture of rabbinic Jewish society in which we need not assume that women were absent from their sons' circumcisions. I will look also at evidence of a birth ritual for girls—not specifically a women's celebration, since it existed for boys as well, but another instance where rabbinic records do not tell us the full story. Finally, we will be in a position to appreciate the involvement of mothers in the "life cycle" rites of their sons. The evidence for their presence, both physical and ritual, in the rite of Pidyon Haben is clear and unambiguous. After exploring their role in that rite, we shall return finally to circumcision, wondering whether women may have had more of a presence there than we usually imagine. Our question will be whether, despite the rabbinic system that excluded them, women (as mothers) were once present anyway; and if so, when, how, and why their right to be present was lost.

Moon Ritual (Dancing, Abstaining from Work, Weaving)

None of the three customs already mentioned—dancing, abstaining from work on the New Moon, and weaving—is part of official rabbinic religion. The Rabbis report them only in passing.

The dancing ritual, which we shall examine in greater detail shortly, is cited as part of a sermonic lesson by Simeon ben Gamaliel.[14] On its own merits, it would have had about as much chance of being included in the Mishnah as a stray article from the *New York Times* would have of being cited in the annual proceedings of a national synagogue body today. Yet it might find a place as anecdotal "lead-in" to the official religious matter under discussion, precisely the case here. As we shall see in a moment, the ritual itself was of no interest to the Rabbi who cites it, or to the final editor of the text who decided to include it, except as a convenient homiletical introduction to the speaker's or the editor's own concern.

Similarly, the custom to avoid work on the New Moon is included in the Talmud, not because of its innate importance to the editor regarding what it has to say about what women do or why they do it, but because, along with other examples, it illustrates a theoretical discussion regarding the extension of Sabbath and festival rules of rest. At issue is whether the already-extant practice by which some women do no work on the New Moon is an acceptable custom or not. The Rabbis rule that it is.[15]

Finally, the account of the weaving women, too, is introduced only for its utilitarian value. It is part of an illustrative comment on the rules governing the divorce of a suspected adulteress. Rabbi Joshua maintained that such a woman could not be legally divorced "until and unless the women who spin their yarn in the moonlight gossip about her."[16]

A common thread does run though all of these narratives on women's rites, but the Rabbis miss it—or, perhaps, just ignore it—with the result that we may miss it, too. All three rites revolve in one way or another around phases of the moon. The women spin their yarn by moonlight (when it is brightest perhaps? the full moon?); they rest on the New Moon; and they dance on the fifteenth of the lunar month, the full moon.

Rosh Chodesh, the New Moon, has lost its centrality for us because we follow Babylonian custom. But for centuries, it was a very important holiday in the Land of Israel. Genizah fragments display a festival sanctification prayer (Kedushat Hayom) declaring the moon's sanctity. That prayer concludes with a eulogy, the most common one being "Blessed art Thou, who sanctify Israel and the new month."[17] This is precisely equivalent to the prayers that have reached us intact and that we do say to inaugurate what we consider the major Jewish holidays—Rosh Hashanah and the pilgrimage festivals. The Palestinian use of a sanctification formula to introduce the New Moon with the same grandeur as was common for other festivals must have continued until Palestinian Jewry was destroyed by the Crusaders, for we find it not just in a few Genizah fragments but in the fifth-century midrash collection Exodus Rabbah and in the Palestinian Talmud. We find it again in an eighth-century Palestinian source, *Massekhet Sofrim,* where an entire ritual called *kiddush levanah* ("sanctification of the moon") is elaborated.[18]

Even aside from the question of what *women* did, *kiddush levanah* is itself an excellent example of popular custom officially unnoticed by the Rabbis. It went unrecognized even though there are rabbinic benedictions for seeing the new moon, so the custom is hardly heretical and not even particularly unrabbinic. The existence and nature of parallel texts in both the Palestinian *Massekhet Sofrim* (eighth century) and the Babylonian Talmud (sixth century) indicate that the ritual predates the final compilation of both documents, though how far back it goes we cannot say. None of the rabbinic references to the moon ritual, however, makes even the slightest mention of the moon in the lives of women. There is, at best, oblique notice given in the *Sofrim* benediction:

> By his [God's] word, He created the heavens, by the breath of his mouth, all of their hosts. He assigned them a law and a *zeman* that they would not alter their heavenly course [*tafkid*]. They [the heavenly bodies that inerrantly follow their own divinely ordained *tafkid*] are workers of truth whose work is truth.[19] To the moon, He said that it should be renewed in brightness,[20] and be a crown of glory to those whose wombs are heavy [*amusei beten*], for they were to be renewed just as it was.[21]

At least some Rabbis then, recognized the feminine symbolism inherent in the periodicity of the moon's cycle. But even they do not say that women kept the New Moon, a practice known to us only by virtue of the chance citations included in the other contexts mentioned above.[22]

Birth Ritual for Girls: Shevua Habat

I turn now to some evidence that there were also birth celebrations for girls in the tannaitic period. These would not have been instances of women's ritual per se, since there were parallel rituals for the birth of baby boys. But they serve once again to demonstrate that the official rabbinic record does not always give us the whole story. They teach us also that as much as gender opposition was part of rabbinic culture, average Jews, even those who followed the Rabbis in their religious life, did not necessarily discriminate against girls as universally as rabbinic rites might suggest. At issue is the custom known as Shevua Haben.

In chapter 3 we looked at the *chavurah,* and observed that this early religious institution served, among other things, as a locus for the celebration of "life cycle" events in the families of the members. In that connection, we hear of *chavurot* in Jerusalem convening for a ceremony known as Shevua Haben, literally, "the week of a boy."[23] Almost universally, and going all the way back to a medieval exegetical tradition,[24] this ceremony has been assumed to be an all-night vigil on the eve of a boy's circumcision, a rite known elsewhere as Yeshua Haben.[25] But Saul Lieberman sums up the textual difficulties that militate against such a construction:

> Our Rabbis, the Rishonim, explained that we have here the day of circumcision which falls at the end of the week. This is an early interpretation [going back to seventh-century sources]. But it is difficult to identify Shevua Haben as the exact day of circumcision, since circumcision falls on the eighth day [after birth, not the seventh, whereas the word *shevua* comes from the Hebrew for "seven," appearing to refer to the whole week between the boy's birth and his circumcision]. From the [talmudic] sources themselves there is no proof [that it was circumcision day], and perhaps the purpose of the Shevua Haben was to let people know that a son had been born.[26]

Shevua Haben was thus a birth ceremony held prior to the circumcision. It may have lasted for the whole week prior to circumcision, hence the name "seven." That, at least, is Lieberman's conjecture, as it is Eliezer ben Yehudah's,[27] both of whom follow earlier German scholarship in concluding that Shevua Haben had nothing whatever to do with circumcision, though by chance it did last seven days, which is to say, right up to circumcision day.[28] The Yeshua Haben, by contrast, is altogether different. It is not ancient at all, but a late medieval custom by which people partied the night before the circumcision.[29] Shevua Haben is an older weeklong birth celebration that ended that very night. Since the last day of Shevua Haben and the night of Yeshua Haben are coterminous, people who celebrated the latter found historical precedent in their textual recollections of the former.

Actually, Shevua Haben was a Jewish adaptation of the Greek custom of celebrating a child's birth for a whole week, a custom that continued among the Arab population and could still be seen among Jews in Arab lands at least as late as the nineteenth century.[30] The question arises, then, as to whether such a celebration existed also for girls. Since Greek society kept a weeklong feast for girls as well as boys, Jews who kept Shevua Haben should have kept Shevua Habat ("the week of a girl") also.

Indeed, they did just that. Though the "official" collections of tannaitic writings—Mishnah and Tosefta—ignore it, several medieval rabbis cite a tannaitic source that read: "If one has to choose between a Shevua Habat and a Shevua Haben, Shevua Haben takes precedence."[31] Shevua Habat can hardly be connected to a circumcision! But neither was Shevua Haben. Both must have been parallel weeklong celebrations marking a child's birth.

We thus have ample evidence of the existence of women's rituals revolving around the cycles of the moon, but carried only obliquely in rabbinic literature, and a probable case for birth ceremonies for girls, about which the Rabbis say nothing, except that a birth ceremony for boys takes precedence if one is invited to both at the same time. It would seem wise, therefore, to hesitate before concluding that what the Rabbis said about circumcision is a complete account of the way things were. I thus want to inquire now as to whether women *as mothers* played any role in their sons' rites of passage. We shall see that women were not absent there in the tannaitic and amoraic periods, and that it took centuries to remove women entirely from the scene.

Pidyon Haben

We get our first and most significant idea of women's involvement in the ritual life of their sons from the Redemption of the Firstborn, or Pidyon Haben, which we have already had occasion to consider.[32] We saw above that on the spectrum of graded holiness, firstborn sons born to a nonpriestly caste are considered too holy for ordinary life and therefore must be redeemed, bought back (literally) from the priest whose domain they inhabit. The rite is demanded in the Bible,[33] and elaborated by the Rabbis.

It will be recalled that redeeming a son is one of the commandments entrusted specifically to the father, not the mother. But the Bible necessarily implicates the mother in that it defines "firstborn" as the child that first opens the womb. Hence it is only the first son born to a mother that matters. If a man marries a woman who has already borne a child, in a prior marriage perhaps, and then with her as the mother he sires his own first child (but her second), that child is *his* firstborn but not *hers,* and therefore does not require redemption. From a legal point of view, it is thus the mother alone who is in a position to testify as to the status of her son. Yet once again, in the official record of the Mishnah, the Tosefta, and the two Talmuds, we find no notice of any role played by the mother.

As with so many instances of women's involvement in ritual, practice and rabbinic theory are at odds here. On the one hand, only men are commanded to redeem children; on the other, only women can say whether a given child requires redemption. We shall see that women were involved at the very least as ritual witnesses, even though rabbinic theory required that their presence be overlooked in talmudic discussion. In the case of Pidyon Haben, we again have an instance where the widespread presence of women was omitted from the Rabbis' reports. The omission may have been inadvertent here, however, since the Tannaim say almost nothing else about the ceremony either, even though they had to have engaged in it.

Pidyon Haben is first reported in an addendum tacked onto the end of a tractate of the Babylonian Talmud.

> Rabbi Simlai happened to be at a Redemption of the Firstborn. They asked him, "It is obvious that for the Redemption of the Firstborn, the father must recite the blessing, ". . . who has sanctified us with thy commandments and commanded us concerning the redemption of the firstborn." But should it be the priest or the father who says [the Shehechiyanu blessing]: "Blessed art Thou . . . who has given us life, sustained us, and brought us to this *zeman*." Should the priest say this, inasmuch as he receives benefit from the occasion [that is, the child is redeemed for silver pieces, which become his possession instead of the child]? Or does the father say it, since it is he who is fulfilling commandment? He [Rabbi Simlai] could not answer the question, so he proposed it at the academy, and was told, "The father says both blessings."[34]

A textual problem regarding the placement of this pericope in the Talmud is that if it has any relationship to what precedes it, even medieval commentators did not know what that relationship was.[35] In all probability, the final editors of the text included it here because they found no more convenient place to put it. That is, though it may play no role in expounding or otherwise enhancing the unit of material in which it has been embedded, it may have been important to the Babylonians in its own right, so much so that they found some relatively arbitrary place to locate it. As we look at the content of the pericope, it becomes clear that it served Babylonian interests in their ritual rivalry with Palestine.

The political role of the material is explainable in the light of two liturgical facts: (1) In the Palestinian custom, the priest, not the father, said the benediction over redeeming the child, whereas in Babylonia, the father said it. (2) The Palestinians did not say the Shehechiyanu benediction at all, whereas the Babylonians did.[36] The report thus serves to demonstrate the validity of the Babylonian custom in both instances. What we have, then, is an anti-Palestinian polemic within the Babylonian Talmud. The Babylonian case rests on an academic tradition that has been passed on by Rabbi Simlai, who, conveniently, is known to have been a Palestinian who migrated to Babylonia. Such a diatribe would be perfectly in keeping with stage one of the geonic era (c. 750–900) when the final editing of the Babli was underway.[37] If this assumption is correct, we may have a very late tale pseudepigraphically connected to Rabbi Simlai (third-century Babylonia).

I have cited the report in toto here, not because I believe it to be an accurate picture of some putative "earliest" redemption ritual known to us, but to indicate the problem we face in basing our findings on the collection of tales that we just happen to have. The canon we receive is the result of a multitude of considerations; it is hardly a true and adequate reflection of the totality of Jewish ritual life. There is always much more going on than we are officially told, including ritualization by women.

Whatever more extended ritual may have existed in tannaitic and amoraic times, and whether mothers were included in it, we simply do not know. But how different the record is by the time we arrive at the geonic period. Not only do we have the whole Babylonian ritual recorded for us in geonic prayer books; we also find isolated geonic responsa on the subject, as well as Genizah fragments citing the Palestinian ceremony from the same period.

What interests us most in all of these reports is a responsum detailing an entire geonic rite, including a benediction that we no longer say and a considerable ritual role for the mother. What follows is the rite as we find it, divided and labeled alphabetically for heuristic purposes.

A. He [the father] brings his son before the priest and says to the priest that he is the firstborn of the womb.

B. The priest takes him, and says to the father, "Do you want your firstborn son? Then give me the five selahs that you need to redeem him."

C. The father replies, "I want my firstborn son. Here are your five selahs. Blessed is God . . . who commanded us concerning the redemption of the firstborn. Blessed is God who has given us life, sustained us, and brought us to this *zeman.*"

D. They mix a cup of wine for the priest and hand him some spices, and he says, "Blessed art Thou . . . who has created the fruit of the vine. Blessed art Thou . . . who has created sweet-smelling trees [*borei atzei besamim*]."[38]

E. He [the priest] also says, "Blessed art Thou who sanctified the fetus in its mother's womb [*bim'ei imo*]. From the tenth day on, He [God] apportions 248 bodily parts, and after that breathes a soul into him, as it says: 'He breathed a living soul into his nostrils and the man became a living being' [Gen. 2:7]. You have clothed me with skin, and intertwined me with bones and sinews, as it is written: 'You have clothed me with skin, and intertwined me with bones and sinews' [Job 10:1]. Through the miracle of his wonders, He feeds him with food and drink, honey and milk, to make him rejoice, and summons his angels to watch over him in his mother's womb, as it is written: 'You granted me life and favor, and your command sustained my soul' [Job 10:12]."

F. The boy's father says, "This is my firstborn son."

G. And his mother says, "This is my firstborn son, for God opened the doors of my womb with him. We are obligated [*nitchayavnu*] to give the priest five selahs as his redemption, as it is written: 'Take as their redemption price from the age of one month and up, the money equivalent to five shekels by the sanctuary weight, which is twenty *gerahs*' [Num. 18:16]. Also it says: 'You shall have the firstborn of man redeemed' [Num. 18:15]. Just as this firstborn has merited redemption, so may he merit Torah, marriage, and good deeds. Blessed art Thou . . . who sanctify the firstborn of Israel in their redemptions [*befidyonam*]."[39]

Several issues merit notice before we turn to the most interesting information regarding the mother. First, there is the troubling eulogy in G. What could it mean to praise God for sanctifying the firstborn "in their redemptions," or, translating the *bet* as a *bet* of means, "through" or "by means of" their redemptions? As we saw above, the whole point of redemption was to *release* the firstborn from the state of innate sanctity into which he was born! In the parallel Palestinian rite, the father is even asked to stipulate that the

money for which he exchanges the child is not holy; the nonholy money becomes holy as it enters the domain of the priest, while the holy child becomes
"everyday" by passing out of the priest's (that is, God's) domain.[40] The eulogy
might therefore more appropriately praise God for permitting relative desanc-
tification through redemption.

There is, however, no reason to accept the *bet* as accurate, since other
extant versions of the same blessing provide us with different prepositions, a
lamed, for instance, so that the sense may be, "Blessed art Thou . . . who
sanctify the firstborn of Israel for the sake of their redemptions [*lefidyonam*]."
We also get the conjunction *vav,* giving us "and their redemptions [*ufi-
dyonam*]." I see no way of knowing for sure which of these, if any, is correct;
we must assume that the original sense, if there was one, was garbled by later
scribes who no longer knew just what was being said. I suspect, however, that
the wording once read *mekadesh yisra'el,* "who sanctify Israel," without the
final reference to redemption at all. That simple two-word eulogy is found also
as a variant wedding blessing, instead of the more complex "Who sanctify
Israel by means of *chuppah* and *kiddushin* [transferral of the bride to the
groom's quarters and the rite of betrothal]," the standard form in which we
have inherited it.[41] It may be, then, that a eulogy referring without specifica-
tion to God's sanctification of Israel was common, and that eventually, someone added an oblique reference to redemption, just as, apparently, someone
also enlarged upon the same blessing for weddings.

Second, in E, we find the full text of the unusual benediction summing
up rabbinic "embryology," which I looked at briefly in my discussion of sanctity from the womb. It begins with ". . . who sanctified the fetus in its mother's
womb." The rest of the blessing is either biblically based, or dependent on a
teaching of the Mishnah, which instructs us on the number of limbs granted
to every human being.[42] The modern-day scholars cited in chapter 7 are not
the first to wonder what it meant to be sanctified from the womb. The notion
puzzled even Rabbenu Asher ben Yechiel (better known as the Rosh), the
famed thirteenth- and fourteenth-century authority who settled in Spain after
emigrating from Germany. Recognizing that the rite celebrated the moment at
which the womb opened to release a firstborn child, he argued that the description of the prior sanctity of the fetus was out of place.

> I do not understand the beginning of this benediction, ". . . who sanc-
> tified the fetus in its mother's womb," since if it is the firstborn's sancti-

fied state that we have in mind, God has made that state dependent on the opening of the womb [but not a prior state that existed before the moment of birth].[43]

Though he does not cite it, he may have seen a variant of the benediction known to us from the Genizah, which has the priest address the child on God's behalf, saying, "When you were in your mother's womb, you were in the domain of your Father in heaven, and in my domain, too, for I am a priest, and in the domain of my brothers, the priests. But your father and your mother want to redeem you from me."[44] It was the doctrine that the womb functions as the domain of God for the firstborn that Rabbenu Asher denied. Indeed, halakhically, the sanctity of a firstborn does derive solely from the physical act of opening the mother's womb for the first time, just as Rabbenu Asher says. However, it is evident that at least some Rabbis believed that the womb was the domain of God for this child, just as the priest and the blessing claim. Halakhah and embryology were not necessarily in agreement.

As we saw above, the claim of prenatal sanctity is remarkably similar to the circumcision benediction, "who sanctified the beloved one from the womb,"[46] and we know that the circumcision blessing is tannaitic. Because it is that old, it was accepted into the official communal practice in both Palestine and Babylonia. Even if we had no tannaitic text displaying it, the very fact that it appears ubiquitously in both Babylonian and Palestinian prayer collections would suggest its early composition, since Amram tended to avoid Palestinian practice except where the antiquity of the material militated against omitting it.

The parallel prayer for redemption (E above), however—including its opening line proclaiming sanctity in the mother's womb—did not make it into Amram. Even Saadiah, who knows of it as an option, as he does a great deal of Palestinian custom, declares it unnecessary (*devarim she'ein lahem ikar*).[46] We know about it as prescribed practice only from the Genizah or from Rishonim, and from the very late gaon Hai, who unlike Amram but like Saadiah incorporates Palestinian material freely.[47] It is tempting, therefore, to conclude that, unlike the circumcision blessing, this redemption blessing is not tannaitic. If we assume that the early circumcision ceremony influenced the later redemption rite, we would then have to revise our earlier conclusion to the effect that prenatal sanctity was in general assumed by the Tannaim, and we would be back where we started, trying to figure out why that quality is asserted only for Abraham.

There is no need to make that assumption, however. Of all our rites, Redemption of the Firstborn is the least documented in rabbinic literature. It will be recalled that the only reference to it is an addendum to a tractate of the Babli, which does not even purport to give us the whole rite but only to discuss specific questions that were matters of debate between Palestine and Babylonia. The Genizah has other blessings that also are not found in official tannaitic and amoraic records, but should not on that account automatically be dated after the codification of the Talmud. Before reciting psalms, for instance, Palestinian congregations praised God "for choosing David, His servant, and for taking pleasure in his sacred songs."[48] Similarly, the morning rubric known as the Shema and its blessings was introduced by a Palestinian blessing praising God "who has sanctified us by his commandments, and commanded us to recite the *Shema* to declare Him King with a full heart, willingly to announce his unity, and happily to serve Him."[49] The Shema and its blessings occupy a good deal of the mishnaic discussion dealing with prayer. Surely we might have expected this blessing to occur there. But we knew nothing about it until the Genizah was discovered. Was this also an innovation after the conclusion of the Yerushalmi? Possibly, but again, not necessarily. The spiritual life of Tannaim and Amoraim was far more variegated than we have been willing to concede. The Mishnah codified some practices, and so did later authorities all the way into the Middle Ages, but many ancient practices survived without codification. Some were eventually admitted grudgingly by authorities even though there was no textual evidence supporting their validity. Others, like the redemption blessing, were rejected, usually on the grounds that no ancient source mentions them, but additionally (in this case) because the implicit anthropology seems to contradict the *halakhah.*

The circumcision blessing, whereby an unnamed "beloved one" was sanctified by God, *is* mentioned by Tannaim. We saw above that the medievals differed in assigning specific biblical persons to the role.[50] Precisely because their texts carried it, they felt obliged to interpret it. The parallel redemption benediction, on the other hand, had never been passed down in Babylonia; it never became part of the Babylonian corpus. When the medievals heard of it, and especially if they found its anthropology objectionable, they could just get rid of it—which is exactly what Asher ben Yechiel did. His son, Jacob ben Asher, recalled his father's ruling on the subject and canonized it in his influential fourteenth-century code of Jewish law, the *Tur:*

In France and Germany, they do not say this blessing. We find that we do not say any blessing that is not mentioned in the Mishnah, the Tosefta, and the Gemara [= the Talmuds]. No blessing was initiated after the [closing of the talmudic canon]."[51]

So the circumcision blessing did not necessarily influence the wording of the redemption blessing. Both blessings may have been equally early. However, it likely did influence the inclusion, in G, of wishes that the boy merit "Torah, marriage, and good deeds,")[52] as well as, perhaps, the insertion of wine and spices into the ritual in D. The latter was evident in *Seder Rav Amram's* circumcision ceremony, and the former was present all along as the standard response to the father of the boy being circumcised. But it will be recalled that the response was originally addressed to the father, not to the boy, and it did not include "good deeds." Our text is late enough to vary in both respects, and thus to convert the original halakhic intent into a general wish for the child's future.

Finally, we turn to the real surprise: the inclusion of the mother in far more than a token capacity. She stands side by side with her husband as together they recite the ritual words that will redeem their son.

F.   The boy's father says, "This is my firstborn son."

G.   And his mother says, "This is my firstborn son, for God opened the doors of my womb with him. We are obligated to give the priest five selahs as his redemption, as it is written: 'Take as their redemption price from the age of one month and up, the money equivalent to five shekels by the sanctuary weight, which is twenty *gerahs*' [Num. 18:16]. Also it says: 'You shall have the firstborn of man redeemed' [Num. 18:15]. Just as this firstborn has merited redemption, so may he merit Torah, marriage, and good deeds. Blessed art Thou . . . who sanctify the firstborn of Israel."

I suspect the biblical verses were not recited in actual practice. Our written texts regularly append biblical verses for one reason or another, so that what we have here is a typical example of a literary conceit overlaid on the report of the rite as it was performed. An analogous case is the women's dancing rite that we mentioned above. As the Mishnah describes it:

A.   Rabban Simeon ben Gamaliel said: there were no better days for Israel than the fifteenth of Av and the Day of Atonement [the tenth

of Tishri], for on those days, Jerusalemite girls . . . would go out
and dance in the vineyards.

B. What did they say? "Fellow, look around and see—choose what
you want! Don't look for beauty, but for family. 'Charm is deceitful
and beauty is vain, but a woman who fears the Lord will be praised'
(Prov. 31:30). And it says, 'Give her of the fruit of her hands and
let her work praise her in the gates' (Prov. 31:31). And likewise it
says, 'Go forth you daughters of Zion, and behold King Solomon
with the crown with which his mother crowned him in the day of
his espousals and in the day of the gladness of his heart' (Song of
Songs 3:11)."

C. "The day of his espousals" refers to the building of the Temple;
"the day of the gladness of his heart" refers to the building of the
Temple. May it be rebuilt quickly in our days. Amen.[53]

That the women danced and called out to the men is quite probable.
That they addressed their potential suitors in full biblical verse resonant of
exactly the modest homebound family image of women that the Rabbis favored is less so. The rite was no longer extant even by Simeon ben Gamaliel's
time. He describes it as something that used to happen, and, as I noted above,
he cites the old practice as an introduction to his sermon on the theme of
hope. Even the sermon, however, may not be his. What we probably have is
an independent tradition of dancing, which an editor has constructed into an
elaborate sermonic text. The topic of Mishnah Ta'anit in general is the destruction of the Temple. So the fabricated sermon serves as a convenient end
to the book: a promise of dancing at the time when the Temple is restored.

The Mishnah's report of what transpired at the dancing rite is another
instance of reconstruction. B imagines what the women used to say, replete
with pious citations; C interprets the citations of B. These interpretations are
the point of the passage as it is finally constituted, the reason it was included
in the Mishnah. Thus the homiletical lesson in C is the only reason we even
know about the women's dancing rite of A. It is possible, I must admit, that
the rabbinic editor who made up the sermon fabricated the whole dancing
event also. However, the image of women dancing to attract men hardly seems
the sort of thing that any Rabbi would willingly concoct. If the point was to
cite biblical verses that might be interpreted to foretell the rebuilding of the
Temple, some other verses tacked onto a different story might have served just

as well. It is more likely, therefore, that the dancing rite did exist, and that the rabbinic editor could make his sermon do double duty. First, he would have an appropriate homiletical ending for his tractate; second, he could clean up the dancing ritual so that the women engaging in it would be remembered as appropriately chaste, their interest no longer being beauty and matters of the flesh, but family, piety, and housework (from Proverbs 31).

Clearly, when the Rabbis wrote up their rites, they felt free to put into people's mouths the requisite biblical bases for what they were doing. Precisely that practice characterizes our report on the redemption of the firstborn. We have every reason to suspect the inclusion of biblical prooftexts. But, at the same time, we have every reason to believe the Rabbis' reports of the prominent involvement of women, since that presence is the last thing they would have invented in a rite that they held to be the exclusive domain of the father (who, it will be recalled, has the sole *legal* obligation to redeem his son). As the Mishnah reports, "All commandments that devolve upon the father with respect to the son are incumbent upon men, but women are exempt from them."[54] These include, among others, "to circumcise him, [and] *redeem him*" (if he is a firstborn).[55]

Yet what does the mother in our ritual say to the priest? After testifying, "This is my firstborn son, for God opened the doors of my womb with him," she says, "*We* are obligated [*nitchayavnu*] to give the priest five selahs as his redemption." Finally, she, not her husband or the priest, prays, "Just as this firstborn has merited redemption, so may he merit Torah, marriage, and good deeds. Blessed art Thou . . . who sanctify the firstborn of Israel."

Moreover, in his report on *how* the ceremony proceeded, the Rosh (thirteenth-century Germany) tells us, "The priest would bless the child, *and hand him back to his father and mother.*"[56] In thirteenth-century Italy as well, we see that the mother was still present and involved in her son's redemption, since the *Tanya*, a work generally attributed to the Italian Rabbi Yechiel ben Yekutiel Anav (d. 1300), tells us: "The priest asks the mother, 'Have you had a miscarriage or have you borne another child previously?'"[57] Only after she testifies to both queries that she has not does the ceremony proceed.

In sum:

1. Despite the law to the contrary, at least in some places, as late as the geonic era, the *rite* of redemption featured the boy's mother saying that she, too, was obligated to redeem her son.

2. A considerable speaking role is attributed to the mother by many parallel sources, and even when her actual speaking goes unreported, she is portrayed as standing with her husband, and at least testifying about her son's firstborn standing.

3. As late as the thirteenth century, we find that she was present in Italian ceremonies of redemption.

4. Exactly how and when she was excluded from the ceremony remains unknown.

What, then, of the mother's participation in her son's circumcision? On the one hand, unlike redemption, which depends on the physical fact of the child being the firstborn of his mother, circumcision need not have anything to do with her. Here is a rite from which we might well expect her to be absent entirely. But, on the other hand, given the dichotomy in the case of redemption between official rabbinic theology and actual practice, we at least ought to look carefully at our sources on circumcision, requiring of them some actual sign of the mother's absence. For even if she had no speaking role, she may well have been at least a physical presence in the ritual action that admitted her son to the male covenant in this otherwise all-male induction ceremony.

chapter 11

Medieval Rabbinism and the Ritual Marginalization of Women

Our survey of the meanings implicit in the rite of circumcision has nearly reached its end. We have traced the rite beyond its biblical foundations to the period of its classical formulation in the second and third centuries, and noted that it was circumcision blood that saved. In part, the debate over salvation was tied to the Jewish-Christian polemic on faith versus works, with the Rabbis seeing circumcision as the saving work par excellence. Both faiths recognized the saving grace of blood. Sacrificial blood, the blood of the paschal lamb, and the blood of the circumcised boy all figure prominently in rabbinic midrash as vehicles of deliverance.

The blood of circumcision thus functioned as an iconic marker in opposition to the blood of menstruation to differentiate the genders in rabbinic Judaism. As circumcision blood saved, menstrual blood polluted. Circumcision blood was culturally mandated and drawn while menstrual blood flowed naturally and uncontrollably; men were thus seen as controlled while women were not.

By the Middle Ages, however, this entire set of public meanings was lost. Never having entered the record as an official meaning of the rite, the nature/culture dichotomy disappeared as a public meaning also. True, the salvific quality of blood remained alive at least as a hypothetical entry in the religious lexicon of literate Jews. Midrashic and talmudic texts referred to blood often enough that the use of blood to save—the lamb in Egypt, the sacrifices in the defunct cult, and the blood of the circumcision covenant—had to have been common intellectual currency among the rabbinic elite. But the underlying iconic value of male blood that is drawn and quickly stanched as opposed to female blood that flows naturally and of its own accord was lost.

What exists in literary records and what passes through people's minds when they ritualize the texts based on those records are two different things. Regardless of what the literary records reveal, blood was probably never *consciously* understood as symbolic of control in men but not in women. I doubt that anyone ever brought their children to be circumcised with that meaning in mind. The capacity of circumcision blood to save, however, was expressly known and taught. It appears in the circumcision liturgy itself. Jews in antiquity certainly understood the salvific meaning implicit in the rite, and probably associated that saving quality with the blood that was drawn. By the Middle Ages, on the other hand, even that meaning may have attenuated to the point where it was a mere textual memory available to the scholarly elite at best.

Nonetheless, circumcision as a male rite that initiated a boy's covenantal journey through life continued to be acted out, and with a distinctively male cast of characters that only added to the male ambience. We saw, for example, that ninth-century Babylonian men and boys engaged in a rite that had as its focus the washing of hands in the blood-water mixture of a male newly initiated into the covenant. The meaning of the blood was expressly given by the geonic text: it was "as if to say, 'This is the blood of circumcision that mediates between God and Abraham our father [*kelomar zeh dam habrit sheben hamakom le'avraham avinu*]."[1] Thus, although details of the public meaning of circumcision evaporated with time, the rite as a public demonstration of male initiation into the covenant did not.

We were led therefore to reconsider what role, if any, women had in the rite through the centuries. Our query arose out of the recognition that today women frequently have no role at all; they may not even be in the same room where the rite unfolds. The geonic responsum by Kohen Tzedek that reports the ritual washing of hands certainly is imaginable without women in attendance. In Luke's first-century pericope, John's mother Elizabeth is present, but plays no ritual role in her son's circumcision. In the second-century midrash of Simeon bar Chalafta, the mother is not even mentioned. The rite calls only for the father to speak, and it is he who admits his son into "the covenant of Abraham our father." So despite the pericope in Luke, which may have had its own reasons for including Elizabeth, at least as a foil for her mute husband, it may be that mothers were not even physically present for the occasion.

The problem with reaching this conclusion on the basis of our texts is the nature of the texts themselves, as we discovered in the last chapter. Ross Shepard Kraemer draws attention not only to authors but to copiers.

Suppose, for instance, an equal number of men and women had been present at circumcisions, and suppose further that they had each recorded their own recollection of what transpired. Would we know any more about women at the rite than if only men had come and only men had documented the occasion? Not necessarily. Kraemer has in mind Christian documents that "survived in the form of Byzantine and medieval copies made and stored in libraries of Christian monasteries." True, only some rabbinic texts got passed along that way, but rabbinic scribes were no kinder to women's religion than Christian monks were. In both cases, Kraemer claims, "if texts are dependent for their survival on being read and copied, *who* reads and *who* copies becomes paramount." So for monks as for rabbis, "the demonstrated misogynism" of the copiers limits what gets copied.[2]

As we saw in the previous chapter, the fact that women were invisible in rabbinic literature did not mean that they were absent from Jewish ritual life. Rabbinic records are silent about women's presence at circumcisions in antiquity, but let us turn to *Seder Rav Amram,* the same ninth-century work that describes adolescent boys washing their hands in the blood-water mixture. Amram includes the mother with a prayer for her health, after which, he reports, "We hand [her] the cup [of wine]."[3] More than a perfunctory motion, this is a *ritual* act as far as Amram is concerned. As we saw in chapter 4, by his time a blessing over wine had been added, so that someone now had to drink from the cup in order to save the rite from a breach of the Rule of Proper Use. Amram's solution was to give it to the mother.

Fortunately, that very point of Jewish law is what allows us to trace the mother's presence, which otherwise might have gone unnoted altogether. Amram, and then Amram's copiers, recognized the legal issue involved, and retained what they correctly took to be a creative legal solution.

As we move beyond Amram, we must contend with the fact that rabbinic literature, though vast, is exceptionally selective, consisting mostly of a series of literary glosses on prior literature rather than firsthand descriptions of actual practice. Regarding circumcision, therefore, one author after another reiterates talmudic and geonic information, stopping only to give his own interpretation of the text. The author of the key French work of the eleventh century, *Machzor Vitry,* for example, copies blessing N from our rite and adds: "Interpretation: 'Who sanctified the beloved'—Isaac is called the beloved; 'from the womb'—before he was born, he was set aside for this commandment."[4] If we considered only this sort of literary tradition, we would never know what people actually did or what words they said. We would be limited to the words already canonized in older texts and therefore a ready subject for subsequent literary commentary.

A frequent exception to the general pattern by which old texts were merely replicated with new running commentary is responsa literature, wherein people explain their actual practice and request guidance. What leads them to ask the authorities anything at all is precisely their habit of doing or saying something for which older texts give no mandate. So we must look to responsa for records of things said or done beyond the literary record already established in the talmudic canon.

A legal quandary faced by eleventh-century rabbis was how to handle the drinking of circumcision wine on a fast day. Since circumcisions are performed on the eighth day after a boy's birth regardless of the day in question, and since fast days were ubiquitous in medieval times, it was relatively common for a community to have to celebrate a circumcision on a day when all eating and drinking was strictly proscribed. But the wine blessing had long been included in the ritual by then, and according to the Rule of Proper Use, someone had to taste at least some of it. A responsum on that subject informs us that the mother was still present, and sets us on the road toward discovering when and how she was removed as well.

Machzor Vitry records a responsum by Isaac ben Judah (d. 1064, in Mainz) to Menachem ben Machir, asking who should drink the wine in the case of a circumcision performed on a fast day. "Do we say a blessing over the wine and give it to the mother to drink, or do we give it to a child [who is not obliged to keep the fast], or should we avoid the blessing completely?"[5] Apparently, the mother still drank the wine in eleventh-century Germany, and in France, too, since the same source later turns to native French custom, saying that first the *mohel* drinks, then he puts wine on the infant's lips, and finally, "We give wine to the mother also, since it is on account of the fruit of her womb that the cup of wine is poured in the first place."[6] The same was true of Italy, where the case of a circumcision on Yom Kippur was solved "by putting the wine aside until Yom Kippur is over, and then giving it to the mother to drink."[7]

The context of the event is all important here. There are exceptions, but circumcision today usually takes place in private homes or, at least, in private gatherings. Its connection to the community at large and to communal events, even religious events, has been severed. It rarely has anything to do with the daily worship service held in the synagogue. But that was distinctly not the case in eleventh- and twelfth-century Europe. Circumcision was a major communal event that occurred among the people gathering for prayer. Only with such an assumption can one make sense out of the literature of the period, which juxtaposes concerns about the circumcision itself with questions about altering the daily prayers. Let us take a closer look at the responsum by Isaac ben Judah.

> We circumcise in the synagogue [says the eleventh-century author of the text in which the responsum is embedded]. . . . Rabbi Isaac ben Judah was asked, "What happens when a circumcision is held on a communal fast day, like the seventeenth of Tammuz or the third of Tishri? Do we say all the supplications and penitential poetry, including the confession and recitation of God's pardoning attributes? And if we say the blessing over wine, who tastes it—the person who says the blessing or the mother of the child? And how much has to be tasted for the taste to count?"
>
> [He answered,] "Where we are, this is what we do on a day when a circumcision is held. If it is also a fast day, we say the penitential poetry and a confession. But we do not recite Vehu Rachum and the supplicatory prayers. [Vehu Rachum is a specific set of daily supplicatory prayers running several pages in length, emphasizing the sinfulness of the human condition.] We do so because the tradition of our ancestors is the Torah by which we live, and [we have the tradition that] they accepted the commandment of circumcision with joy. We therefore still keep it with joy. . . . So we omit the supplicatory prayers including Vehu Rachum. It is enough to make do with some of the day's penitential liturgy. The person leading the communal prayers [the word used is *sheliach tzibbur,* the normal term for the functionary who leads the daily service in the synagogue] says the blessing over the wine, but does not taste it. Again, custom becomes "Torah" eventually, and we have the custom that you do not have to drink it on a fast day. You don't give it to a child to drink, since he might be led into sin [thinking that drinking is acceptable on fast days] . . . and you don't give it to the baby's mother to drink either, since she has to fast.[8]

Clearly, the circumcision took place in the middle of the daily service. We even know at what point: Zedekiah ben Abraham (thirteenth-century

Rome) cites a responsum from Worms to the effect that a circumcision on Yom Kippur takes place immediately after the morning Torah reading: "We go out immediately after the Torah is read, but before we begin the Additional Service [Musaf]; then we do the circumcision, and come back into the sanctuary to finish the service."[9] That was on Yom Kippur. But if the practice on Yom Kippur was the same as on any other day, we need only ask what prayer follows the liturgy at the point where the Additional Service occurs on Yom Kippur. The answer from about the fourteenth century on is the Alenu. Though originally a prayer to introduce a section of Rosh Hashanah liturgy, the Alenu had by then been added as a daily concluding prayer.[10]

Now we know why it eventually became customary to include the Alenu at the end of the circumcision rite. As we saw in chapter 4, the rite as we have it ends with the following instructions (S): "Then they say Alenu, after which they wash their hands, say the blessing over bread, and eat the meal." Nowadays, when the rite is normally scheduled for a convenient time having nothing to do with daily worship and takes place in a private home rather than the synagogue, the inclusion of Alenu is perplexing, since Alenu is a statutory daily prayer having no apparent connection to circumcision. It must have become associated with the rite because when circumcision was a synagogal event, Alenu was the prayer that followed it. Later, when it was moved to the home, Alenu went with it, so that the rite still calls for Alenu as the official completion of the ceremony.

So the circumcision of a boy was once a communal event, inserted into a prayer service that preceded and followed it. It was even orchestrated, says *Sefer Hapardes,* not by the *mohel,* but by the *sheliach tzibbur,* the leader of the service. An account from Germany concurs, saying, "The father says [the father's blessing] and the *chazan* sings the blessing over wine."[11] This was probably the norm in France, Germany, and Italy—that is, throughout Ashkenaz—as late as 1300.

Circumcision did not universally take place in the synagogue, since Isaac ben Sheshet Perfet (1326–1407) knew of a circumcision performed at home, but that custom was rare enough that he noted the anomaly, saying "the custom of the city was [not to] circumcise in a synagogue."[12] He does not tell us what city he has in mind, however. (Synagogues were used in Isaac's native Barcelona just as they were in Ashkenaz—Rabbenu Nissim [1290–1375] assumes it in his own discussion about drinking the wine). For our purposes here, however, we need note only that the issue involved saying the blessing wine at the synagogue, and then delivering the wine to the mother eft at home.[13]

Synagogue circumcisions in the context of daily worship were thus the norm in both Ashkenazi and Sephardi circles going back all the way to the geonic period, when the synagogue as locus was known to the Gaon Kohen Tzedek (838–48). He tells his respondents expressly that he has no objection to their using the place for circumcision, since the rite is a sacred event.[14] From his time on the synagogue continued to be the normal milieu for public circumcision celebrations. If the circumcision did not take place in the sanctuary itself, it at least occurred in an anteroom *with the mother present.*

But the mother was soon to be dismissed. On that we can have no doubt, because our texts are explicit. Our primary witness for the about-face regarding the presence of women is Samson ben Tzadok (known generally as the Tashbetz), an illustrious German authority who died around 1285. A more remarkable statement on the issue is hard to find:

> I am not at all in favor of the technically permissible custom that one finds in most places: namely, that a woman sits in the synagogue among the men, and they circumcise the baby in her lap. Even if the *mohel* is her husband, or her father or her son, it is not appropriate to allow a beautifully dressed-up woman to be among the men and right there in the presence of God. [The implication is that the event occurred in the sanctuary, in which case the mother may have been sitting with the men during the service as well.] This is exactly what they object to in the Talmud, when they ask, "Could it be that women were allowed in the Temple courtyard?" [Kid. 52b]. The reason [for excluding women from the courtyard] is that they were afraid that the young priests would compete for her. Besides, with respect to the principle of circumcision, *she* is not commanded to circumcise even her own son. Scripture says, ". . . which [God] commanded *him*"—that means "*him*" [the father], not "*her*" [the mother]. If so, how could it possibly be that they circumcise children on their mothers' laps, thus snatching away the commandment from the men. Anyone who gets the opportunity to prevent such goings-on should do so. May people who act stringently in this case find blessing and peace. [This is a communication of] Meir ben Rabbi Barukh, may he rest in peace.

When my teacher wrote this, I cried out for many days, but no one paid any attention to me, since it seemed very cruel to them. I grant that [during the act of circumcision] the people pay strict attention to their work, and do not let their thoughts wander along sinful paths. But still, people who see them will be suspicious, even if it is a case of a husband [who is the *mohel* performing the operation on his own son] and wife. Moreover, not everyone knows that she is his wife. Is it for nothing that the Temple had a separate courtyard just for the women? Without it, [the sacrifices of the Temple] would have appeared like commandments that are carried out only at the cost of sin, a circumstance that Scripture warns against when it says, "To obey is better than to sacrifice" [1 Sam. 15:22]. Every man who fears the word of God is obliged to walk out of the synagogue [if they try to circumcise babies on their mothers' laps], lest he give the false impression of aiding and abetting sinners. My teacher, Rabbenu Tuviah Yekutiel bar Moses, may he rest in peace, warned us about this, and I agree with him, adding only this [advice of Rabbi Yochanan, from the Talmud], "It is better to walk behind a lion than behind a woman" [Ber. 61a].[15]

Rabbi Samson could not be clearer. Speaking partly for his teacher and partly for himself, he bemoans the fact that everywhere he goes people are circumcising children on their mothers' laps, right in the middle of the synagogue. Women must have been coming and sitting with the men, possibly throughout the service. That would be bad enough. But Samson also worries about impure thoughts that he thinks are bound to occur to people who see a beautifully dressed woman and a man bent over her lap. Besides, his teacher had taught him that only men, not women, are commanded to circumcise. How dare the women snatch the commandment away from the men? To buttress his case, Rabbi Meir had cited a talmudic discussion of the reason for excluding women from the Temple courtyard, giving it a negative spin by including the explanation that women would disrupt the young priests at work. Actually, he takes the question out of context and does not tell us what he surely must have known: that the prominent French Tosafist Rabbenu Tam (d. 1171) differed with the Talmud here, arguing that women *were* permitted to enter the courtyard.[16] In this statement we have a picture of two men, teacher and student, living in fear that men like themselves might become sexually aroused by a woman at a circumcision, and imputing similar sexual arousal to young priests in the time of the Temple.

Neither Samson nor his teacher Meir had experienced success in eliminating women from the rite, even though Meir surely ranks among the few most influential rabbis in all of German history. Known by the acronym Maharam, Meir ben Barukh of Rothenberg directed the fortunes of Ashkenazi Jewry for half a century, from his return to Rothenberg in 1242 after many years of study with the grand talmudic masters of the prior generation until his imprisonment and death at the hands of Emperor Rudolph I in 1293. No wonder Samson was appalled by the equanimity with which people ignored his teacher, Meir. But they paid no attention to Samson either; nowhere in his outcry does he indicate that things have begun to change in his favor.

The next word on the matter comes from another giant in German Jewish history, the Maharil, that is, Jacob Moellin (1360?–1427). What the Maharam was to the thirteenth century, the Maharil was to the fourteenth and fifteenth. By then, the center of Jewish life had moved eastward into Bohemia and Austria. Those who were destined to become the leading rabbis of these newly burgeoning eastern cities came to study with the Maharil in Mainz, just as a hundred years earlier Samson ben Tzadok and his circle had attended the academy of the Maharam in Rothenberg. The Maharam's advice, carried so diligently by his avid pupil Samson, apparently reached the Maharil, who was remembered as ruling further on it:

> Regarding a woman who is the *ba'alat brit* [a technical term to which we shall return], the Maharam wrote that she should take the child from its mother in order to bring him to the synagogue for his circumcision. She should bring him as far as the synagogue door, but should not go inside to be his *sandek* [the person who holds the child on his lap], since the child should not be circumcised in her lap. A woman should not walk among the men, on account of the need to maintain modesty.[17]

Actually, the Maharil—or his student—had an apocopated and somewhat garbled version of the evolution of the custom. The fourteenth-century master had actually moved beyond the stand taken by the Maharam a century earlier. Though we do not know whether Samson ben Tzadok lived to see it, he and his successors had eventually won the day. No longer does the Maharil worry about mothers in the synagogue service. The point of contention has now become whether the mother can come even as far as the synagogue door, and whether women in general can enter the synagogue sanctuary where the celebration will be held. The Maharil uses the Maharam to argue negatively on both matters. His position is that the mother should stay home, and that another woman, who became known as the *ba'alat brit,* should be appointed to deliver the baby boy from his mother to the synagogue door. There a man known now as the *sandek* takes the boy to the *mohel,* who circumcises him on the *sandek*'s lap rather than on the mother's.

Moses Mat (c. 1551–c. 1606) in Galicia had a more reliable explanation of what had occurred:

> Samson ben Tzadok wrote that a woman should not enter the syna-
> gogue to be among the men in order to be the *sandek* and have the
> child circumcised on her lap; for even if the *mohel* is her husband, it is
> not seemly for a beautifully dressed-up woman to be among men. The
> Maharil wrote that a logical extension of the seriousness of the Mahar-
> am's approach would be that a woman should not enter the anteroom
> of the synagogue with the men, and similarly, that a man should not
> enter the place where the women are in order to get the child from his
> mother. Rather, the woman who is the *ba'alat brit* should take the
> child from the mother and bring him to the door of the synagogue, but
> not enter, and the *ba'al brit* [her male equivalent] should take the child
> from her.[18]

We need to pause for a moment over the introduction of these newly developing ritual roles, the *ba'al brit,* the *ba'alat brit,* and the *sandek.* What exactly did these people do, and when and why were these roles invented in the first place? The evidence is complex, but its tortuous path is worth traversing, since we will see exactly when and how women were removed from the circumcision rite, and just how completely a series of men who played the various ritual roles came to dominate it.

Let us review the evidence thus far. A *ba'alat brit* is mentioned first by either Meir of Rothenberg or by the Maharil—depending on which version of the report we believe, the Maharil himself, who says it was the former, or Moses Mat, who thinks it was the latter. Either way, the *ba'alat brit* comes into being sometime during the century or so marked at either end by these two Ashkenazi giants, the Maharam and the Maharil, that is to say, somewhere in the thirteenth or fourteenth century. But her role is so new that the rabbis who report her existence feel constrained to explain what she does.

The *ba'alat brit* was the answer to the perceived impropriety of having the mother present at her son's circumcision. The mother could be segregated at home while the *ba'alat brit* took the child to the synagogue, where she handed him over to the man on whose lap the circumcision would take place. To obviate the possibility that we simply exchange one woman for another in the ritual act of holding the boy, the *ba'alat brit* was explicitly barred from doing that job.

But we have some confusion regarding the two men who are mentioned, the *sandek* and the *ba'al brit*. Neither in his citation of the Maharam nor in his own coda to the Maharam's ruling does the Tashbetz mention either one. The Maharil, however, quotes the Maharam as forbidding the *ba'alat brit* from serving as the *sandek,* and it is clear that he knows exactly what the *sandek* does. Moses Mat, too, quotes his predecessors as knowing that the man who holds the child is a *sandek*. The problem is that he also knows of a man who takes the child from the *ba'alat brit* and presumably delivers him to the *sandek*. If so, the child gets passed from *ba'alat brit* to *ba'al brit* to *sandek*.

Unfortunately, things are not that simple. Elsewhere, Rabbi Isaac of Corbeil (d. 1280) wrote a halakhic compendium known as *Amudei Hagolah,* which later became a popular guide known as *Sefer Mitzvot Katan.* His disciple, Peretz of Corbeil (d. 1295), composed glosses on the work. Peretz tells us:

> When the father is not in town [for the day of his son's circumcision, which must occur on the eighth day, even if the father, say, is on a business trip and unable to return in time for it], the universal custom is that the *sandek* says [the father's blessing]. The *sandek* is the *ba'al brit,* and maybe that is because he is a sort of agent of the court.

For Peretz, obviously, the title *ba'al brit* is older and better known than *sandek,* since Peretz explains *sandek* in terms of it. The fact that he has to tell people what the *sandek* is implies that it must be quite new indeed. In France, then, the introduction of the term *sandek* can be dated to the thirteenth century.

But outside of France, the term is older than that. In the eleventh century, Nathan ben Yehiel of Rome composed a medieval dictionary called the *Arukh.* He includes an entry for *sandek* or, as he spells it, *syndekos,* saying that he is not the first to use the word. He read it in the *Midrash on Psalms,* which said, "I will be a *syndekos* at the time of circumcision." Nathan explains, "In Greek and Latin that means *patron* or *praklit*." [19] The *Midrash on Psalms* (in the present edition) contains material dating from the third all the way to the thirteenth century. The entry Nathan cites in his *Arukh* must predate the eleventh century when he lived, but it is unclear how much farther back it goes. At any rate, the midrashic fragment in question is a gloss to Psalm 35:

> David said to God, I shall praise you with every organ of my body. . . .
> With my knees: With my knees I bow in prayer. With my knees: with
> my knees I become a *syndeknos* for children who are being circum-
> cised on my knees.[20]

So although the term *sandek* was a novelty in thirteenth-century France, it had already enjoyed at least two hundred years of familiarity in the Mediterranean countries where the *Midrash on Psalms* was composed and where Nathan also lived. But this text was read by rabbis in the north as well, including a thirteenth-century German halakhist and mystic, Rabbi Eleazer of Worms (d. 1238). Like Isaac of Corbeil (also an Ashkenazi, but a member of the next generation and living in neighboring France), Eleazer decided he had to explain this new word to his readers. He wrote, "The *Midrash on Psalms* says, 'With my knees I serve as *sandeknim* for children. It means the *ba'al brit*."[21] We now have several versions of the actual word: *syndekos* (from Nathan), *syndeknos* (from our printed edition of the *Midrash*), and now *sandeknim* (from Eleazer). As we shall see, the word is of Greek derivation and therefore apt to be misheard, misread, and miscopied by rabbinic tradents. Our authors disagree on how it is pronounced, but they concur on what it means: it means the *sandek* who holds the child during the circumcision.

Eleazer's comment also confirms that the term *sandek* was new to northern Europe in the thirteenth century. Both Eleazer in Germany (sometime before 1238) and Peretz in France (sometime before 1295) explain the new term *sandek* in terms of *ba'al brit*. There were apparently two terms in use in different parts of Europe: (1) the Greek derivative, used in Rome and southern Europe, known variously as *syndekos, syndeknos,* and the plural, *sandeknim,* as well as other variations; and (2) the Hebrew *ba'al brit,* which was commonly used in thirteenth-century Germany and France, and (as we shall see) utilized in northern Italy also.

We know whence the Greek term came. It means exactly what Nathan says, a *patron,* but intended in a specialized ritual way, namely, the sponsor who admitted Christian children to baptism.[22] The editor of the standard edition of *Midrash on Psalms,* Solomon Buber (1827–1906), gives us this etymology in his notes, crediting the discovery to "the great rabbi and scholar, our master and teacher, Doctor Perles."[23] He means Joseph Perles (1835–94), who says he got it from none other than the founder of the modern study of Jewish liturgy, Leopold Zunz. Zunz had mentioned the Christian institution of the godfather along with such things as the Neoplatonic doctrine of emanation and the practice of astrology as instances in which Judaism had borrowed from its host culture. Characteristic of much of his work, Zunz makes his claim without argument, including only a brief note of his primary sources. In his note he cites some of the authorities given above, including the *Midrash on Psalms,* saying that the Jewish godfather is called "*sandek* or *sandekos.*"[24] Zunz's interest was historical; Perles enjoyed etymology. So Perles considers the actual Greek alternatives available, deciding that "*sandek* is either a shortened form of *syndeknos* or it comes from *anadokos,* to which a preceding 's' has been added."[25] As evidence of the latter possibility, Perles cites other loan words to which "s" has been prefixed. Because the option of *syndeknos* obviated the need to posit an added "s" Buber altered his text to read *syndeknos* (not *anadokos,* Perles' other possibility), without telling us, however, what his original manuscript read.

The history of the Christian godparent is well known.[26] An institution dating from the third century, the godparent appears in the West as a sponsor in infant baptism, necessitated by the fact that infants are too young to affirm their promise to live a Christian life. In the East, however, by the fourth century, godparents do more than promise for the child. Adult baptism was still the norm there. People would spend three years in general preparation and only then enter an intensive period of study prior to being baptized. The godparent acted as a guarantor for and guide to prospective catechumens as they left the three-year period and began the year of proximate mystagogic instruction.[27] Godparents were given various names in the West. They are called *sponsores* by Tertullian (c. 200), but the usual Latin title until the fifth century was *offerentes* (those who offer the child for baptism). For infant baptism in the West, parents usually served as the *offerentes* until the fifth century, but thereafter a distinction was made between biological parenthood—which implied raising a child born in the state of sin—and spiritual parenthood, a parent who mirrors God's relationship to the child. Only a spiritual parent was allowed to present the child for baptism. Hence the need for spiritual parents in addition to the biological ones—that is to say, godparents.

Actually, however, spiritual godparents were already the rule in the East by the fourth century. They are mentioned in the fifth century by Theodore of Mopsuestia, John Chrysostom, and Dionysius the Areopagite. Gregentius Tapharensis knows them one century later, and in the seventh century they are also known to Leontius Abbas.[28] It seems, therefore, that as a result of its new theology, the West adopted the eastern custom of having someone other than the natural parents present the person to be baptized, except that in the West that person was a child.

In the East, the standard Greek word for godfather was *anadekomenos,* from *anadekomai,* meaning one who undertakes, promises to do, or stands surety for.[29] It is used that way by John Chrysostom (d. 404) in Constantinople and by Theodore of Mopsuestia (d. 429) one hundred miles or so outside of Antioch.[30] Given the evidence from Chrysostom and Theodore, however, and given also the appearance of the vowel "a" in *sandek,* I suspect Buber's preference for *syndeknos* is misguided. Jews who spoke no Greek apparently shortened *anadekomenos* to *anadek,* and then dropped the second vowel to get *andek.*[31] As with the other examples cited by Perles, an opening "s" was added, probably because the definite article *ha* when prefixed to *andek* would have come out with two adjacent "a" sounds, *ha-andek,* a difficult oral construction. Linguistically, a consonant to divide the vowels would have been preferable. As it happens, however, normal church instructions utilized the plural, speaking of godparents in general. Moreover, the term is found in the accusative case, so that "the godparents" comes out *tous anadekomenos.* Jews who did not speak Greek may have borrowed the final "s" from the Greek *tous* and arrived at *sandek.*

Whichever Greek form they heard, Jews in the Mediterranean must have been familiar with the Christian rite of baptism and the role of the godparents who offered the child for initiation into the church. Recognizing the similarity between baptism and circumcision, they borrowed the technical term used by the church and applied it to the man who offered a Jewish boy to the *mohel;* in the process, they transformed the Greek into a variety of words, eventually arriving at *sandek.*[32] So *sandek* is indeed a loan word from the Greek that entered the Mediterranean Jewish lexicon somewhere before the eleventh century. It was recorded at that time in *Midrash on Psalms,* where it was identified as the man who holds the baby boy on his knees, offering him for circumcision as an act of praise to God. In Northern Italy and Ashkenaz generally, the word in use was *ba'al brit,* but by the thirteenth century, authorities in France and Germany had borrowed *sandek* for their own use and were using it interchangeably with the Hebrew *ba'al brit.*

But where did the term *ba'al brit* come from? If the mother commonly held the child, why was there any need for a *ba'al brit?* Apparently, there were at least two customs. We know from the outcry of Meir of Rothenberg that the mother held the child. But we know as well (from Peretz, for instance, who died in 1295, only two years after Meir) that elsewhere a man known as the *ba'al brit* was already doing that. Two thirteenth-century Italian sources carry this information:

> The father of the baby gives the baby to his great *ba'al brit* [*ba'al brito hagadol*] . . . the *ba'al brit* sits down with the child on his lap. The *mohel* stands up [and proceeds with the liturgy and the operation]. After the operation, the *mohel* takes the child from the *ba'al brit* and then hands him to the father, who gives him to another *ba'al brit,* who puts the child in his lap while the blessings are being concluded.[33]

The mother was still present; she was given wine to drink after the operation was over.[34] But she did not hold the baby.[35]

In sum, at least in Italy, a *ba'al brit* and a *sandek* were in fact the same thing but known by different names, the former in the north and the latter in the south. Both held the child and both were agents of the court, that is, people charged with making sure the boy was properly admitted into the covenant. Both thereby mirrored the Christian *anadekomenos.* A *ba'al brit* also existed in Germany. We do not know for sure that he held the baby the way his namesake did in Italy, but it is probable that he did, since both Eleazer of Worms and Peretz of Corbeil identify him as doing what the *sandek* does in *Midrash on Psalms*—holding the boy on his knees.

But in the German areas known to Meir of Rothenberg and his students, it was the mother who held the boy. Here a genuine novelty is introduced, for we have a new female role, the *ba'alat brit,* a female equivalent of the normal Ashkenazi *ba'al brit.* The Maharil expressly forbids the *ba'alat brit* to serve also as the *sandek.* He decries the continued presence of a woman on whose lap the circumcision takes place.

It is the German rabbis from Maharam to Maharil, then, who successfully ended the ritual role of mothers once and for all. Meir, Samson ben Tzadok, and the Maharil all fought to remove mothers from the scene of the cir-

cumcision, thus necessitating someone (another woman) who would b
child from the mother (who now stayed at home) to the synagogue (wh
circumcision occurred as part of the morning service, at which the me
expected to be already present). We find yet a third agent, a man who would
conduct the child from the woman who stayed outside the synagogue to another man who would serve as the *sandek*.

In sum, removing the Ashkenazi mother from her old role as the one
who held the child during circumcision gave rise to new functionaries. First,
and originally, there had been a *ba'al brit,* whom thirteenth-century authorities correctly identified as their northern equivalent of the southern *sandek*.
But when women still insisted on carrying their sons to the synagogue—and
possibly also, once they were already there, holding them during the circumcision rather than giving them up to one of the men—a *ba'alat brit* was instituted. Now she, not the mother, brought the child to the synagogue doors.
Finally, a *ba'al brit,* who did not necessarily also serve as the *sandek,* conducted the child from the arms of the *ba'alat brit* to the waiting arms of the
sandek.

If we now combine what we know about the synagogue locus of the
circumcision and the rise of functionaries who carried the child, called the
ba'al and *ba'alat brit,* we can readily trace the disappearance of mothers from
their sons' circumcision rites. Since circumcisions almost always took place in
the synagogue, someone had to take the child there from his home. Originally
it was the mother, who also held her baby on her lap during prayer services
and throughout the operation. Thirteenth- and fourteenth-century Ashkenazi
authorities were scandalized by the image of women sitting with men during
synagogue services; they were even more horrified at seeing a male *mohel*
leaning over a mother while performing the circumcision. Speaking for this
school of thought, Meir of Rothenberg initiated the movement to dismiss
women from the ritual. Even though he managed to achieve only limited
success in his lifetime, the next hundred years saw his exploratory efforts
reach fruition. By the time of the Maharil, women had effectively been left
at home.

With the Maharil, the circumcision had finally become exclusively male.
A male *mohel* circumcised a male child on the lap of a male *sandek,* who had
taken the child from a male *ba'al brit* in the male synagogue milieu, during
services where only males came to pray. The only woman who came to the
synagogue (the *ba'alat brit*) gave up the child outside the synagogue doors.

Theology now entered to raise the new male role of *sandek* to an appropriate new height. Recall that the *Midrash on Psalms* had said, "David said to God, I shall praise you with every organ of my body," leading its author to cite the use of the knees to hold the circumcised baby boy. Eleazer of Worms also read and cited the midrash in question, indicating that his pietistic Ashkenazi tradition associated the *mitzvah* of circumcision with using the knees to praise God. It turns out that Eleazer is probably thinking of a larger tradition, one that sees not just the knees but every bodily organ as properly commanded to serve God rather than to engage in bodily sin. The German pietists who developed this tradition devised a series of daily blessings, one for each bodily organ that serves God. A manuscript of the German pietist school, dated to 1326–27, roughly a century after Eleazer died and a full generation after the death of Meir of Rothenberg, contains a fairly exhaustive list of bodily parts that serve God, usually in their everyday function, like, "Praised be Thou, Lord, for my eyes and their sight."[36] The bodily parts mentioned correspond neither to a full listing of talmudic information on the body nor to medieval anatomical information. What we have instead is an ad hoc list of body parts. Thus it is significant, I think, that the knees go unmentioned. We can say, then, that as late as 1326–27, the tradition of seeing the *sandek*'s role as a bodily commandment had yet to be integrated into a larger theological context.

However, the Maharam had already called the holding of a boy during circumcision a commandment, complaining that women had the audacity to "snatch away the commandment from the men." His spiritual successor, the Maharil, took the next step by developing the theological consequences implicit in the Maharam's line of reasoning. He combines (1) the larger tradition of the bodily parts serving God; (2) the notion that where such an act is a commandment dependent on time, women are to be prohibited from it; and (3) the theology of sacrifice. Acting as a *sandek* emerges as more than an ordinary commandment. It is nothing less than a replication of the ancient sacrificial cult, with the *sandek* serving as priest!

> When Maharil was appointed as *ba'al brit* (which is called *sandek* in the language of the sages),[37] he used to bathe himself in order to bring the child to his circumcision while he himself was in a state of purity. He said that the commandment of being a *ba'al brit* is greater than the commandment performed by the *mohel,* since his knees are likened to an altar as if he were offering incense to heaven.[38]

This teaching enters Jewish law in the sixteenth-century gloss of Isserles.

> The *sandek* takes precedence over the *mohel* in being called to the Torah, since a *sandek* is likened to someone who offers incense at the altar. . . . Thus a woman may not serve as a *sandek,* because that would constitute brazenness [*peritsut*], although she may help her husband take the boy to the synagogue where the man takes him from her and becomes the *sandek.* However, a man may do the whole thing without a woman, and that is what the Maharil would do.[39]

In sixteenth-century Poland, then, a mother need no longer remain at home, as the Maharil had insisted. She could now act as the *ba'alat brit* and join her husband in delivering the child to the synagogue. In addition, her husband often became the *sandek.* But the mother stopped outside the synagogue doors. The husband's decision to serve as *sandek* was no doubt occasioned by the new theology that saw the *sandek*'s role as equivalent to offering God a sacrifice. The *sandek*'s knees were the altar. It was only a matter of time until the *sandek* role was expanded ritually as would befit the man serving as a priest before God. Before the circumcision, he would have his hair cut and take special pains to wash so as not to make an offering of the child while in an unclean state.[40]

Circumcision had been transformed from a family event with mother, father, and child at the center into a male-only ritual, almost sacramental in both public and official meaning. That mothers had once brought their children, held them during the rite, had prayers said for their recovery from childbirth, and drunk some of the wine intended for their recuperation would soon be forgotten.

Brit or Milah? Circumcision in American Culture

This book was largely finished in 1987. I had been teaching my life-cycle course for a decade, slowly but surely collecting material and formulating hypotheses. Then came a sabbatical, time to put those hypotheses together into a coherent account for publication. I already had the biblical and rabbinic conclusions intact, and I had discovered the basic documents on the medieval marginalization of women as well. The tannaitic text had been reconstructed, and the symbolic use of blood had been discovered and explored against the backdrop of Christian-Jewish debate. I already knew and had written up the key insight—the element of control, symbolized by the blood of men but not of women—and that realization had led me to the consequent foray into Jewish cosmology as an explanation of women's exemption from positive time-bound commandments. I had shared these conclusions at two scholarly conferences and could have published the book by 1988. But I didn't, and I now wonder why not.

To begin with, the manuscript sat in my computer untouched for months. When I finally decided to turn to it, I discovered that I had somehow (inadvertently?) erased the whole thing! And if that was not bad enough, for the first and only time in twenty years of writing, I had misplaced the only hard copy. One does not lose the product of an entire sabbatical easily, but the consequences were especially disastrous in this case, since except for my class notes, which did not include any secondary literature, I had no records or outline from which I might reconstruct the work. Oddly enough, however, I simply went on to other things, thinking that the manuscript would turn up someday, or reasoning that this was just the way it was meant to be. I am not by nature a fatalist. My dispassionate acceptance of so much labor lost stands out as something important to explain.

Eventually, of course, the hard copy did materialize, and I paid my daughter to sit by the computer reentering it word by word. It was 1990. I could have taken up the book immediately. But again I temporized, finding any number of other projects that took precedence. Meanwhile, I continued teaching my findings to my students and sometimes to rabbinic colleagues, all of whom annoyed me by asking, "When will you publish this?" By 1991 I was lecturing on it to university audiences with similar results, until finally I realized how ambivalent I was about what I had discovered. Maybe part of me didn't want to publish this book.

Once upon a time, we were all taught to keep facts and values strictly separate: facts were objectively given data that were true as opposed to false, whereas values were thought to be mere opinions. Scholarship was about facts, not values; it was a method to ingest data and spew out conclusions. Researchers could safely ignore the motivations that brought them to their work in the first place, as they could the unsettling observation that the everyday world of the media, politics, advertising, and business regularly uses what scholars discover in unforeseen and undesirable ways.

Responsible scholars nowadays no longer delude themselves into thinking that scholarship is only "true facts." At the very least, we are to some extent accountable for what we unleash in the marketplace of ideas. Facts and values, moreover, are more intertwined that we ever imagined. A growing number of philosophers hold that they are known in roughly the same way, and that, in fact, they are the same kind of thing, so that what we study has an impact upon what we know about the way the world is and the way we ought to act within it.[1] Many social scientists concur, explaining the so-called objective stance of the observer as a vestige of academic colonialism and its consequent disregard for the culture it studies.[2] Rabbinic Judaism is the culture that I investigate, and there are modern-day inheritors of rabbinic Judaism around today—myself among them. What I say about my subject matters, not just to scholars who will review my claims as part of the way they make a living, but to practicing Jews who live with circumcision as part of their own cultural heritage. Do they have to know the extreme sexist symbolism of this rite that has initiated a male lifeline, that once called on boys entering puberty to wash their hands in a mixture of circumcision blood and water, that contrasted male blood that saves with female blood that pollutes, and that became the dominant male ritual from which women were eventually forcefully excluded, even though the infants they nursed were required to undergo it?

As I said in the introductory chapter, however, I made the commitment to finish what I had begun. I decided that it is better to come to terms with the crawly creatures in the basement than to pretend that they are not there. My own commitment to feminism and egalitarian causes should be evident by now. I am equally committed to my liberal version of rabbinic tradition. It is not true that these two sets of commitments are necessarily in unremitting opposition. In the case of circumcision, it remains to be seen how we will iron out the creases—whether (unlikely) we will give up circumcision after all or whether (more probably) we will emend the practice and its surrounding ritual in ways that address our modern discomfort with it. In any case, it seemed right to append this conclusion, both to give an account of this work and to add a summary of our current problems with an age-old ritual that has defied all attempts to end it.

First, we should be clear on why American Jews practice circumcision and the extent to which they do so. We saw that by the nineteenth century circumcision had become problematic for Jews who lived in countries where the host Christian culture did not observe the custom. Even so, when lay-people tried to do away with it, a unified rabbinic front successfully opposed them. The result was that, unlike many medieval or even ancient ritual practices that German Reform Jews jettisoned, circumcision was brought to North America and practiced. Thus, even among those Reform Jews whose revised form of Judaism hails from Germany, circumcision is generally the norm.

This is not to say that all or even the majority of North American parents actually see to it that a ritually correct version of the operation is performed. I will return shortly to people who decide against it on religious or moral grounds. For the moment, let us concentrate on parents for whom ideological concerns are not primary. Only 30 percent of all American Jews belong to congregations,[3] and might reasonably expect a hospital visit from a rabbi urging circumcision for their newborn boy whether they had originally planned it or not. The remaining 70 percent, who are unaffiliated and have no rabbi, might be just as loyal to Jewish tradition as the synagogue-going 30 percent, but might also find themselves with less social pressure to celebrate circumcision in a traditional way. In any event, since even non-Jewish boys are systematically operated on before they leave the hospital, both groups of Jews now have the option of a nonritual circumcision performed there, so that they are spared what they may consider the undesirable onus of arranging a ritual circumcision on the eighth day in their home. Most of those who opt out of the home ceremony do so simply because it is the easy thing to do.

As in Germany one hundred years ago, however, the rite of circumcision has not lost its power to move people. Not too long ago I received a phone call from a woman whose daughter, like herself, maintained no official tie with any Jewish organization, including a synagogue. The daughter had given birth to a boy and was prepared to have him circumcised like most other boys in America: not ritually, but by a doctor in the hospital before taking him home with her. The woman had argued strenuously that her daughter should wait until the eighth day, but nothing would convince her to do so. Finally, however, she agreed at least to have a rabbi present so that "it should feel Jewish." The woman placed several calls to Jewish organizations, including the New York national office of the Reform Movement, where, for some unknown reason, someone gave her my name. Could she "hire" me for an hour to attend the medical procedure in the hospital? In the course of the conversation, I declined, she pleaded, and I declined again. Finally she acknowledged that she would just have to call another rabbi, whose name, she professed, she would attain simply by calling back the "agency."

A woman who belongs to no synagogue, who raised children with little or no Jewish consciousness, who has (at best) tenuous memories of what Jews do, and who is sufficiently alienated from contemporary Jewish life as to think she has been in contact with a hire-a-rabbi agency is not someone with particularly deep attachments to things Jewish. But not to have her grandson circumcised in at least a marginally Jewish way seemed to her tantamount to apostasy. Leslie Fiedler, reflecting on the fact that neither he nor any of his eight children are married to Jews, is widely quoted as declaring himself not just a minimal Jew, but a "terminal Jew, the last of a 4,000 year line."[4] I suspect that the possibility of becoming a terminal Jew herself was the heretical possibility that sent the woman scrambling for a rabbi's presence at least briefly in her extended family's life.

If even a marginally Jewish grandmother is reluctant to give up circumcision as a ritual practice, highly identified religious Jews consider it an enduring Jewish duty. Indeed for vast numbers of Jews, circumcision remains what it always has been—an absolute requirement with ritual force comparable to baptism for Christians. The Christian question has not been *whether* to baptise, but only when, how, and whom. To suggest publicly that there is something inherently and unalterably wrong with circumcision has seemed unimaginable. As of late, however, liberals have been attacking almost every sacred institution across the spectrum of American culture: American Thanksgiving, for instance, which is seen as an affront to Native Americans; Columbus Day, for the same reason; even Memorial Day, which has fallen from grace since W. Lloyd Warner described it as "an American sacred ceremony" in 1953.[5] Now parades, wreaths, and cemetery visits have given way to department store sales (for a generation that cannot recall exactly what war is) and antiwar protests (for the generation that reclaims the memory of war only to object to the military-industrial complex that lives off it).

In this culture backdrop, circumcision has not emerged unscathed. I turn now to the real subject of this chapter: not the people who pass over circumcision as irrelevant to their attenuated Jewish identity, nor those who want their boys circumcised but avoid the troublesome details of organizing an eighth-day home ritual, but the increasing number of people plagued by ambivalence over an age-old Jewish duty that is no longer an unmitigated blessing.

Current uneasiness with the rite falls into three categories:

1. *Ritual:* Circumcision is inherently sexist. It conflicts with the higher value of promoting egalitarian Judaism and thus cannot be justified any longer as a desirable Jewish ritual.

2. *Medical:* Far from being medically beneficial (as it was once thought to be), circumcision is at best medically neutral, and maybe even dangerous, so that we can no longer justify it on nonritual but rational grounds relating to hygiene or health.

3. *Moral:* Removed from both ritual and medical grounds of justification, circumcision emerges as nothing more nor less than a classic instance of genital mutilation practiced on helpless children. As such, it should not be countenanced.

I want to turn to each of these charges, and then suggest some ways in which people today are altering the rite of circumcision so as to respond to them.

1. The Ritual Argument

This entire book has provided the details of the argument on ritual grounds, so that a summary of my findings will suffice here. We have seen the series of developments by which circumcision came to symbolize a boy's initiation into a sacrosanct male lifeline. In priestly society, it underscored patrilineal descent. For the Rabbis, male blood was salvific. Geonim assembled three generations of men: fathers, boys entering puberty, and newborns; fathers drew the blood from infant boys and mixed it with water in which adolescents washed. Ashkenazi authorities expelled women from the ceremony and multiplied ritual male roles. Nowhere do any of these Rabbis ever consider a covenant ritual for girls. The sign of the covenant can be made only on the male sexual organ. Women thus remain covenanted only through the male who is so stamped and in whose domain they have their official socially recognized existence. They are portrayed as uncontrolled, and therefore relegated to the margins of Jewish responsibility.

In this age of heightened feminist consciousness, it will surely be said that my thesis underscores the extent to which rabbinic Judaism has been a religion for men more than for women. Not everyone cares, of course, but vast numbers of Jews do find this androcentrism troubling, and this study is just further evidence of exactly how troubled these critics should be.

On the other hand, the general observation that traditional rabbinic Judaism is male-dominated is hardly new. Substantial feminist literature exists regarding ways to correct for female experience. Later I will describe how a covenant ceremony has been provided for girls as well as how the circumcision aspect (the *milah*) has been played down while the covenant perspective (the *brit*) has been foregrounded in the customary boys' rite.

2. The Medical Argument

In recent years debate has resurfaced as to whether circumcision is desirable from a medical perspective. For example, in 1985 Jane Brody summarized some common mythology surrounding circumcision in her widely read column in the *New York Times,* "Personal Health." She noted the spate of new medical pronouncements that had arisen within the decade and a half prior to her writing.

> In 1971 and again in 1975 the American Academy of Pediatrics concluded that routine circumcision of all male babies was not medically warranted. The Academy committee found little evidence to justify routine circumcision as a means of preventing venereal disease, cancer or other disorders. Nor does circumcision prevent masturbation or

premature ejaculation. . . . In 1978, the American College of Obstetricians and Gynecologists joined the pediatricians in opposing routine circumcision.[6]

As Brody makes clear, circumcision as a standard procedure for all males in the United States has been associated with a variety of claims, most of them hardly imaginable today. It was instituted in the 1870s as part of America's fling with what Sydney Ahlstrom calls the age of "sentimental moralism."[7] By the 1870s, doctors adopted circumcision because they believed it would discourage masturbation, which Presbyterian minister Sylvester Graham had posited as a prime cause of insanity.[8] In the course of time, other benefits were added to the list.[9] But the 1980s and 1990s were different. Now, without actually opposing circumcision, doctors were at least reported as not favoring it.

Yet American boys are still being circumcised as a matter of course, and doctors continue to debate the issue. Those in favor of circumcision emphasize the fact that the same 1975 report by the American Academy of Pediatrics, which had concluded that there was insufficient reason for the practice, also noted that circumcision prevents carcinoma of the penis; moreover, other evidence links circumcision to a lower rate of urinary tract infections.[10] The opposition responds that simple hygiene works equally well to mitigate against these diseases.[11]

Given the medical debate, it does seem difficult to justify automatic circumcision, even though it continues to be the norm in hospitals across the entire continent. Jewish parents have the added difficulty of negotiating the ritual debates. If they decide to circumcise but feel uncomfortable with the ritual, they can still do what non-Jewish parents do: circumcise their sons medically in the hospital.

While American Jews are ambivalent over the blatant sexist implications of circumcision and over the fact that they cannot explain their decision to circumcise by any rational appeal to medicine, above all they are uneasy about charges that circumcision is really a case of genital mutilation.

3. The Moral Argument

Opponents of circumcision generally cite Edward Wallerstein or Rosemary Romberg.[12] The former provides a passionate anticircumcision argument that even Brody, who liked the book enough to recommend it to her readers, called "biased." The latter is a particularly thorough rejection of the practice as part of a larger ideological argument for retaining the body in its natural condition with a minimum of meddling physicians. One reviewer describes it as "lengthy, impassioned, and at times unpleasant." [13] Jewish critics who rely on these two treatments or who advance their own arguments, usually from firsthand experience, are vocal and growing in number.

Lisa Braver Moss may be taken as representative. She cites recent evidence that infants feel pain as much if not more than adults, that they remember pain (with disastrous consequences), and that if they do not cry during the operation it may be because they are "withdrawing into a state of neurogenic shock in response to sudden, massive pain." She briefly considers the possibility of local anesthesia, consisting of a dorsal penile nerve block, but she rejects that solution on the grounds that the injection itself involves some pain. While she avers that uncircumcised boys might suffer Jewish ostracism later in life, she nonetheless advocates abandoning the ritual on the grounds that the physical pain has worse consequences, and that, in fact, there is even an outside chance that the baby will die. [14]

Naturally, Braver Moss is not without her critics. These range from outright denials of whatever she says to attempts to modify her claims in such a way as to leave room for circumcision as long as preliminary care is taken to avoid the kind of pain that she describes. Esther Raul-Friedman, for instance, acknowledges the pain, but says that trauma occurs only when a clamp rather than a knife is used. "Unlike the knife which cuts the foreskin," she says, "the clamps completely crush and sever the skin, the nerve endings and the blood vessels." That is why, she concludes, "all rabbinic authorities prohibit the use of clamps." She therefore advocates that we return to the traditional methods so as to do away with undue pain. [15] Raul-Friedman's argument is part of a larger conservative polemic against using a clamp on ritual and religious grounds. [16] Doctors, who generally choose one of the many clamps on the market, presumably disagree with her assessment. To back up her argument for ritual circumcision, Raul-Friedman claims that there *are* medical benefits to circumcision (so that the medical justification ought to be retained), and that because circumcision is a command from God, ritual is justified by theology. In fact, she says, "The external circumcision activates an internal commitment to God." [17]

Daniel Landes and Sheryl Robbin provide a sophisticated blend of tradition and social science in their response to Braver Moss. They turn first to nonmedical considerations, saying, "Circumcision has compelling meaning for the spiritual, ethical, communal, and sexual dimensions of life."[18] It symbolizes the unity of the covenant between God and Abraham that made the Jewish people what it is. They cite Maimonides to the effect that "it provides all [*sic*] Jewish people with a common bodily sign," thereby fostering community, solidarity, and commitment. Since it is an act that we perform on ourselves, it constitutes a symbolic rejection of Sartre's notion that Judaism is a status ascribed by a hostile outer world intent on labeling Jews as different. And it is a sacrifice both theologically and physically, demonstrating the reality that, as a serious and mature religion, Judaism demands personal sacrifice. In addition, it promotes endogamy because to be circumcised is to remember that all sexual activity must take place within the Jewish group. It also constitutes an affirmation of *tikkun olam,* "correcting the world" to make it better, because (contra Romberg) it is a demonstration of the fact that, far from being perfect, the state of nature exists only to be corrected so as to bring about a messianic age. As to the medical argument, they correct the record by citing a later pediatric report "which states that there is a slight advantage to having an infant boy circumcised and that physicians should discuss this topic with the parents."[19]

None of this speaks to the issue of pain, however, which the authors turn to only at the end of their rebuttal. They cite rabbinic authorities who differ on the permissibility of anesthetic. Meir Arik of Galicia (1855–1926) prohibits anesthesia because he believes we should actually value the pain. In his view, children and converts to Judaism should put themselves in Abraham's position, experiencing what he did. It may even be that, in the divine calculus of reward and punishment, it is precisely the willingness to undergo pain that will be recompensed. Subsequent responsa deny the value of pain but generally prohibit anesthesia anyway, sometimes because it is an innovation (innovations are generally regarded suspiciously by Orthodox authorities). It also may be that we value the child's actual involvement in the ceremony; he should know what is going on, not be shielded from it. Landes and Robbin take issue with Braver Moss's assumption that pain is necessarily bad. To begin with, if there is any pain at all, it is minimal in a child whose neural connections are not well developed. Besides, we regularly impose minor pain on our children for their own benefit, by immunizing them, for instance. Finally, they claim that the risks entailed in a dorsal penile block are sufficiently serious as to make us loath to use it.

I have only touched the surface of the debate, but what I have cited is enough to illustrate the depth of emotion with which this issue is charged—again, something one would have predicted simply from the precedent of the Frankfurt Society for the Friends of Reform. But in this instance, opposition is slowly growing, and for the first time in history, it includes outspoken rabbis as well. It will be recalled that even Holdheim, who despised circumcision as barbaric, arrayed himself publicly with the conservatives on the issue, as did the more moderate Geiger. Recall that Geiger wrote his real feelings about the rite to Zunz but refused to make them public. What has changed is that some rabbis are less resistant to admit their ambivalence over circumcision; more and more of them are voicing their misgivings, at least to each other, and often in print.

Again an anecdote proves useful. A number of years ago, I sat around a table with some fifteen rabbis with whom I was studying, both men and women. They were all of child-rearing age; indeed, most already had at least one child and were planning to have others. The topic for the day was a consideration of the texts I had discovered on circumcision, and my evolving understanding of the rite that I had already written up into the first draft of this book. At the end of the session, conversation turned to circumcision today, and people began telling stories. As we went around the room, several of these young rabbis related the case of their own son's circumcision, about which, it turned out, they frequently harbored intense rage—rage at themselves for allowing it to happen, and in some cases rage at the *mohel* who had done it and botched the job. Only here, in the intimacy of a class composed in large part of close friends, did they feel comfortable telling their tales. Stories proved cathartic; at one point people cried.

"Then maybe we should get rid of circumcision," one voice suggested.

Silence ensued. I broke it by adding, "But we haven't. Is there anyone here who has had a son but not circumcised him?"

Silence became anger. In a way, I had no right to participate in the debate. It was true, as someone there charged, "It's easy for you to talk. You have already had all your children. We still have to worry about it." Besides, as an academician, I could afford the comfort of theoretical discourse. But these were rabbis in congregations who faced the dilemma of circumcision every time a baby boy was born to one of their members, not to mention to themselves.

Though unaware that any such meeting had taken place, Rabbi Michael

Herzbrun was to echo the opinions expressed there in a widely read article published in the professional journal for Reform rabbis. As we saw above (p. 2), recalling his son crying during his circumcision, Herzbrun concludes that he had "betrayed" his own infant boy, even smiling at the people assembled in the room and reassuring them silently that everything was all right, when he knew that it was not. Nevertheless, he asserts, "Despite the cutting of the flesh and the pain inherent in the circumcision procedure, the *brit milah* appears destined to remain an inviolate rite."[20]

Emphasis has therefore been placed on altering the nature of the rite so as to continue it in such a way as to meet the objections mounted against it. Primary in the efforts to make sure that is the case, liberal Jewish movements have begun training doctors in the religious side of the circumcision ritual, thus ensuring the existence of a network of *mohalim* (and now, *mohalot,* the feminine plural), who favor both the liberalization of the operation and ceremonial innovation.[21] These *mohalim/ot* (as they refer to themselves) are more apt to utilize local anesthesia, despite the traditional hesitancy to do so. And having women as well as men perform the ritual operation has muted its male bias.

A final word should be said about new liturgies for the occasion. An abundance of ad hoc home-produced mimeographed and word-processed services can be found, some of them relatively traditional, others completely novel, some omitting any surgical procedure whatever.[22] One trend that I expect to continue is a conscious effort to reshape the liturgy so that, as much as possible, it becomes egalitarian. I do not mean, of course, that anyone seriously recommends introducing a parallel operation for girls, but mothers and fathers now say together what was once just the father's blessing, and the same prayers are said both for sons and for daughters in a rite that is no longer called "the covenant of circumcision" (*brit milah*) but simply, "covenant" (*brit*).[23] Thus, on the eighth day after their birth, both boys and girls are initiated into the "covenant of our People Israel" (instead of the traditional "covenant of Abraham our father") by their mother and father.[24] If the child is a boy, ritual circumcision with anesthesia may occur at the same time, but in the background rather than as the ritual focus of the ceremony. The operation thus takes a backseat to the liturgy, thereby emphasizing the theological notion of covenant and playing down the actual surgical procedure.

I said at the outset that this book would explore the public meanings of circumcision. Circumcision as an act of drawing blood that saves is a meaning that was lost a long time ago. Even Orthodox Jews would find such elements in the rabbinic symbol system hard to fathom nowadays. For most Reform Jews, salvation in terms of a life after death, or even a world to come where the messiah reigns, has been transformed into a vague belief in a better messianic age toward which Jews as well as their non-Jewish neighbors work. Salvation by blood would make no sense to them at all.

But the official meaning of circumcision remains the same. It is the rite of initiation into the covenant; hence its new name in Reform circles: "covenant service";[25] hence also the presence of a parallel liturgy for girls, who now are covenanted directly with God, just as their brothers are.

I can only guess at current public meanings. Remember the woman who wanted me to witness her grandson's circumcision in the hospital? On the basis of anecdotal evidence as well as some of the newly composed "creative" liturgies where authors explain their rationale for having some sort of ceremony, albeit not necessarily the traditional one, I suspect that circumcision is seen primarily as a manifest assertion of Jewish continuity with the past. For some, it is a decision to remain true to Judaism even after the Holocaust. Others hold fast to circumcision as one of the few things they still do in a lifestyle that has already jettisoned practically everything else that is Jewish. At least they will mark their children as Jews. There are also people like Herzbrun who, although they lead rich and active Jewish lives, cannot bring themselves to admire this particular rite. Nevertheless, they continue it, albeit with anesthesia and updated liturgy, out of a sense of obligation to Jewish tradition and a sign of their belief that the covenant with God continues. Distasteful as it seems to them, they will go through with the initiation rite, since not to do so is unthinkable. Others circumcise their sons as proudly as their ancestors did, seeing their act not simply as something they have to do, but as something they want to do as well. They may point to the modernization strategies that I have elucidated as evidence that for them, at least, even this age-old and problematic rite can be reclaimed. And finally, there are the critics of the critics, like Landes and Robbin, for whom the whole debate on modernization is irrelevant in that it is the official meaning of circumcision that matters, and that hasn't changed in two thousand years.

Notes

Chapter One

1. *The Jerusalem Report,* 9 September 1993, p. 8.

2. "Message from Dr. David James," in *National Directory of Mohalim/ot,* ed. Lewis M. Barth and Judith Schindler (April 1993), p. iv.

3. Michael B. Herzbrun, "Circumcision: The Pain of the Fathers," *CCAR Journal* 38, no. 4 (Fall 1991): 1.

4. See Allen S. Maller, "Pain and Circumcision," *CCAR Journal* 39, no. 2 (Summer 1992): 70, and Herzbrun, "Pain and Circumcision," *CCAR Journal* 40, no. 1 (Winter 1993): 61–62.

5. Joshua J. Hammerman, "About Men: Birth Rite," *New York Times Magazine,* 13 March 1994, p. 28.

6. See Ismar Schorsch, "Emancipation and the Crisis of Religious Authority: The Emergence of the Modern Rabbinate," in *Revolution and Evolution: 1848 in German-Jewish History,* pp. 205–45.

7. See Michael A. Meyer, *Response to Modernity: A History of the Reform Movement in Judaism* (New York: Oxford University Press, 1988), p. 122.

8. Schorsch, "Emancipation and the Crisis of Religious Authority."

9. See Jakob J. Petuchowski, "Abraham Geiger: The Reform Jewish Liturgist," in *New Perspectives on Abraham Geiger* (Cincinnati and New York: Hebrew Union College-Jewish Institute of Religion and Ktav Publishing, 1975), pp. 42–54.

10. In keeping with recent taxonomy in the field of ritual studies, I identify circumcision as a rite rather than a ritual. "The term 'rite' (from the noun *ritus*) denotes specific enactments located in concrete times and places. . . . 'Ritual' (from the Latin adjective *ritualis*) refers here to the general idea of which a rite is a specific instance. . . . Ritual is an idea scholars formulate. . . . Ritual is what one defines in formal definitions and characterizations; rites are what people enact" (Ronald L. Grimes, *Ritual Criticism: Case Studies on Its Practice, Essays on Its Theory* [Columbia: University of South Carolina Press, 1990], pp. 9–10).

11. The following objections are cited by Meyer, "*Berit Milah* within the History of Reform Judaism," in *Berit Milah in the Reform Context,* ed. Barth (New York: Central Conference of American Rabbis, 1990), pp. 143–44.

12. See literature cited by Meyer in *Response to Modernity,* pp. 423–24 n. 86.

13. Cited in David Philipson, *The Reform Movement in Judaism* (1907; reprint, New York: Ktav Publishing, 1967), p. 136; my emphasis.

14. Contemporary Roman Catholic theology tends to define sacraments as "sacred signs by which spiritual effects are signified and are obtained by the intercession of the Church." The scholastic model, which was still the norm in Frankel's day, emphasized not the sign value of a liturgical act but the objective action that effected an invisible result. See *The New Dictionary of Sacramental Worship,* s.v. "Sacramental Theology after Vatican II" and "Sacramentals."

15. See Meyer, "*Berit Milah* within the History of Reform Judaism," p. 145.

16. Cited in Philipson, *The Reform Movement in Judaism,* p. 154.

17. See Michael Signer, "To See Ourselves as Others See Us," in *Berit Milah in the Reform Context,* pp. 116–19.

18. Ant. 2.16.7.

19. M. Sotah 7 : 8.

20. See Solomon Zeitlin, *The Rise and Fall of the Judean State,* 3 vols. (Philadelphia: Jewish Publication Society, 1967), 2 : 202.

21. M. Ned. 3 : 11.

22. See Elliot R. Wolfson, "Circumcision and the Divine Name," *Jewish Quarterly Review* 78 (1987): 77–112, and Wolfson, "Circumcision, Visionary Experience, and Textual Interpretation: From Midrashic Trope to Mystical Symbol," *History of Religions* 27 (1987): 189–215.

23. Known as Wachtnacht in German lands, Veglia in Italy, and detailed by Elliott Horowitz in "The Eve of Circumcision: A Chapter in the History of Jewish Nightlife," *Journal of Social History* 23 (1989): 45–69. Social aspects overshadowed pietistic practice until the eighteenth century, despite the Zohar's idealized version of the evening as a time of prayer. The first printed edition of prayer and study material for the occasion is *Divrei Haberit* (Venice, 1707). Current equivalents abound. See, for example, *Kol Bo Le'inyanei Berit Milah* (Brooklyn: M. A. Zigelman, n.d.), and *Sefer Otsar Haberit: Entsiklopediah Le'inyanei Milah* (Jerusalem: Machon Torat Haberit, 1986). The former replicates *Sefer Berit Yitzchak* which has enjoyed many printings since the eighteenth century; the latter summarizes Jewish law on the subject and appends a course of study.

24. See Lawrence A. Hoffman, "What Is a Liturgical Tradition?" in *The Changing Face of Jewish and Christian Worship in North America,* ed. Paul F. Bradshaw and Hoffman (Notre Dame, Ind.: University of Notre Dame Press, 1991), pp. 3–25.

25. See *The Invention of Tradition,* ed. Eric Hobsbawm and Terence Ranger (Cambridge: Cambridge University Press, 1983).

26. Hobsbawm, "Mass-Producing Traditions: Europe, 1870–1914," in *The Invention of Tradition,* pp. 277, 271.

27. For further consideration of the method by which rites can be used to reveal culture, see Hoffman, "Reconstructing Ritual as Identity and Culture," in *The Making of Jewish and Christian Worship,* ed. Bradshaw and Hoffman (Notre Dame, Ind.: University of Notre Dame Press, 1991), pp. 22–41.

28. On which, see, for example, Susan Handelman, *The Slayers of Moses:*

The Emergence of Rabbinic Interpretation in Modern Literary Theory (Albany: State University of New York Press, 1982).

29. James A. Sanders, *Canon and Community* (Philadelphia: Fortress Press, 1984), pp. xvii, 38–39.

30. Nancy Jay, *Throughout Your Generations Forever* (Chicago: University of Chicago Press, 1992), p. xxv.

31. There are several publics in any complex society, each with its own somewhat discrete set of meanings. See David Tracy, "The Three Publics of Theology: Society, Academy, and Church," in *The Analogical Imagination: Christian Theology and the Culture of Pluralism* (New York: Crossroad Press, 1986), pp. 6–31.

32. The *Union Prayer Book* was the standard prayer book used by Reform Jews in the United States and Canada since 1894. The Sabbath volume appeared in 1895; it was revised in 1924 and again in 1940. The candle-lighting ritual in question first appeared in the 1940 edition and was therefore common fare for Reform Jews who attended synagogue from 1940 to 1975, the year the *Union Prayer Book* was replaced by the current Reform liturgy, *Gates of Prayer.*

33. For actual examples of women's ritual and its meaning for the women who practice it, see Susan Starr Sered, *Women as Ritual Experts* (Oxford: Oxford University Press, 1992).

34. See above, note 31.

35. See, for example, the now classical discussion by Victor Turner, *Forest of Symbols* (Ithaca, N.Y.: Cornell University Press, 1967), 19–47.

36. See ibid., and Turner, "Symbols in African Ritual," *Science,* 16 March 1972, pp. 1100–1105, reprinted in *Perspectives in Cultural Anthropology,* ed. Herbert Applebaum (Albany: State University of New York Press, 1987), pp. 488–501.

37. Susanne K. Langer, *Philosophy in a New Key: A Study in the Symbolism of Reason, Rite and Art* (Cambridge, Mass.: Harvard University Press, 1942).

38. Michael Krausz, *Rightness and Reasons: Interpretation in Cultural Practices* (Ithaca, N.Y.: Cornell University Press, 1993), p. 67.

39. "Right," that is, as used by Nelson Goodman in *Ways of Worldmaking* (Indianapolis: Hackett Publishing Company, 1978), and *Of Mind and Other Matters* (Cambridge, Mass.: Harvard University Press, 1984). For Goodman there are many worlds—the physicists' world of waves and particles, for instance. The question one must ask is, "What makes a world right?"—that is, "How does its composition cohere?" Ritual, too, is many things; the question is how to arrive at a useful, coherent picture of one of them.

40. For discussion, see Renato Rosaldo, *Culture and Truth* (Boston: Beacon Press, 1989), esp. pp. 48–54.

41. For further consideration of the method by which rites can be used to reveal culture, see Hoffman, "Reconstructing Ritual as Identity and Culture."

42. Daniel Boyarin, *Carnal Israel: Reading Sex in Rabbinic Culture* (Berkeley: University of California Press, 1993), p. 240.

43. Ibid., p. 243.

44. Ibid., p. 242.

45. Ibid.

46. Ibid., p. 243. Though Boyarin does not cite him, he undoubtedly has Marvin Harris in mind. See Harris, *Cultural Materialism* (New York: Vintage Books, 1980).

Chapter Two

1. See especially the work of Harry M. Orlinsky, for example, "The Biblical Concept of the Land of Israel: Cornerstone of the Covenant between God and Israel," in *The Land of Israel: Jewish Perspectives,* ed. Lawrence A. Hoffman (Notre Dame, Ind.: University of Notre Dame Press, 1986), 27 – 64.

2. Julian Morgenstern, "The 'Bloody Husband' (?) (Exod. 4:24–26) Once Again," *Hebrew Union College Annual* 34 (1963): 39. For earlier literature, see the citations in ibid., pp. 38–39. The most recent claim that circumcision is a sacrifice of the part for the whole comes from Stanley F. Chyet and Norman B. Mirsky, "Reflections on Circumcision as Sacrifice," in *Berit Milah in the Reform Context,* ed. Lewis M. Barth (New York: Central Conference of American Rabbis, 1990), pp. 59–68.

3. Eric Isaac, "Circumcision as a Covenant Rite," *Anthropos* 59 (1964): 452.

4. See W. Gunther Plaut, *The Torah: Genesis* (New York: Union of American Hebrew Congregations, 1964), p. 118; Th. C. Vriezen, *The Religion of Ancient Israel* (Philadelphia: Westminster Press, 1967), p. 151; and Roland de Vaux, *Ancient Israel,* 2 vols. (New York: McGraw Hill, 1965), 1:47–48.

5. For classical theory that reduces the "meaning" of circumcision to castration anxiety, see Otto Fenichel, *The Psychoanalytic Theory of Neurosis* (New York: W. W. Norton, 1945). For alternative, but equally reductionist, views, see Frank Zimmerman, "Origin and Significance of the Jewish Rite of Circumcision," *Psychoanalytic Review* 38 (1951): 103–12, and Herman Nunberg, "Circumcision and the Problem of Bisexuality," *International Journal of Psychoanalysis* 28 (1949): 145–79. More recently, see Bruno Bettelheim, *Symbolic Wounds: Puberty Rites and the Envious Male* (New York: Collier, 1962), where the etiology of the rite is explained not as castration anxiety but as womb envy, just the reverse.

6. For a thorough statement of this possibility, see Joseph Blenkinsopp, *The Pentateuch,* Anchor Bible Reference Library (New York: Doubleday, 1992).

7. E. A. Speiser, who attributes Genesis 34 to J, admits that "P has received the majority vote" among scholars who see the hand of P in the editorializing (Speiser, *The Anchor Bible: Genesis* [Garden City, N.Y.: Doubleday and Company, 1964], p. 266).

8. S. R. Driver, *An Introduction to the Literature of the Old Testament* (Cleveland and New York: Meridian Books, 1956), p. 11.

9. Ibid., p. 28.

10. Ibid., p. 42.

11. Ibid., pp. 121, 106.

12. Ant. 5.20ff.

13. Uwe Glessmer and Heinz Fahr, *Jordandurchzug und Beschneidung als Zurechtweisung in einem Targum zu Josua 5,* Orientalia Biblica et Christiana 3 (Glueckstadt: J. J. Augustin, 1991).

14. Howard Eilberg-Schwartz, *The Savage in Judaism* (Bloomington: Indiana University Press, 1990), p. 174.

15. Speiser, *The Anchor Bible: Genesis,* p. 126.

16. 1962 Jewish Publication Society translation.

17. See M. Ned. 3:11 and B. T. Ned. 32a, Rashi *ad loc.,* and midrashic sources cited by Barth in *Berit Milah in the Reform Context,* pp. 105–6, and repeated in Michael B. Herzbrun, "Circumcision: The Pain of the Fathers," *CCAR Journal* 38 (Fall 1991): 2–4. For the pietists, see Elliot R. Wolfson, "Circumcision and the Divine Name," *Jewish Quarterly Review* 78 (1987): 89.

18. Circumcision as covenant would then be common to exilic Isaiah and to P proper. Both worry about boundary issues, though against the more stringent version of the latter (Ezra/Nehemiah) the former polemicizes that circumcision and Shabbat are the two covenantal signs that mark one as in rather than out.

19. S. David Sperling, "Rethinking Covenant in Late Biblical Books," *Biblica* 70, no. 1 (1989): 50–72; on Isaiah particularly, see pp. 70–72.

20. M. Ned. 3:11.

21. J. Duncan Derrett ("Circumcision and Perfection: A Johannine Equation [John 7:22–23]," *Evangelical Quarterly* 63, no. 3 [1991]: 211–24) attempts to conflate rabbinic commentary on this Mishnah and elsewhere so as to enlarge the meaning of *tamim,* "perfect," to include moral stature as well as physical form. His interest is John 7:23, where Jesus justifies his healing of a paralytic on the Sabbath (John 5:1–18) by saying, "You circumcise a man on the Sabbath. If on the Sabbath a man receives circumcision . . . are you incensed with me because on the Sabbath I healed a man's whole body?" "It is ridiculous to say that circumcision affects merely the male organ," claims Derrett. "It was instituted to affect the whole person," including bodily wholeness and "moral perfection." Thus Jesus was offering the sick man genuine wholeness, both of body and of soul, and that is why he urges him (5:14), "See, you have been made well! Do not sin any more, so that nothing worse happens to you." For Derrett, then, wholeness is a matter of one's "spiritual condition" (pp. 214, 216, 217). John 7 refers back to the healing incident in John 5:2–18. Neither passage refers to anything spiritual or moral. I think it is likelier, therefore, that Jesus, like the Rabbis, is reading *tamim* as "physically whole." God cured Abraham of what he was lacking; Jesus cured a paralytic in the same way. Both were rendered physically "whole."

22. Paula Fredriksen, "Judaism, the Circumcision of Gentiles, and Apocalyptic Hope: Another Look at Galatians 1 and 2," *Journal of Theological Studies,* n.s. 42, no. 2 (1991): 536–37, nn. 11 and 12.

23. Josh. 5:9, assuming it to be authentically D. See discussion above.

24. Howard Eilberg-Schwartz, *The Savage in Judaism,* pp. 141–76. Murray Wax reviews this book in *Journal for the Study of Religion* 30, no. 3 (1991): 328–329. See ensuing debate in this journal: Eilberg-Schwartz's objections in 31, no. 2 (1992): 224–25, and Wax's response immediately following on pp. 226–27.

25. Eilberg-Schwartz calls it a symbol, saying, "A symbol differs from a sign in that it has properties that make it appropriate for the content which it signifies" (*The Savage in Judaism,* p. 146). The literature on signs and symbols is so diverse that there is no agreed upon taxonomic usage; see Edmund Leach, *Culture and Communication* (Cambridge: Cambridge University Press, 1976), pp. 9–16. Liturgically, I prefer the term "icon" for what Eilberg-Schwartz call "symbol," so I agree wholeheartedly with his analysis in substance, though I substitute my own term

here, as defined by Jaroslav Pelikan in *The Vindication of Tradition* (New Haven, Conn.: Yale University Press, 1984), p. 55.

26. Eilberg-Schwartz, *The Savage in Judaism,* p. 146.

27. Ibid., pp. 149–54.

28. Karen Ericksen Paige and Jeffrey M. Paige, *The Politics of Reproductive Ritual* (Berkeley: University of California Press, 1981), p. 48.

29. Ibid., pp. 49, 78.

30. Ibid., pp. 147–57.

31. See, for example, Ezra 8.

32. Eilberg-Schwartz, *The Savage in Judaism,* 167–73.

33. E. H. Gombrich, *Art and Illusion* (Princeton, N.J.: Princeton University Press, 1960), pp. 83, 82.

34. Harold Bloom, *The Anxiety of Influence: A Theory of Poetry* (Oxford: Oxford University Press, 1973), pp. 31, 30.

35. Bloom, *A Map of Misreading* (Oxford: Oxford University Press, 1975), p. 65.

36. The popular misconception that the rabbinic system replaced patrilineal with matrilineal requirements derives from the rabbinic rule that a child born to a Jew and a non-Jew follows the mother's religious identity. Actually, the rule of patrilineality holds, since a child born to two Jews inherits the status of the father and is known as the son/daughter of the father. But when an illicit union produces offspring, exceptions to the system occur. The matrilineal exception to a fundamentally patrilineal system has been traced to several factors: the influence of Roman law; a basic aversion to mixed breeding in plant and animal life, to which mixed marriages were likened; and the possibility of female conversion, which was introduced sometime in the second century C.E. See Shaye J. D. Cohen, "The Origins of the Matrilineal Principle in Jewish Law," *AJS Review* 10, no. 1 (1985): 19–54.

37. Savina J. Teubel, *Sarah the Priestess: The First Matriarch of Genesis* (Athens, Ohio: Swallow Press, 1984); Nancy Jay, "Sacrifice, Descent, and the Patriarchs," *Vetus Testamentum* 38, no. 1 (1988): 52–70, and, more extensively, *Throughout Your Generations Forever* (Chicago: University of Chicago Press, 1992). For earlier literature dealing with putative early matrilineality, see Cohen, "The Origins of the Matrilineal Principle in Jewish Law," pp. 50–51.

38. Jay, "Sacrifice, Descent, and the Patriarchs," p. 57.

39. Jay, *Throughout Your Generations Forever,* pp. 98–99.

40. Ibid., p. 106.

41. Jay, "Sacrifice, Descent, and the Patriarchs," p. 54.

42. Ibid., p. 70.

43. Cohen, "The Origins of the Matrilineal Principle in Jewish Law," p. 21.

44. Mary Douglas, *Purity and Danger: An Analysis of the Concepts of Pollution and Taboo* (London: Routledge and Kegan Paul, 1966), p. 140. The best exposition of Douglas's ideas on purity and their application to the Bible is Jerome H. Neyrey, "The Idea of Purity in Mark's Gospel," *Semeia* 35 (1986): 91–128.

45. Douglas, *Purity and Danger,* p. 142.

46. Ibid., pp. 142, 143.
47. Ibid., pp. 145–46.

Chapter Three

1. Nancy Jay, *Throughout Your Generations Forever* (Chicago: University of Chicago Press, 1992), p. 96.

2. In fact, the circumcision ceremony even made use of sacrificial language, as if the ritual circumcision *was* the cult. See below, chapter 4.

3. Peter L. Berger, *The Sacred Canopy: Elements of a Sociological Theory of Religion* (New York: Doubleday/Anchor, 1967), p. 45. See also Berger, "Some Second Thoughts on Substantive Versus Functional Definitions of Religion," *Journal for the Scientific Study of Religion* 13 (1974): 125–33, where he maintains, "I have never liked functional definitions of religion of this kind," that is, when "religion is defined in terms of what it does" (p. 127). Despite the disclaimer, Berger's functionalism is evident throughout his discussion in *The Sacred Canopy.* Yet his "second thoughts" are directed "not against Luckman, Geertz or Bellah, but against the uses to which their approaches have been put by others in the marketplace of ideas," more specifically, "the *ideological uses*" (ibid.). Berger wants to identify an essentialist definition of what counts as religion, and then to study what it does, rather than arbitrarily assume that anything that does a particular thing is necessarily religion. His essentialist tendency is derived from Weber, he says, and from the phenomenological mandate toward *Verstehen.* So far so good. But he also accepts Otto's essentialist definition, and I take issue with him there. See Lawrence A. Hoffman, *Beyond the Text* (Bloomington: Indiana University Press, 1987), pp. 149–71. The term "plausibility structure" is his own, suggested, he says, by "some key understandings of Marx, Mead, and Schutz" (*The Sacred Canopy,* p. 192 n. 20). He also regularly records his indebtedness to Durkheim, whom he recasts, however, in a Meadian context (for example, in ibid., p. 191 n. 12).

4. Berger, *The Sacred Canopy,* pp. 45–46.

5. Personal communication from Harry M. Orlinsky, who says that when the Jewish Publication Society retranslated the Bible, he even argued for the translation of the ambiguous *banim,* which usually means "children," as "sons."

6. Philo, *Questions and Answers on Genesis* 3.48–50.

7. For dating, see Jacob Neusner's work. A synopsis can be found in his *Understanding Seeking Faith: Essays on the Case of Judaism,* vol. 2 of *Literature, Religion and the Social Study of Judaism* (Atlanta: Scholars Press, 1987), pp. 143–48.

8. Joseph Heinemann, *Prayer in the Talmud,* trans. Richard Sarason (1966; Berlin and New York: Walter de Gruyter, 1977).

9. See Ellis Rivkin, "Ben Sira and the Non-existence of the Synagogue," in *In a Time of Harvest: Essays in Honor of Abba Hillel Silver on the Occasion of His 70th Birthday,* ed. Daniel Jeremy Silver (New York: Macmillan, 1963), pp. 320–55.

10. See the discussion in Heinemann, *Prayer in the Talmud,* pp. 218–21.

11. Ibid., p. 220.

12. Ibid., p. 221.

13. *Sefer ben Sira Hashalem,* ed. M. S. Segal, 2d ed. (Jerusalem: Mossad Bialik, 1949), p. 355.

14. Solomon Schechter, "Genizah Specimens," *Jewish Quarterly Review* o.s. 10 (1898), reprinted in Jakob J. Petuchowski, *Contributions to the Scientific Study of Jewish Liturgy* (New York: Ktav, 1970), pp. 375–76.

15. See Philip Birnbaum, *Ha-siddur Ha-shalem: Daily Prayer Book* (New York: Hebrew Publishing Company, 1949), p. 89.

16. Walter J. Ong, *Orality and Literacy* (1982; reprint, London and New York: Routledge, 1988), p. 21.

17. See Heinemann, *Prayer in the Talmud.* Heinemann seems to accept the notion that Ben Sira is already a form of Tefillah, however.

18. This issue has once again become the center of scholarly debate following an influential article by Ezra Fleischer, "Lakadmoniut Tefillot Hachovah Beyisrael," *Tarbiz* 59 (1990): 397–445. Fleischer takes the position I advocate here, not about circumcision liturgy per se, but about dating statutory prayer after 70. The older position (all the way from Zunz to Heinemann), which posits such liturgy as early as Ben Sira, is continued in a modified way by Stefan Reif, who responded to Fleischer ("Al Hitpatchut Hatefillah Hakadumah Beyisrael," *Tarbiz* 60 [1991]: 677–81), and published his view in extended form in his *Judaism and Hebrew Prayer* (Cambridge: Cambridge University Press, 1993). For the latest view of what happened after 70—that is, in the canonical work of Gamaliel II—see Na'ami Cohen, "Shimon Hapakuli Hisdir Shemoneh Esrei Berakhot," *Tarbiz* 52 (1983): 547–55.

19. See Neusner, *Understanding Seeking Faith,* pp. 150–51, for a superior summary and citation of literature.

20. See, for example, insistent testimony from Apollonius (second century): "A sacrifice bloodless and pure I too and all the Christians bring unto almighty God." Both Tertullian and Cyprian (third century) feel the need to develop a technical vocabulary for sacrifice. Christian apologists had previously argued that God did not need sacrifices, but finding themselves continually on the defensive nonetheless, they found it necessary to speak as if sacrifice were part and parcel of their new faith. See the synopsis of texts and discussion in Joseph Jungmann, *The Mass: An Historical, Theological and Pastoral Survey* (Collegeville, Minn.: Liturgical Press, 1976).

21. Peter Brown, "St. Augustine's Attitude toward Religious Conversion," *Journal of Religious Studies* 54 (1964): 109.

22. On the *chavurah,* see, for example, Heinemann, "Birkath Ha-Zimmun and Havurah Meals," *Journal of Jewish Studies* 13 (1962): 23–29; Neusner, *Fellowship in Judaism* (London: Vallentine, Mitchell and Co., 1963); Pinchas Ha-Cohen Pelli, "The Havurot that Were in Jerusalem," *Hebrew Union College Annual* 55 (1984): 55–74; Shmuel Safrai, "Kehillah Kadisha Devirushalayim," *Zion* 22, no. 1 (1957): 183–93; Solomon J. Spiro, "Who Was the *Haber?* A New Approach to an Ancient Institution," *Journal for the Study of Judaism* 11, no. 2 (1980): 186–216.

23. See Marc J. Belgrad, "Table as Altar: Tannaitic Table-Fellowship as the Locus of Spirituality" (Master's thesis, Hebrew Union College-Jewish Institute of Religion, 1986).

24. See, for example, Neusner, *From Politics to Piety* (New York: Ktav, 1979), p. 67.

25. Ramsay MacMullen, *Paganism in the Roman Empire* (New Haven, Conn.: Yale University Press, 1981), pp. 38–39.

26. Brown, *The Cult of the Saints* (Chicago: University of Chicago Press, 1981), pp. 39–41.

27. The notion that the benediction is prototypically biblical is explored in a classic essay by Jean-Paul Audet, "Esquisse historique du genre littéraire de la bénédiction juive et de l'eucharistie chrétien," *Revue Biblique* 65 (1958): 371–99. It is accepted by Heinemann, who cites many more such instances of biblical blessings (*Prayer in the Talmud*, p. 82). But both authors overrate the significance of the biblical connection. To be sure, biblical and rabbinic worshippers blessed God for this or that, but the use of the phrase "Blessed be" in the former context is altogether different from its use in the latter, where it becomes the central hallmark of rabbinic liturgy. What psalms and associated phrases like *Hodu l'adonai* are to the Bible, benedictions are to the Rabbis.

28. The issue is complex. The earliest strata generally cited are the Hillelite/Shammaite debates, which Neusner has effectively discredited as necessarily accurate measures of the time of which they purport to speak. See his *Rabbinic Traditions about the Pharisees before 70* (Leiden: Brill, 1971). An authentic early account, on the other hand, is probably M. Ta'an. 2:1–4, which knows the concept of a benediction, and even benediction strings, probably with concluding summary eulogies (though the eulogies we have may be a later gloss on the original text). See Hoffman *Beyond the Text*, pp. 9–11 and notes cited, for synopsis of textual difficulties. So there was *some form* of benediction very early, but exactly what it was, whether there were several alternatives, and how central benedictions were to rabbinic prayer we do not know. On the *ma'amad*, see M. Ta'an, 2:1–4. The daily sacrifice, or *tamid*, is said to have been overseen by lay representatives drawn from representative geographical sectors of society, each known as a *ma'amad.*

Chapter Four

1. See especially Paul F. Bradshaw, "Ten Principles for Interpreting Early Christian Liturgical Evidence," in *The Making of Jewish and Christian Worship,* ed. Bradshaw and Lawrence A. Hoffman (Notre Dame, Ind.: University of Notre Dame Press, 1991), pp. 3–21; and, more recently, Bradshaw, *The Search for the Origins of Christian Worship* (New York and Oxford: Oxford University Press, 1992), chap. 1, where the limits to what we can know about early Jewish liturgy are explored.

2. Julius Wellhausen, *Prolegomenon to the History of Ancient Israel* (1878; reprint, New York: Meridian Books, 1957), pp. 297–98. In keeping with his own lofty conception of biblical spirituality, Wellhausen located the P author's concern in his desire to provide a "cosmogonic theory" in order to transcend a mythical analysis by postulating an elementary scientific one. Other views emphasize political realities: the exilic returnees' need to emphasize that since God created the entire world, God rightly rules everywhere, even the land to which they had been transported.

3. See Genesis Rabbah 1:1.

4. Rashi to Genesis 1:1, on which, see Michael A. Signer, "The Land of Israel in Medieval Jewish Literature," in *The Land of Israel: Jewish Perspectives,* ed. Hoffman (Notre Dame, Ind.: University of Notre Dame Press, 1986), pp. 225–27.

5. See, for example, James A. Sanders, *Canon and Community* (Philadelphia: Fortress Press, 1984), pp. 3, 5 ("Biblical criticism has locked the Bible into the past"); and Sanders, *From Sacred Story to Sacred Text* (Philadelphia: Fortress Press, 1987), p. 84, where he urges us to see the Bible as "a paradigm of God's work . . . out of which we can construct paradigms of our own, rather than a jewel box of ancient wisdom to be perpetuated."

6. See Hoffman, *Beyond the Text* (Bloomington: Indiana University Press, 1987), for methodological discussions.

7. Hyman E. Goldin, *Hamadrikh: The Rabbi's Guide: A Manual of Jewish Religious Rituals, Ceremonies and Customs,* rev. ed. (New York: Hebrew Publishing Company, 1956).

8. Ibid., author's "Introduction" page.

9. Philip Birnbaum, *Ha-siddur Ha-shalem: Daily Prayer Book* (New York: Hebrew Publishing Company, 1949).

10. Goldin, *Hamadrikh,* pp. 33–37; Birnbaum, *Ha-siddur Ha-shalem,* pp. 742–44.

11. The motif of sacrifice is itself a significant public meaning that I have chosen not to emphasize, because even though it does go back to rabbinic sources it becomes central only with the Zohar. See Geza Vermes, *Scripture and Tradition in Judaism* Leiden: E. J. Brill, 1983), pp. 178–92, and Elliot R. Wolfson, "Circumcision and the Divine Name," *Jewish Quarterly Review* 78 (1987): 99.

12. *Pirkei deRabbi Eliezer,* end of chap. 29. See discussion in chapter 6.

13. Both blessings are cited as tannaitic in Shab. 137b and T. Ber. 6:12. The possibility that these attributions are suspect is discussed below.

14. M. Ber. 6:1.

15. See Ismar Elbogen, *Der Jüdische Gottesdienst in seiner Geschichtlichen Entwicklung* (1913; reprint, Hildesheim: Georg Olms, 1962), p. 80; Joseph Heinemann, *Prayer in the Talmud,* trans. Richard Sarason (1966; Berlin and New York: Walter de Gruyter, 1974), pp. 270–74.

16. See Kenneth Pike, *Language in Relation to a Unified Theory of the Structure of Human Behavior* (Glendale, Calif.: Summer Institute of Linguistics, 1955), p. 48.

17. Peter Brown, *The Cult of the Saints* (Chicago: University of Chicago Press, 1981), pp. 33–35.

18. Yoram Bilu, "Dreams and Wishes of a Saint," in *Judaism Viewed from Within and from Without,* ed. Harvey Goldberg (Albany: State University of New York Press, 1987), p. 290.

19. Thomas O'Meara, "Field of Grace," *Notre Dame Magazine* 20 (Autumn 1991): 12–13.

Chapter Five

1. Shab. 137b.

2. See *Dikdukei Sofrim, ad loc.*

3. See mss. in T. Ber. 6:13; P.T. Ber. 9:3; discussion in Saul Lieberman, *Tosefta Kifshutah,* 7 vols. (New York: Jewish Theological Seminary, 1955), 1:114.

4. See Lawrence A. Hoffman, *Canonization of the Synagogue Service* (Notre Dame, Ind.: University of Notre Dame Press, 1979).

5. See *Seder Rav Amram Gaon,* ed. E. D. Goldschmidt (Jerusalem: Rav Kook, 1971), p. 179, and *Siddur Rav Saadiah Gaon,* ed. Simchah Assaf, Israel Davidson, and Issachar Joel, 2d ed. (Jerusalem: Mekitsei Nirdamim, 1963), p. 98.

6. See textual alternatives discussed by the Geonim in Hoffman, *Canonization of the Synagogue Service,* p. 137.

7. See, for example, the celebrated *baraita* in B.T. Yeb. 12b, meaning either that certain categories of women "may" or "have to = must" use a contraceptive, and therefore (by logical extension), that all other women either "may not" or "do not have to, but may" practice birth control. See discussion in David M. Feldman, *Birth Control in Jewish Law* (New York: New York University Press, 1968).

8. P.T. Ber. 9:3.

9. See the parallel *Rabbah* texts above, pp. 126–31.

10. See P.T. 1:7; B.T. Kid. 29a–30a.

11. M. Kid. 7:1.

12. See Fred O. Frances, "The Baraita of the Four Sons," *Journal of the American Academy of Religion* 42 (1974): 280–97. Some modern Haggadot mistranslate deliberately as "four children," but the original meaning is "sons."

13. Bertinoro, *ad loc.*

14. See Ber. 33a.

15. See the responsum by Israel Schepansky in *Or Hamizrach* 31, no. 2 (1983) and 31, nos. 3–4 (1983).

16. See T. Ber. 4:1; Ber. 35a.

17. *Sefer Ha'eshkol, Hilkhot milah,* sect. 40.

18. Ket. 7a. See Rashi's evident difficulty in explaining why the rule does not hold here.

19. See form-critical analysis introduced by Joseph Heinemann, *Prayer in the Talmud,* trans. Richard Sarason (1966; Berlin and New York: Walter de Gruyter, 1977); summarized in Hoffman, *Canonization of the Synagogue Service,* pp. 3–4.

20. Even so, as late as the tenth century, Saadiah listed blessings that differ from the list as the Talmud gives it. See *Siddur Rav Saadiah Gaon,* p. 108.

21. The claim is most avidly put forward by Avigdor Aptowitzer in connection with the work of Eliezer ben Joel Halevi (Germany, c. 1140–c. 1225), who claimed explicitly to have seen such a source. See Aptowitzer, *Sefer Haravyah Lerabbenu Eliezer Berabbi Yoel Halevi* (Jerusalem: Mekitzei Nirdamim, 1931), cited in Daniel Sperber, *Minhagei Yisrael: Mekorot Vetoldot* (Jerusalem: Rav Kook, 1990), p. 63 n. 9.

22. Sperber, *Minhagei Yisrael,* p. 62.

23. *Sefer Chemdah Genuzah* (republished, Jerusalem, 1963), p. 31a.

24. *Seder Rav Amram Gaon,* p. 179.

25. *Sefer Chemdah Genuzah,* p. 21a.

26. 1 Cor. 11:25–27; translation of *New Revised Standard Version* (1989).

27. Shab. 19:2.

28. Shab. 133b.

29. *Tur,* Y.D. 264; S.A., Y.D. 264:3; Maimonides, *Sefer Ahavah, milah* 2:1.

30. I know of one other text where wine and blood commingle in a cup. See Mordecai Margaliot, *Sefer Harazim* (Jerusalem: American Academy for Jewish Research, 1966), p. 73; discussion p. 10. "Behold, in your hand is the cup with blood and wine in it." The translation "by your blood" rather than "in your blood" here is a deliberate attempt to employ the ablative of means, the grammatical usage intended here. See above, p. 182.

31. On the synagogue, see the summary article by Marilyn J. S. Chiat and Marchita B. Mauck, "Using Archeological Sources," in *The Making of Jewish and Christian Worship,* ed. Paul F. Bradshaw and Hoffman (Notre Dame, Ind.: University of Notre Dame Press, 1991), pp. 69–106. Chiat's *Handbook of Synagogue Architecture* (Chico, Calif.: Scholars Press, 1982), still the best source for the remarkable variation in synagogue architecture, belies any simplified developmental model of how the synagogue grew.

32. M. Shab. chap. 2.

33. *Seder Rav Amram Gaon,* pp. 179–80.

34. See Jacob Mann, "Rabbinic Studies in the Synoptic Gospels," *Hebrew Union College Annual* 1 (1924): 324, 329, for the marshalling of data.

35. See Hoffman, *Canonization of the Synagogue Service,* pp. 161–64, for details.

36. See *Siddur Rav Saadian Gaon,* pp. 98–99.

37. *Seder Rav Amram Gaon,* p. 179.

38. In fact, in fourteenth-century Spain Abudarham still used them interchangeably, Amram's prayer being reserved for occasions when the father was not still alive, since it does not explicitly mention him among those who are to be blessed with the son's growth. See Abudarham, *Milah uvirkhoteha,* p. 352.

39. *Ravyah* 1:360.

40. See note 21 above, and Sperber, *Minhagei Yisrael,* pp. 62–63, for medieval sources other than the *Ravyah* for such a Palestinian provenance.

Chapter Six

1. Daniel Boyarin seeks to separate the drawing of blood in such cases from the issue of actual bodily circumcision, since he sees the latter as a symbolic "feminizing [of] the male," to open him to "the divine speech and vision of God" (Boyarin, "'This We Know to Be the Carnal Israel': Circumcision and the Erotic Life of God and Israel," *Critical Inquiry* 18 [Spring 1992]: 495). It follows, then, that the actual drawing of blood must be a separate issue (p. 496 n. 65). Indeed it is, as my own treatment here indicates. Male blood in itself was salvific.

2. See excellent summary of data as well as theories regarding circumcision in Karen Ericksen Paige and Jeffery M. Paige, *The Politics of Reproductive Ritual* (Berkeley: University of California Press, 1981).

3. Victor Turner, *The Forest of Symbols* (Ithaca, N.Y.: Cornell University Press, 1967), p. 31.

4. See David Weiss Halivni, *Midrash, Mishnah, and Gemara: The Jewish Predilection for Justified Law* (Cambridge, Mass.: Harvard University Press, 1986).

5. Turner, *The Forest of Symbols,* p. 19.

6. Invariance as a necessary part of ritual has received considerable treatment. See, for example, essays reprinted in Maurice Bloch, *Ritual, History and Power* (London: London School of Economics, 1989) esp. pp. 19–45, on language; a response to Bloch (among other things) by Stanley Jeyeraja Tambiah, "A Performative Approach to Ritual," in *Culture, Thought and Social Action* (Cambridge, Mass.: Harvard University Press, 1985), esp. pp. 154–56; and Roy A. Rappaport, *Ecology, Meaning and Religion* (Berkeley, Calif.: North Atlantic Books, 1979), esp. pp. 173–221 on "The Obvious Aspects of Ritual."

7. Turner, *The Forest of Symbols,* pp. 29–30, 31.

8. Ibid., pp. 30–32, 20.

9. All quotes below are from *Pirkei deRabbi Eliezer,* chap. 29.

10. Literally, "the fourth kingdom," taken to mean the Roman Empire, under which Jews believed they would remain until final messianic deliverance.

11. See Shalom Spiegel's classic, *The Last Trial* (Philadelphia: Jewish Publication Society, 1967).

12. *Seder Rav Amram Gaon,* ed. E. D. Goldschmidt (Jerusalem: Rav Kook, 1971), p. 180. Attributed to Rav Tzadok Gaon; see alternative attribution to the Gaon Kohen Tzedek by the *Tur.*

13. See Lawrence A. Hoffman, *Canonization of the Synagogue Service* (Notre Dame, Ind.: University of Notre Dame Press, 1979), p. 187.

14. *Teshuvot Hageonim: Sha'arei Tzedek,* part 3, p. 11. There were two recensions of the same account. This one can be found also in *Orchot Chaim, Hilchot Milah,* Schlesinger ed. (Berlin: 1902), part 2, p. 14. The Amram text, on the other hand found its way into the *Tur* and the *Eshkol;* see note by Schlesinger, *ad loc.*

15. The list of differences circulated widely and is cited in part here and there by most Western European authorities. This version is from *Sefer Ha'eshkol, Hilchot milah,* Auerbach ed. (Halberstadt, 1868), p. 131.

16. Joel Mueller, *Chilluf Minhagim bein Bavel Ve'eretz Yisra'el* (Vienna, 1878; reprint, Jerusalem: Makor Press, 1970), pp. 18–19.

17. See discussion by Auerbach, *Sefer Ha'eshkol,* p. 131 n. 1.

18. Generally still considered a tannaitic midrash. Its final editing may fall somewhat later, but not exceptionally so, despite late dating claimed by Ben Zion Wacholder. See Wacholder, "The Date of Mekilta de-Rabbi Ishmael," *Hebrew Union College Annual* 29 (1968): 117–44.

19. *Mekhilta Bo,* chap. 5.

20. Shab. 137b.

21. *Exodus Rabbah* 15 : 12, beginning and end.

22. See *Haggadah shel Pesach Vetoldoteha,* ed. E. D. Goldschmidt (Jerusalem: Bialik Institute, 1960), p. 83.

23. P.T. Pes. 10:3.

24. See Hoffman, "Does God Remember?" in *Remembrance in Jewish and Christian Tradition,* ed. Lawrence Cunningham and Michael A. Signer (forthcoming, University of Notre Dame Press).

25. W. Jardine Grisbrooke, "Anaphora," in *The New Westminster Dictionary of Liturgy and Worship,* ed. J. G. Davies (Philadelphia: Westminster Press, 1986), p. 18.

26. See Philip Birnbaum, *Machzor Shalem: High Holyday Prayer Book* (New York: Hebrew Publishing Company, 1951), pp. 385–89.

27. Usually translated as "the birthday of the world," but "conception" is preferable. See Hoffman, *Gates of Understanding*, 2 vols. (New York: Central Conference of American Rabbis, 1984), 2:102–4.

28. Birnbaum, *Machzor Shalem,* pp. 388–89.

29. On early Christian and Jewish symbols of salvation, see Hoffman, "A Symbol of Salvation in the Passover Haggadah," *Worship* 53, no. 6 (1979): 519–37.

30. See Herbert Chanan Brichto, "On Slaughter and Sacrifice, Blood and Atonement," *Hebrew Union College Annual* 47 (1976): 19–55 for survey of sources in *Tanakh.* See pp. 51–53 for a short discussion on post-*Tanakh* sources in New Testament and in Talmudic literature.

31. See T. Pes. 10:12, and the more familiar account in the Haggadah (Birnbaum, *The Passover Haggadah* [1953; reprint, New York: Hebrew Publishing Company, 1976], p. 65). The latter cites "Rabbis Eliezer, Joshua, Elazar ben Azaryah, Akiba, and Tarfon [who] were celebrating the seder together in B'nai B'rak"; the former gives us "Rabban Gamaliel and the elders . . . in Lydda."

32. See M. Pes. 10:1 for earliest rabbinic account of seder, discussed in some detail by Baruch M. Bokser, *The Origins of the Seder* (Berkeley: University of California Press, 1984), chaps. 3 and 4.

Chapter Seven

1. See David de Sola Pool, *The Old Jewish Aramaic Prayer, The Kaddish* (Leipzig: R. Haupt, 1909), and more recently, Joseph Heinemann, "The Background of Jesus' Prayer in the Jewish Liturgical Tradition," in *The Lord's Prayer and Jewish Liturgy,* ed. Jakob J. Petuchowski and Michael Brocke (New York: Seabury, 1978), pp. 81–89.

2. The summary statement of the problem usually cited is Joachim Jeremias, *The Eucharistic Words of Jesus,* rev. ed. (1964; reprint, Philadelphia: Fortress Press, 1976). More recently, see the up-to-date survey of the influence of Jewish liturgy on Christian liturgy by Paul F. Bradshaw, *The Search for the Origins of Christian Worship* (New York and Oxford: Oxford University Press, 1992), pp. 1–29.

3. On the calendar in general, see Thomas J. Talley, *Origins of the Liturgical Year* (New York: Pueblo Publishing Co., 1986).

4. Lawrence A. Hoffman, "The Jewish Lectionary, the Great Sabbath, and the Lenten Calendar: Liturgical Links between Christians and Jews in the First Three Christian Centuries," in *Time and Community: In Honor of Thomas Julian Talley,* ed. J. Neil Alexander (Washington, D.C.: The Pastoral Press, 1990), pp. 3–20.

5. Pioneering work by Eric Werner (*The Sacred Bridge,* vol. 1 [New York: Columbia University Press, 1959]; vol. 2 [New York: Ktav Publishing, 1984]) has been reevaluated, and supplemented by novel research, by Edward Foley, *Foundations of Christian Music* (Bramcote and Nottingham: Grove Books, 1992). A summary of Christian musical development in the early period comes from Margot Fassler and Peter Jeffery, "Christian Liturgical Music from the Bible to the Renais-

sance," in *Sacred Sound and Social Change,* ed. Hoffman and Janet R. Walton (Notre Dame, Ind.: University of Notre Dame Press, 1992), pp. 84–123.

6. See Reuven Kimelman, "*Birkat Haminim* and the Lack of Evidence for an Anti-Christian Prayer in Late Antiquity," in *Aspects of Judaism in the Greco-Roman Period,* ed. E. P. Sanders, vol. 2 of *Jewish and Christian Self-Definition* (Philadelphia: Fortress, 1981), pp. 226–44, notes on pp. 391–403; and response by Lawrence H. Schiffman, *Who Was a Jew?* (Hoboken, N.J.: Ktav, 1985), pp. 53–61, notes on pp. 94–97.

7. See *The Sabbath in Jewish and Christian Tradition,* ed. Tamara C. Eskenazi, Daniel J. Harrington, S. J., and William H. Shea (New York: Crossroad, 1991), esp. John F. Baldovin, S. J., "Sabbath Liturgy: Celebrating Sunday as a Christian," pp. 95–208.

8. *Mekhilta Bo,* chap. 5.

9. See Amy Ross Scheinerman, "Circumcision as an Index of Jewish-Christian Argumentation Regarding Covenant and Salvation in the First Two Christian Centuries" (Rabbinic ordination thesis, Hebrew Union College-Jewish Institute of Religion, 1984), for an excellent collection of sources and an overall excellent treatment of the subject.

10. *Mekhilta Beshalach* 4 (Lauterbach ed.), p. 218.

11. *Mekhilta Beshalach* 7, pp. 252–54.

12. Daniel Boyarin, "'This We Know to Be the Carnal Israel': Circumcision and the Erotic Life of God and Israel," *Critical Inquiry* 18 (Spring 1992): 474–505.

13. Clement of Alexandria, "The Stromata or Miscellanies," and Tertullian, "An Answer to the Jews," in *The Ante-Nicene Fathers,* ed. Alexander Roberts and James Donaldson, 10 vols. (Grand Rapids, Mich.: William B. Eerdmans Publishing Co., 1962), 2:538 (Clement) and 3:154 (Tertullian). These and other Church Fathers are discussed in Scheinerman, "Circumcision as an Index of Jewish-Christian Argumentation."

14. Sidney Hoenig, "Circumcision: the Covenant of Abraham," *Jewish Quarterly Review* 53 (1962–63): 322–34.

15. See above, pp. 181–84, where the blessing is discussed more fully.

16. Rashi and Tosafot on the Babli passage, 137b, d.h. *yedid,* are generally cited, but the most comprehensive treatment is *Orchot Chaim,* Schlesinger ed., p. 10. See also Saul Lieberman, *Tosefta Kifshutah,* 7 vols. (New York: Jewish Theological Seminary, 1955), 1:114.

17. See, for example, Hoffman, *Beyond the Text* (Bloomington: Indiana University Press, 1987), pp. 40–41.

18. David Flusser and Shmuel Safrai, "Who Sanctified the Beloved in the Womb," *Immanuel* 11 (1980): 46–55.

19. For other texts on the apotropaic function of circumcision, see Elliot R. Wolfson, "Circumcision and the Divine Name," *Jewish Quarterly Review* 78 (1987): 79–80 nn. 6 and 7.

20. Cf. Hoenig, "Circumcision," pp. 330–31; Flusser and Safrai, "Who Sanctified the Beloved in the Womb," p. 55.

21. See also the second blessing of the Grace after Meals, in which God is thanked "for your covenant which you stamped in our flesh," among other things

(Philip Birnbaum, *Ha-siddur Ha-shalem: Daily Prayer Book* [New York: Hebrew Publishing Company, 1949], p. 762). Hoenig ("Circumcision," p. 332) explains this insertion in a blessing over the Land of Israel by noting Justin Martyr's claim that Jews had forfeited their rights to it; the Rabbis responded linking circumcision (the covenant act par excellence) with the Land (the covenant space).

22. See discussion in Hoffman, *Canonization of the Synagogue Service* (Notre Dame, Ind.: Notre Dame University Press, 1979), p. 137; Naphtali Wieder, "Correction of a Corrupted Responsum of Hai Gaon," *Sinai* 53 (1964): 285–89; and Flusser and Safrai, "Who Sanctified the Beloved in the Womb."

23. See Eruv. 19a.

24. Since Saadiah and Sar Shalom have a version that reads "May it be our lot that our children be saved . . . ," I argued in 1979 that the original sense of the blessing was petitionary, with at least two early alternative forms extant by the ninth century: the geonic "May it be our lot . . . ," and our version with the verb "command" in the imperative. I thus discounted Hai Gaon's insistence that the correct reading is the third-person perfect, "commanded." That now seems to me less likely than the hypothesis developed here. See Hoffman, *Canonization of the Synagogue Service,* pp. 136–39.

25. *Mekhilta Bo,* chap. 5.

26. The debate that one still finds on occasion with regard to whether sacrifice in fact did continue for some time and in some circles outside the Temple precinct after the Temple was destroyed is beside the point. Whether it did or not, the overwhelming rabbinic opinion that it should not had clearly prevailed by the time the Mishnah was composed. The official texts treated here all presuppose the system in which sacrifice is indeed impossible regardless of what some sectarians or minority groups might have been doing temporarily.

27. See, for example, *Leviticus Rabbah* 30:2: "David says to God, 'Let me know which gate goes to everlasting life.'"

28. The text is corrupt at this point. It adds a second quality of some sort, possibly either "distinguished-looking" or "fat." See the standard translation by Abraham Cohen, *Soncino Midrash, Ecclesiastes Rabbah,* p. 77, and commentary by Luzzatto, *Chiddushei Harashdal, ad loc.*

29. Or "Repeat after me." The text is corrupt.

30. The verb is רחץ (*r.ch.ts*), literally, "to petition." It is used also in the sense of "having trust in."

31. In DR, the editor shortens this part of the tale by omitting the ritual response. He also translates the technical Aramaic word for a wedding feast as *simchah,* which might mean any joyous occasion, thus leaving it unclear whether he means a wedding feast or not. But the Aramaic original employs *mishtuta,* a word that occurs elsewhere for weddings. See citations in Marcus Jastrow, *A Dictionary of the Targumim, the Talmud Babli and Yerushalmi, and the Midrashic Literature* (1903; reprint, New York: Judaica Press, 1971), p. 859.

32. From DR; ER reads "messenger of creatures," a euphemism for the same thing.

33. Again, רחץ (*r.ch.ts*), literally, "petitioning," but rendered here colloquially as "trusting in the power of."

34. Or "be able to avoid": עובר על (*over al*).

35. Deutoronomy Rabbah 12:1.
36. See Hoffman, *Canonization of the Synagogue Service,* chap. 11.
37. M. Avot 4:16, 22.
38. M. Sotah 9:15.
39. M. San. 10:1, 3.
40. Ramsay MacMullen, *Paganism in the Roman Empire* (New Haven, Conn.: Yale University Press, 1981), p. 55.
41. Ibid., p. 49.
42. Ibid., p. 51.
43. Ibid., pp. 52, 55.

Chapter Eight

1. See, for example, M. Shab. 2:6, 7. The three "women's commandments," of which Sabbath preparation is one, have been discussed ubiquitously. See, however, recent comments by Judith Romney Wegner, *Chattel or Person* (New York and Oxford: Oxford University Press, 1988), pp. 155–56, and Ross Shepard Kraemer, *Her Share of the Blessings* (New York and Oxford: Oxford University Press, 1992), pp. 99–105.

2. M. Ta'an. 2:1–4. See discussion in Lawrence A. Hoffman, *Beyond the Text* (Bloomington: Indiana University Press, 1987), pp. 8–13.

3. On the *ma'amad* and the synagogue, see, for example, Martin A. Cohen, "Synagogue: History and Tradition," in *The Encyclopedia of Religion,* ed. Mircea Eliade, 16 vols. (New York: Macmillan, 1987), 14:211.

4. Joseph Gutmann, "Sherira Gaon and the Babylonian Origin of the Synagogue," in *Occident and Orient: A Tribute to the Memory of A. Scheiber,* ed. Robert Dan (Leiden: Brill, 1988), p. 209.

5. For an early instance, see George Foot Moore, *Judaism,* 3 vols. (Cambridge, Mass.: Harvard University Press, 1927), 1:283, and Wilhelm Bacher's classic article, "Synagogue," in the *Jewish Encyclopedia,* ed. Isidore Singer, 12 vols. (New York, 1901), 11:619.

6. Louis Isaac Rabinowitz, "Synagogue: Origins and History," in *Encyclopedia Judaica,* ed. Cecil Roth and Geoffrey Wigoder, 16 vols. (Jerusalem: Keter Publishing House, 1972), 15:580; my emphasis.

7. See Ellis Rivkin, "Ben Sira and the Non-Existence of the Synagogue," in *In the Time of Harvest: Essays in Honor of Abba Hillel Silver on the Occasion of his 70th Birthday,* ed. Daniel Jeremy Silver (New York: Macmillan, 1963), esp. pp. 351–54; Solomon Zeitlin, "The Origin of the Synagogue, *Proceedings of the American Academy of Jewish Research* 1 (1940–41): 69–81; and Martin Hengel, "Proseuche und Synagoge," in *The Synagogue, Studies in Origin, Archeology and Architecture,* ed. Gutmann (New York: Ktav, 1975), pp. 27–54. The most recent attempt to place the fledgling synagogue in the Diaspora is Stefan C. Reif, *Judaism and Hebrew Prayer* (Cambridge: Cambridge University Press, 1993), pp. 71–75.

8. Lee I. Levine, *The Synagogue in Late Antiquity* (Philadelphia: American Schools of Oriental Research, 1987), p. 14.

9. Ibid., p. 19.

10. Hengel, oppositely, sought liturgical origins in praying places outside the Land and thus had to assume that the *proseuche* of the Diaspora was a general

and altogether different phenomenon that gave rise to rabbinic liturgy and then spread its influence into Palestine. See Hengel, "Proseuche und Synagoge."

11. See L. Roth-Gerson, *Greek Inscriptions from Palestinian Synagogues* [Hebrew], cited in Ezra Fleischer, "*Lakadmoniut Tefillot Hachovah Beyisra'el,*" *Tarbiz* 59 (1990): 407.

12. Fleischer, "*Lakadmoniut Tefillot Hachovah Beyisra'el,*" p. 412. See also the response by Reif, "*Al Hitpatchut Hatefillah Hakadumah Beyisra'el*" *Tarbiz* 60 (1991): 677–81. Reif's views are now also available in his *Judaism and Hebrew Prayer,* chap. 3.

13. See Jonathon Z. Smith, *Imagining Religion* (Chicago: University of Chicago Press, 1982), pp. 15–18.

14. For a summary of the synagogue from this perspective, see Shaye J. D. Cohen, *From the Maccabees to the Mishnah* (Philadelphia: Westminster Press, 1987), pp. 111–15, 223.

15. See, for example, Wayne A. Meeks, *The First Urban Christians: The Social World of the Apostle Paul* (New Haven, Conn.: Yale University Press, 1983), pp. 23–25, 70–71.

16. Bernadette J. Brooten, *Women Leaders in the Ancient Synagogue: Inscriptional Evidence and Background Issues* (Chico, Calif.: Scholars Press, 1982); summarized nicely in Ross S. Kraemer, *Her Share of the Blessings* (New York: Oxford University Press, 1992), pp. 117–23.

17. Kraemer, *Her Share of the Blessings,* pp. 93–127.

18. See Wegner, *Chattel or Person,* p. 189, in connection with women's role in the synagogue.

19. In addition to Brooten, *Women Leaders in the Ancient Synagogue,* see also Kraemer, "A New Inscription from Malta and the Question of Women Elders in the Diaspora Jewish Communities," *Harvard Theological Review* 78 (1985): 431–38.

20. They are collected in Mordecai Hakohen, *Mikdash Me'at* (Jerusalem: Yad Ramah, 1975).

21. See the Theodotus inscription in Brooten, *Women Leaders in the Ancient Synagogue,* p. 24.

22. On the later period in Babylonia, see David Goodblatt, *Rabbinic Instruction in Sasanian Babylonia* (Leiden: E. J. Brill, 1975). For Palestine, see Levine, *The Rabbinic Class of Roman Palestine in Late Antiquity* (New York: Jewish Theological Seminary, 1989), pp. 26–29. Levine finds "the evidence of a *bet hamidrash* (in the Pharisaic-rabbinic sense) in the second Temple period . . . problematic" (p. 26). The institution arose largely after 200, although by the late first century the term was being used in the sense of a study circle surrounding a particular sage and dependent on his charisma—exactly as it was in Goodblatt's Babylonia.

23. Levine, "The Sages and the Synagogue in Late Antiquity: The Evidence of the Galilee," in *The Galilee in Late Antiquity,* ed. Levine (New York: Jewish Theological Seminary, 1992), pp. 201–22.

24. See Marc J. Belgrad, "Table as Altar: Tannaitic Table-Fellowship as a Locus of Spirituality" (Rabbinic thesis, Hebrew Union College-Jewish Institute of Religion, 1986).

25. Noted already by Gedaliah Alon, *Mechkarim Betoldot Yisra'el,* 2 vols. (Israel: Hakibbutz Hame'uchad, 1957), 1:287.

26. See the list in T. Meg. 5:14: "Rabbi Eleazer ben Rabbi Tzaddok said: This is what the *chavurot* in Jerusalem did. Some were for celebration, and some for mourning; some for a meal to celebrate betrothal, and some for a meal to celebrate a marriage; some to celebrate the week of a son's birth, and some to gather the bones of the deceased for a second burial."

27. See, for example, M. Pes. 7:3; T. Pes. 7:6–8.

28. See M. Pes. 7:3; T. Y.T. 2:7–8.

29. M. Pes. 8:7. However, we find reference to the presence of a bride at the *chavurah* meal celebrating the marriage (M. Pes. 7:13). Women may have been in attendance at the other meals also, but they did not count, and could not join in the Grace.

30. M. Ber. 7:2. On the Grace after Meals as a *chavurah* institution, see Joseph Heinemann, "Birkath HaZimmun and Havurah-meals," *Journal of Jewish Studies* 13 (1962): 23–29.

31. See M. Demai 2:3, 2:14.

32. See Jacob J. Neusner, *Fellowship in Judaism* (London: Valentine Mitchell and Co, Ltd., 1963), and Neusner, *From Politics to Piety* (New York: Ktav, 1979).

33. See T. Demai, chap. 2, esp. 2:14.

34. For summary, see Zeitlin, "The Origin of the Synagogue," p. 77.

35. Marcus N. Tod, *Sidelights on Greek History: Three Lectures on the Light Thrown by Greek Inscriptions on the Life and Thought of the Ancient World* (Oxford: Basil Blackwell, 1932), chap. 3. Women also may have had their own *chavurot* as they did elsewhere in the Hellenistic world. My thanks to S. Blake Leyerle for directing me to this source.

36. See the survey in B. G. Walker, *The Woman's Encyclopedia of Myths and Secrets* (New York: Harper & Row, 1983), s.v. "menstrual blood."

37. Nancy Jay, *Throughout Your Generations Forever* (Chicago: University of Chicago Press, 1992), p. 107.

38. Leonie J. Archer, "Bound by Blood: Circumcision and Menstrual Taboo in Post-Exilic Judaism," in *After Eve,* ed. Janet Martin Soskice (London: Collins Marshall Pickering, 1990), pp. 38–61.

39. See Judith Baskin, "The Separation of Women in Rabbinic Judaism," in *Women, Religion, and Social Change,* ed. Yvonne Yazbeck Haddad and Ellison Banks Findly (Albany: State University of New York Press, 1985), pp. 8–9 (following Michelle Zimbalist Rosaldo), and Jerome H. Neyrey, "The Idea of Purity in Mark's Gospel," in ibid., pp. 91–105 (following Mary Douglas).

40. Rahel Wasserfall, "Menstruation and Identity: The Meaning of *Niddah* for Moroccan Women Immigrants to Israel," in *People of the Body: Jews and Judaism from an Embodied Perspective,* ed. Howard Eilberg-Schwartz (Albany: State University of New York Press, 1992), p. 318.

41. Jacob Milgrom, *The Anchor Bible: Leviticus 1–16* (New York: Doubleday, 1991), pp. 904–05. Verse 31 is probably by a different hand than the rest of this closely constructed unit.

42. Ibid., p. 907. The root *zuv* refers in general to that which "oozes." It may be used positively, as in the expression "a land flowing with milk and honey" (Num. 13:27). See p. 906.

43. Ibid., pp. 910–11.

44. See, for example, the opening chapter on the subject in M. Kelim 1:1.

45. See David P. Wright, *The Disposal of Impurity* (Atlanta: Scholars Press, 1987), pp. 179–219, summarized nicely as "The Communication of Impurity" in Milgrom, *The Anchor Bible: Leviticus 1–16*, pp. 953–57.

46. Howard Eilberg-Schwartz's paper at the 1986 Minnesota symposium was entitled "The Language of Jewish Ritual: An Anthropological Approach to the Menstrual Taboo in Judaism." He has since published a somewhat redefined perspective in *The Savage in Judaism* (Bloomington: Indiana University Press, 1990), pp. 177–94. See also interchange between Eilberg-Schwartz and Murray L. Wax in *Journal for the Scientific Study of Religion* 30, no. 3 (1991): 328–29, and 31, no. 2 (1992): 224–27.

47. Rachel Adler, "Tum'ah and Toharah: Ends and Beginnings," *Response* 18 (1973): 117–24; Emanuel Feldman, *Biblical and Post-biblical Defilement and Mourning* (New York: Yeshiva University Press, 1977); Raphael Patai, *Sex and Family in the Bible and Middle East* (Garden City, N.Y.: Doubleday, 1959).

48. Eilberg-Schwartz, *The Savage in Judaism,* pp. 184–85.

49. Eilberg-Schwartz, "The Language of Jewish Ritual," p. 20.

50. Eilberg-Schwartz, *The Savage in Judaism,* p. 187.

51. Eilberg-Schwartz, "The Language of Jewish Ritual," p. 31 n. 54.

52. Ibid., p. 21.

53. Eilberg-Schwartz, *The Savage in Judaism,* p. 187.

54. Ibn Ezra to Lev. 15:18.

55. M. Nid. 2:5.

56. M. Nid. 9:11.

Chapter Nine

1. *Seder Rav Amram Gaon,* ed. E. D. Goldschmidt (Jerusalem: Rav Kook, 1971), p. 180.

2. M. Avot 4:1.

3. See, in general, claims by Jacob Neusner, reiterated in his work on system, for example, *First Principles of Systemic Analysis* (Lanham, Md.: University Press of America, 1987).

4. *Kodesh/chol* is the basic binary opposition on which rabbinic Judaism rests. See Lawrence A. Hoffman, *Beyond the Text* (Bloomington: Indiana University Press, 1987), chap. 2, for analysis.

5. Émile Durkheim, *The Elementary Forms of the Religious Life,* trans. Joseph Ward Swain (1915; reprint, New York: Free Press, 1965), p. 52.

6. Rudolf Otto, *The Idea of the Holy* trans. John W. Harvey (1917; Oxford: University of Oxford Press, 1958).

7. Mircea Eliade, *The Sacred and the Profane: The Nature of Religion,* trans. Willard R. Trask (New York: Harcourt, Brace and World, 1959).

8. Neusner, *The Idea of Purity in Ancient Judaism* (Leiden: Brill, 1973), p. 124.

9. Jerome H. Neyrey, "The Idea of Purity in Mark's Gospel," *Semeia* 35 (1986): 92.

10. Mary Douglas, *Purity and Danger: An Analysis of the Concepts of Pollution and Taboo* (London: Routledge and Kegan Paul, 1966), p. 49.

11. T. Ber 4:1, and elsewhere. See Barukh M. Bokser, "*Ma'al* and Blessings over Food: Rabbinic Transformation of Cultic Terminology and Alternative Modes of Piety," *Journal of Biblical Literature* 100 (1981): 558–70.

12. For detailed treatment, see the introduction to *The Land of Israel: Jewish Perspectives* ed. Hoffman (Notre Dame, Ind.: Notre Dame University Press, 1986).

13. M. Kelim 1:6–9.

14. See the normal benediction wording in Philip Birnbaum, *Ha-siddur Ha-shalem: Daily Prayer Book* (New York: Hebrew Publishing Company, 1949), p. 552, and the altered version in Birnbaum, *The Passover Haggadah* (New York: Hebrew Publishing Company, 1953), p. 59.

15. Popular apologists for Sabbath observance, but sometimes scholars too, may plead the case that the Sabbath is the holiest time of the year, but I do not see how that claim can be sustained. Neyrey ("The Idea of Purity in Mark's Gospel," p. 99) bases his claim on the order of the tractates in the Mishnah, but their order is due to their relative size, the largest coming first and the shortest coming last.

16. T. Kelim B.K. 1:7.

17. T. Kelim B.K. 1:8.

18. See W. M. Feldman, *Rabbinical Mathematics and Astronomy,* 3d ed. (New York: Hermon Press, 1978); J. H. Charlesworth, "Jewish Astrology in the Talmud, Pseudepigrapha, the Dead Sea Scrolls and the Early Palestinian Synagogue," *Harvard Theological Review* 70 (1977): 183–200. The most widespread account of astrological calculation in late antiquity (*Tetrabiblos,* by Claudius Ptolemeus, second century) was in fact the source of *Baraita de Mazzalot* (sixth–eleventh century). See Andrew Sharf, *The Universe of Shabbetai Donnolo* (New York: Ktav, 1976), summarizing work of G. B. Sarfati, "An Introduction to 'Barayta de Mazzalot,'" *Annual of Bar Ilan University* 3 (1965): 56–82.

19. Pes. 113b.

20. Shab. 75a.

21. Shab. 53b.

22. See stories gathered in Shab. 156 a/b.

23. See Birnbaum, *Ha-siddur Ha-shalem,* pp. 709–10, 725–26; for original sources, see Shab. 23b, Meg. 21b.

24. See Ber. 59b; *Entziklopediah Talmudit,* s.v. "birkat hazeman"; Birnbaum, *Ha-siddur Ha-shalem,* pp. 775–76, 599–600, 709–10, 725–26; and Nancy Flam, "Birkat Hazeman: The Radical Blessing of Thanks" (Ordination thesis, Hebrew Union College-Jewish Institute of Religion, 1989).

25. *Mekhilta* Bo, ed. Horowitz, p. 67.

26. See current version of prayers in Birnbaum, *Ha-siddur Ha-shalem,* p. 600.

27. Judith Romney Wegner, *Chattel or Person* (New York and Oxford: Oxford University Press, 1988), p. 152.

28. I use the Lévi-Straussian terminology loosely. It is true that rabbinic

metaphors do include images of women as "raw," but these are scattered. See, for example, women as ripening figs (Nid. 5:7, T. Nid. 6:1) and women as vines containing wine (M. Nid. 9:11). A close study of rabbinic midrash and *halakhah* might well turn up closer affinities, but I am content to argue for the culture/nature duality.

29. Sherry B. Ortner, "Is Female to Male as Nature Is to Culture?" in *Women, Culture and Society,* ed. Michelle Zimbalist Rosaldo and Louise Lamphere (Stanford, Calif.: Stanford University Press, 1974), pp. 67–88.

30. Maurice Bloch and Jean H. Bloch, "Women and the Dialectic of Nature," in *Nature, Culture and Gender,* ed. Carol MacCormack and Marilyn Strathern (Cambridge: Cambridge University Press, 1980), p. 39.

31. Carol P. MacCormack, "Nature, Culture and Gender: A Critique," in *Nature, Culture and Gender,* p. 7.

32. Ibid., pp. 12, 11.

33. See M. Kid. 1:1, 2:1.

34. In the realm of marriage and divorce, we *do* get idioms reminiscent of Lévi-Strauss's raw/cooked dichotomy. The best example is probably M. Gitin 9:10. The house of Shammai says, "A man should divorce his wife only if he has found grounds for it in unchastity." The house of Hillel holds, "*Even if she spoiled his dish.*" The Hebrew is unclear here, so it is hard to know exactly how she spoiled it, but that she is accused of misusing cooking and thus ruining food is undebated. There have been many unsuccessful attempts to explain this curious idiom. As many have suggested, this image, along with other images of eating applied to marriage relationships, may be a euphemism for sex. From a Lévi-Straussiam perspective, however, it may also function to say that if a man's wife oversteps her bounds by misusing culture, he may divorce her and thrust her back into her innate "raw" state of nature.

35. Claude Lévi-Strauss, *The Raw and the Cooked,* trans. John and Doreen Weightman (1964; Chicago: University of Chicago Press, 1983), p. 28.

36. Frederick Turner, *Beyond Geography* (New Brunswick, N.J.: Rutgers University Press, 1983).

37. *Sifra to Leviticus,* 160:4:3.

38. *Yalkut Shemoni* #146; my emphasis.

39. See, for example, *Tanchuma Vayeshev* 9; *Genesis Rabbah* 87:6; Sotah 36b.

40. *Genesis Rabbah* 87:4.

41. From Louis Ginzberg, *Legends of the Jews,* 7 vols. (Philadelphia: Jewish Publication Society of America, 1961), 2:50–51; my emphasis. Carried in many sources: cf. James L. Kugel, *In Potiphar's House* (New York: Harper San Francisco, 1990), pp. 28–65.

42. See *Avot deRabbi Natan,* version A, perek 16, and *Pesikta Rabbati,* addendum 3. Joseph himself had shown the way, since Potiphar's wife used to visit him in jail, where she "would go so far as to hold an iron fork under his neck, so that he would have to lift up his eyes to look at her, yet nonetheless *he would not look at her* (*Genesis Rabbah* 87:10); my emphasis).

43. *Genesis Rabbah* 87:7. The explicit sexual imagery of a taut bow comes from Genesis 49:22, where Joseph is described in his father's blessing as follows:

"Archers bitterly assail him . . . yet his bow stays taut." Clearly the exegesis in the *Rabbah,* though citing the verse in question, reverses meaning, preferring to imagine that Joseph was impotent. The interpretation continued into the Middle Ages; see *Sefer Hatosafot Hashalem, ad loc.*

44. *Genesis Rabbah* 87:7; Sotah 36b.

45. See discussion by Tishbi in *Pirkei Hazohar,* 2:212–14; and Zohar itself, *vayeshev,* 215–16.

46. See Howard Eilberg-Schwartz, *The Human Will in Judaism: The Mishnah's Philosophy of Intention* (Atlanta: Scholars Press, 1986).

47. See M. Ket. 7:6; T. Ket. 7:6–7.

48. Nid. 31a.

Chapter Ten

1. T. Ber. 6:18 = Men. 43b. For parallel sources, see Saul Lieberman ed., *ad. loc.* Lieberman describes the Greek origin of the blessings in question, in his *Tosefta Kifshutah,* 7 vols. (New York: Jewish Theological Seminary, 1955), 1:120. For secondary literature, see Lawrence A. Hoffman, *Canonization of the Synagogue Service* (Notre Dame, Ind.: Notre Dame University Press, 1979), pp. 128–29.

2. *Abudarham Hashalem* (Jerusalem, 1963), p. 42.

3. See Philip Birnbaum, *Ha-siddur Ha-shalem: Daily Prayer Book* (New York: Hebrew Publishing Company, 1949), pp. 17–18.

4. See *Tur,* O.H. 46.

5. *Shulchan Arukh,* 46:4.

6. But see Mordecai Jaffe's *Levush,* which does have it (*Hilkhot Birkhot Hashachar,* sect. 46:5).

7. See George Jochnowitz, "Who Has Made Me a Woman," *Commentary,* April 1981, pp. 63–64.

8. For Yiddish *tkhines,* see Chava Weissler, "Traditional Yiddish Literature: A Source for the Study of Women's Religious Lives," The Jacob Pat Memorial Lecture, Harvard University, Cambridge, Mass., 1987, and a small anthology now available in translation: *The Merit of Our Mothers: A Bilingual Anthology of Jewish Women's Prayers,* ed. Tracy Guren Klirs (Cincinnati: Hebrew Union College Press, 1992). Italian equivalents have yet to be studied sufficiently, but a successful beginning can be found in *Out of the Depths I Call to You: A Book of Prayers for the Married Jewish Woman,* trans. and ed. Nina Beth Cardin (Northvale, N.J.: Jason Aronson, 1992), and, most recently, in Paula Feldstein, "Eighteenth-Century Italian Women's Prayer Books" (Rabbinic ordination thesis, Hebrew Union College-Jewish Institute of Religion, 1993), a study of prayers connected to childbirth, taken from twenty-nine eighteenth- and nineteenth-century manuscripts. The best English example is Hester Rothschild's *Imrei Lev: Prayers and Meditations,* which was completed in 1855, printed in New York (Buegeleisen Press) in 1915, and revised in 1982. It was "translated and adapted from a little volume in French entitled, 'Prières d'un Coeur Israelite' published by the 'Société Consistoriale de Bons Livres'" (from the preface to the New York edition). A typical prayer is: "Lord of all the world, in your hand is blessing. I come now to revere your holiness, and I pray you to bestow your blessing on the baked goods. Send an angel to guard

the baking, so that all will be well-baked, will rise nicely, and will not burn . . . as you blessed the dough of Sarah and Rebekah our mothers" (cited in Weissler, "Traditional Yiddish Literature," p. 1).

9. Weissler, "Traditional Yiddish Literature," p. 2.

10. On *tkhines* as source of women's spirituality, see ibid., and Weissler, "Traditional Piety of Ashkenazic Women," in *Jewish Spirituality from the Sixteenth-century Revival to the Present,* ed. Arthur Green (New York: Crossroads, 1986), pp. 245–75. For a study of spirituality among Sephardic women in Israel, see Susan Starr Sered, *Women as Ritual Experts* (Oxford: Oxford University Press, 1992).

11. M. Ta'an. 4:8: "Rabban Simeon ben Gamaliel said, 'There were no better days for Israel than the fifteenth of Av and the Day of Atonement [the tenth of Tishri], for on those days, Jerusalemite girls . . . would go out and dance in the vineyards."

12. P.T. Ta'an. 1:6, Pes. 4:1: "As for the custom that women have, not to work. . . ."

13. M. Sotah 6:1.

14. M. Ta'an. 4:8.

15. P.T. Pes. 4:1 = P.T. Ta'an. 1:6.

16. M. Sotah 6:1.

17. See, for example, Ezra Fleischer, *Tefillah Uminhagei Tefillah Eretz-Yisra'eliyim Bitekufat Hagenizah* (Jerusalem: Magnes Press, 1988), pp. 62, 66. Note that *piyyutim* were composed for the occasion. But as with other Palestinian liturgical staples, the wording of the eulogy varied. Elsewhere, we get only ". . . who sanctify the new month" or even ". . . who renew the months." Some special New Moons were mentioned by name; thus, for example, "On Rosh Chodesh Nisan, one must say, '. . . the first of the new moons'" (*Massekhet Sofrim* 19:3).

18. *Exodus Rabbah* 15:24; P.T. Ber. 9:3; *Massekhet Sofrim* 19:10.

19. In the Platonic sense of the astronomical laws being inerrant and thus the ideal example of mathematical form in action, pure reason at its best. See A. E. Taylor, *Plato: The Man and His Work* (London: Methuen, 1926), pp. 498–501.

20. I assume a word play based on the deliberate use of Job 31:26, where "moon" and *yakar* as "brightness" is used.

21. *Massekhet Sofrim* 19:10; see San. 42a.

22. The ritual was prescribed for any time from the first sighting of the new moon until its fullness, which was taken in various ways, including the talmudic ruling of fourteen to sixteen days, that is, roughly until the full moon is reached and begins to wane (see P.T. Ber. 9:3; B.T. San. 41b–42a). The dance on Yom Kippur may be a separate custom, or it may be the moon dance moved forward to a few days prior to the full moon, in the light of the ruling that such a custom would be in order any time within the first half of the moon's cycle.

23. T. Meg. 3:15; see P.T. Ket. 1:6; B.T. San. 32b., B.K. 80a.

24. See Rashi to B.K. 80a, B.B. 60b, San. 32b, *Arukh,* s.v. "sheva."

25. The *Arukh* (eleventh-century Rome), however, knew the two ceremonies differed, although its author incorrectly thought that Shevua Haben was the watchnight prior to the circumcision and Yeshua Haben was the first night after a boy's birth, when people came "to congratulate the father on the good news that a

male child had been born to him." For current customs, see *Encyclopedia Judaica,* s.v. "circumcision: folklore." On what did become a celebration of the eve of a boy's circumcision, see Elliott Horowitz, "The Eve of Circumcision: A Chapter in the History of Jewish Nightlife," *Journal of Social History* 23 (1989): 45–69.

26. Saul Lieberman, *Tosefta Kifshutah,* 7 vols. (New York: Jewish Theological Seminary, 1962), 5:1186.

27. See Eliezer ben Yehudah, *Dictionary,* s.v. "shavua."

28. They both cite Judah Bergman, "Shebua Haben," *Monatschrift für Geschichte und Wissenschaft des Judentums* 76 (1932): 465–70. Bergman quotes yet earlier studies by Leopold Löew (1811–75) and Samuel Krauss (1866–1948).

29. Also called Veglia and Wachtnacht.

30. Bergman, "Shebua Haben," p. 465.

31. See *Sha'arei Simchah* of Rabbi Isaac Giat, ed. Manberger, *Hilchot avel,* p. 38; Nachmanides' *Torat Ha'adam,* 2:109; *Massekhet Semachot,* ed. Higger, p. 231.

32. For current ceremony, see Hyman E. Golden *Hamadrikh: The Rabbi's Guide: A Manual of Jewish Religious Rituals, Ceremonies and Customs,* rev. ed. (New York: Hebrew Publishing Company, 1956), pp. 51–54; Birnbaum, *Ha-siddur Ha-shalem,* pp. 749–52.

33. Num. 18:15; see Num. 3:40–51, 8:16, and Ex. 13:2.

34. Pes. 121b.

35. See Rashbam to Pes. 121b, s.v. "Rabbi Simlai happened to be. . . ." He recognizes the irrelevance of our pericope to what has just gone before, but tries to save the integrity of talmudic logic by connecting the story, however feebly, to the Mishnah it follows.

36. See "Addendum" by Israel Ta-shema, in Margoliot, *Hilkhot Eretz Yisra'el,* p. 32.

37. See Lawrence A. Hoffman, *Canonization of the Synagogue Service* (Notre Dame, Ind.: University of Notre Dame Press, 1979), pp. 161–64.

38. The use of spices is another old Palestinian custom that we discover merely by accident. It is taken for granted in P.T. Betsah 5:2. The benediction and the spices drop out of the rite eventually, but in thirteenth-century Italy, both were still being used. See *Tanya,* sect. 94. However, Zedekiah ben Abraham no longer knows why they did it! He says explicitly, "As for our custom to say a blessing over spices, I do not know the reason for it. But the custom is to leave myrtle branches in synagogues to let people know a circumcision is taking place, and since we have the myrtle lying ready at hand, we say the blessing over it" (*Shibbolei Haleket, Hilkhot Milah,* sect. 4).

39. B. M. Lewin, *Otsar Hageonim,* 3:130, citing *Tsedah Laderekh,* but cited elsewhere also by many Rishonim and available now in Genizah form accredited to Hai Gaon. See Ta-Shema, "Addendum," pp. 34–37, for variants.

40. For extended treatment, see Hoffman, "Life-Cycle Ceremony as Status Transformation," in *Eulogema: Studies in Honor of Robert Taft, S.J.,* ed. E. Carr et al. (Rome: Centrò Studi S. Anselmo, 1993), pp. 161–77. Primary texts of the Palestinian order of service can be found in Ta-Shema, "Addendum," pp. 32–36.

41. See discussion in Hoffman, *Canonization of the Synagogue Service,* pp. 141–45.

42. M. Ohalot 1:8.

43. Rosh to Kid., chap. 1.

44. T-S J 3/23 Cambridge, cited by Margoliot, *Hilkhot Eretz Yisra'el,* p. 16.

45. The normal word for womb is *rechem;* the circumcision benediction uses *beten,* which refers more exactly to "stomach" than to "womb." The redemption blessing also avoids *rechem,* using *me'ei imo* ("intestines of his mother") rather than *beten.* Although the wording is not exactly the same, the concept is.

46. *Siddur Rav Saadiah Gaon,* ed. Simchan Assaf, Israel Davidson and Issachar Joel, 2d ed. (Jerusalem: Mekitsei Nirdamin, 1963), p. 100.

47. For the difference among geonim with regard to Palestinian material, see Hoffman, *Canonization of the Synagogue Service,* chap. 11.

48. Fleischer, *Tefillah Uminhagei Tefillah Eretz-Yisra'eliyim Bitekufat Hagenizah,* p. 181.

49. Jacob Mann, "Genizah Fragments of the Palestinian Order of Service," *Hebrew Union College Annual* 2 (1925), reprinted in Jakob J. Petuchowski, *Contributions to the Scientific Study of Jewish Liturgy* (New York: Ktav, 1970), p. 396.

50. From the circumcision rite. See above p. 117.

51. Cited by Ta-Shema in "Addendum," p. 33. The *Tur* is basically correct, with one exception—the blessing over kindling Sabbath lights. The Geonim invented this blessing as a polemic against the Karaites, but implied that their creation was not wholly novel by basing it on the blessing for Chanukah candles, which the Talmud does designate, as if to say that nothing new was involved here. See Hoffman, *Canonization of the Synagogue Service,* pp. 86–89.

52. Saadiah objected to the benediction in toto on the grounds that it introduces extraneous subject matter, recited moreover (contrary to the Babylonian Talmud's dictates) by the priest, not by the father. He therefore also omitted the accompanying response in G ("May he merit Torah, marriage, and good deeds"). Instead he inserted a wish from the priest to the father, "Just as you merited the performance of this commandment, so may you merit performing all the commandments in the Torah." This is in keeping with his inclusion of the second-person address to the father in the parallel circumcision wish, "Just as you brought your child to circumcision [he uses *lamilah* instead of the usual *labrit*], so may you bring him to Torah, the marriage, and good deeds." Saadiah's redemption ceremony is also dependent on the circumcision ritual, but uses a different ritual script as its basis. See *Siddur Rav Saadiah Gaon,* pp. 98, 100.

53. M. Ta'an. 4:8.

54. M. Kid. 7:1.

55. Kid. 29a.

56. Rosh to Kid., chap. 1; my emphasis.

57. *Tanya Rabbati,* sect. 48; cited (in part) in Ta-Shema, "Addendum," p. 36.

Chapter Eleven

1. *Seder Rav Amram Gaon,* ed. E. D. Goldschmidt (Jerusalem: Rav Kook, 1971), p. 180.

2. Ross Shepard Kraemer, *Her Share of the Blessings* (New York and Oxford: Oxford University Press, 1992), pp. 6–7.

3. *Seder Rav Amram Gaon,* p. 180.

4. *Machzor Vitry,* 2 vols. (Nuremberg: Mekitzei Nirdamim, 1923), 2:623.

5. *Machzor Vitry,* 2:625. See *Sefer Hapardes, Inyan Milah;* and *Sefer Ma'asei Hageonim,* ed. Jacob Freiman (Berlin: Mekitzei Nirdamim, 1915), p. 60.

6. *Machzor Vitry,* 2:627.

7. *Shibbolei Haleket, Hilkhot Milah,* sect. 4. See *Tanya Rabbati,* sect. 95.

8. *Sefer Hapardes,* ed. H. L. Ehrenreich (Budapest, 1924), p. 76.

9. *Shibbolei Haleket, Hilkhot Milah,* sect. 4.

10. For the history of Alenu, see Ismar Elbogen, *Jewish Liturgy: A Comprehensive History,* trans. Raymond P. Scheindlin (Philadelphia and New York: Jewish Publication Society and the Jewish Theological Seminary of America, 1993), pp. 71–72; and Joseph Heinemann, *Prayer in the Talmud,* trans. Richard Sarason (1966; Berlin and New York: Walter de Gruyter, 1977), s.v. "Alenu leshabe'ach." Ordinarily, Tachanun would have been recited before Alenu, but, as we saw, Tachanun was omitted as not being in keeping with the festive nature of the circumcision. On this very point, see *Tanya Rabbati,* sect. 95 (end): "In synagogues where a circumcision occurs, they do not say Tachanun." The Alenu was still reserved for Rosh Hashanah at the time when our responsum was issued, but when it was added to the daily service, it would have followed the circumcision rite in synagogues.

11. Moshe Herschler, *Siddur Rabbenu Shlomo Meyuchas Lerabbenu Shlomo ben Rabbi Shimshon Megarmaise* (Jerusalem: Chemed, 1971), p. 282.

12. *She'elot Uteshuvot Rabbenu Nissim ben Reuven Gerondi,* ed. Herschler and Aryeh Feldman (Jerusalem: Moznaim Publishing Co., 1984), p. 414; see nn. 1–2.

13. Ibid., pp. 256–58.

14. *Sha'arei Tzedek* 3:5:11.

15. Tashbetz, #397.

16. See T. Kid. 52b., s.v. "vekhi ishah ba'azara minayin."

17. *Rabbi Meir ben Rabbi Barukh Merotenburg: Teshuvot, Perushim, Uminhagim,* ed. Isaac Ze'ev Kahana 31 vols. (Jerusalem: Mossad Harov Kook, 1960), 2:262, #211.

18. *Sefer Matei Moshe, Inyanei Milah,* 4:5.

19. *Arukh,* s.v. "sindekos."

20. *Midrash Tehillim Hamekhuneh Shocher Tov,* ed. Buber, p. 248. The citation may not be original, however. Every part of the body is mentioned in this midrash, but "knees" is mentioned *twice,* as if someone added our line as an afterthought, or as a late gloss on a text that had the knees originally only as bowing to praise God. Nevertheless, the line was apparently there by the eleventh century, even if the rest of the psalm is from an earlier date.

21. *Rokeach,* sect. 107.

22. This etymology has been taken for granted since 1873, when it was offered by Joseph Perles. See Perles, *Zur Rabbinischen Sprach- und Sagenkunde* (Breslau, 1873), p. 33. It is cited as obvious, for instance, by Hayyim Schauss, *The Lifetime of a Jew* (Union of American Hebrew Congregations, 1950), p. 38, and by Marcus Jastrow, *A Dictionary of the Targumim, the Talmud Babli and Yerushalmi, and the Midrashic Literature* (1903; reprint, New York: Judaica Press, 1971), p. 983.

23. Solomon Buber, "Notes and Emendations," in *Midrash on Psalms* (Vilna, 1891), p. 248 n. 8. Buber cites Perles, *Zur Rabbinischen Sprach- und Sagenkunde,* p. 33, but in fact the discussion is taken from Perles, "Miscellen zur rabbinischen Sprach und Alterthumskunde," *Monatschrift für Geschichte und Wissenschaft des Judentums* 21 (1872): 367.

24. Leopold Zunz, *Ritus der synagogalen Gottesdienstes* (Berlin: J. Springer, 1859), p. 4 n. a.

25. Perles, "Miscellen zur rabbinischen Sprach und Alterthumskunde," p. 367.

26. See Derrick Sherwin Bailey, *Sponsors at Baptism and Confirmation* (London: Society for Promoting Christian Knowledge, 1952), and, specifically on the Greek nomenclature, R. F. G. Burnish, "The Role of the Godfather in the East in the Fourth Century," *Studia Patristica* 17, no. 2 (1982): 558–64.

27. Burnish, "The Role of the Godfather in the East in the Fourth Century," p. 560.

28. My thanks to S. Blake Leyerle for directing me to sixth- and seventh-century citations.

29. Liddell and Scott, *Greek-English Lexicon,* s.v. "anadekomai."

30. Burnish, "The Role of the Godfather in the East in the Fourth Century," *Studia Patristica* 17, pt. 2 (1982): 560; *Commentary of Theodore of Mopsuestia on the Lord's Prayer and on the Sacrament of Baptism and the Eucharist,* trans. A. Mingana (Cambridge: W. Heffer & Sons, 1933), p. 25; *Jean Chrysostome: Huit Catechesis Baptismales,* ed. Antoine Wenger (Paris: Du Cerf, 1957), p. 141. My thanks to Gilbert Ostdiek for directing me to Wenger.

31. *Andek* would have occurred in Hebrew without the vocalization anyway. A vowel prior to the "n" would have been required, but the second one would easily have dropped out of oral usage.

32. Eleazer of Worms's *sandeknim* turns out to have been closer to the original than scholars have imagined in that it retains the correct initial vowel.

33. *Tanya Rabbati,* sect. 96; *Shibbolei Haleket, Hilkhot Milah,* sect. 8.

34. *Tanya Rabbati,* sect. 94.

35. From the thirteenth-century report of Eleazer of Worms we learn that two cups of wine were poured simultaneously, one for Elijah the prophet and one for the *ba'al brit* (see *Rokeach,* sect. 450). The *ba'al brit,* not the *mohel,* administered the wine to the child. The offering to Elijah derives from Malachi 3, where he is referred to as *malakh habrit* ("angel of the covenant"), and thereafter accorded his own chair of authority at the primary covenant event of circumcision. The *ba'al brit* or *sandek* sat there holding the child. The chair is first encountered under the title *moshav kavod* in *Pirkei deRabbi Eliezer,* chap. 29 (end). Its more familiar title, *kisei eliyahu,* appears first in Italian literature of the thirteenth century (*Tanya Rabbati* and *Shibbolei Haleket*). As we would expect, patent messianism is evoked by the chair of Elijah. The child is welcomed by the messianic *barukh haba*—"Blessed be he who comes." See David Daube, *He That Cometh* (London: Council for Jewish-Christian Understanding, 1966). Our rishonic authors argue as to whom the welcome should be addressed, and they seem (on the face of it) to be ignorant of its messianic portents. But the heightened messianism as part of the post-Crusade mentality in Europe is well known (see, for example,

Norman Cohn's classic *The Pursuit of the Millenium* [Oxford and New York: Oxford University Press, 1961]), and the heightened concern with Elijah's appearance in Jewish ritual generally seems to be a Jewish response to their environment. Our texts themselves add the telling information that "the *mohel* shouts [to the child], 'Be a brother to seven,' and the congregation adds, 'And a father to eight'" (*Tanya Rabbati,* sect. 94)—a reference, we may assume, to David, who had seven brothers, or at least to Jesse, the father of eight (1 Sam. 17:12). Elijah's cup seems to be a short-lived addition to the circumcision rite (although it endures in the Passover seder, where it likewise welcomes the prophet destined to announce messianic good tidings). The second cup contained the wine used normally during the service.

36. Malachi Bet Aryeh, "Birkhot Ha'evarim," *Tarbiz* 56, no. 2 (1987): 265–72.

37. We saw above that Peretz of Corbeil (d. 1295) knew the term *ba'al brit* and explained the term *sandek* by means of it, saying, "The *sandek* is the *ba'al brit.*" Now we see the two terms being used together again, this time by a disciple of Maharil (d. 1427) over a century later. *Ba'al brit* still seems to be the better-known word, since his recollection is that "When Maharil was appointed as *ba'al brit . . . ,*" not "When Maharil was appointed as *sandek. . . .*" Still he glosses his account so that the word *sandek* is introduced as the preferable term, for it is in "the language of the sages." I suspect that he has seen the earlier material from *Midrash on Psalms* and assumed it to be ancient. He therefore passes on his own tradition in the usual northern Ashkenazi lexicon, but fulfills what he takes to be his responsibility to let his respondents know what the "language of the sages" is as well.

38. *Sefer Maharil, Hilkhot Milah.*

39. S.A. to Y.D. 265:11.

40. See citations in *Kol Bo Le'inyanei Brit Milah* (Brooklyn: Rabbi A. Ziglman, 1986), p. 124. The sacrificial imagery is kabbalistic. See *Sefer Sheloh, Massekhet Chulin* (Jerusalem, 1959 ed., p. 11) which cites (among others) the sixteenth-century work, *Tola'at Ya'akov,* by Meir ibn Gabbai.

Afterword

1. See, for example, Hilary Putnam, *The Many Faces of Realism* (LaSalle, Ind.: Open Court Publishers, 1987), esp. pp. 63–86.

2. See, for example, Renato Rosaldo, *Culture and Truth* (Boston: Beacon Press, 1989); Ronald L. Grimes, "Liturgical Supinity, Liturgical Erectitude: On the Embodiment of Ritual Authority," *Studia Liturgica* 23 (1993): 51–69; Catherine Bell, *Ritual Theory, Ritual Practice* (Oxford: Oxford University Press, 1992).

3. Sidney Goldstein, *Profile of American Jewry: Insights from the 1990 National Jewish Population Survey* (New York: The Graduate School and University Center, City University of New York, 1993), p. 138.

4. Ibid., p. 77 n. 2, citing *New York Times Book Review,* August 4, 1991, p. 3.

5. W. Lloyd Warner, "An American Sacred Ceremony," in *American Life: Dream and Reality* (Chicago: University of Chicago Press, 1953), reprinted in Russel E. Richey and Donald G. Jones, *American Civil Religion* (New York: Harper & Row, 1974).

6. Jane E. Brody, "Personal Health," *New York Times,* 14 August 1985. The pediatricians' statement is cited in *Berit Milah in the Reform Context,* ed. Lewis M. Barth (New York: Central Conference of American Rabbis, 1990), appendix B, p. 212.

7. Typified by Dwight Lyman Moody (1837–99) and William Ashley (Billy) Sunday (1863–1935). See Sydney E. Ahlstrom, *A Religious History of the American People* (New Haven, Conn.: Yale University Press, 1972), p. 747.

8. Cited in Martin E. Marty, *Pilgrims in Their Own Land* (New York: Penguin Books, 1984), p. 321.

9. Details on American practice can be found in Edward Wallerstein, *Circumcision: An American Health Fallacy* (New York: Springer Publishing Company, 1980). Brody relies on Wallerstein. See also summary in Shirley Kesselman, "The Circumcision Decision," *American Baby's Childbirth* 86, pp. 78–81.

10. See Thomas Goldenberg, "Medical Issues and *Berit Mila,*" in *Berit Mila in the Reform Context,* pp. 192–96.

11. Recent discussion of the medical debate can be found in "Report of the Task Force on Circumcision," *Pediatrics* 84, no. 4 (August 1989): 388–90; T. Wiswell, "Routine Neonatal Circumcision: A Reappraisal," *American Journal of Family Practice* 41, no. 3 (March, 1990): 859–63; "Sounding Board" *New England Journal of Medicine* 322, no. 18 (May 3, 1990): 1308–15; "Circumcision of the Newborn," *New York State Journal of Medicine* (May 1990): 231–32, 243–46. William E. Brigman looks at the medical data from a legal point of view in "Circumcision as Child Abuse: The Legal and Constitutional Issues," *Journal of Family Law* 23, no. 3 (1984–85): 337–57. Popular discussion, including the moral argument, can be found in an ongoing "Forum," *Moment* (December 1992, June 1992, April 1993).

12. Wallerstein, *Circumcision,* and Rosemary Romberg, *Circumcision: The Painful Dilemma* (South Hadley, Mass.: Bergin and Garvey Publishers, 1985).

13. Harriet Lyons, review of *Circumcision: The Painful Dilemma,* by Rosemary Romberg, *Journal of Ritual Studies* 1, no. 2 (1987): 123.

14. Lisa Braver Moss, "Circumcision: A Jewish Inquiry," *Midstream* 38, no. 1 (1992): 20–23. See also Braver Moss, "Current Debate: Circumcision Decision," *Tikkun* 5, no. 5 (1990): 70–71.

15. Esther Raul-Friedman, "A Rebuttal—Circumcision: A Jewish Legacy," *Midstream* 38 (1992): 32.

16. For summary and literature, see Isaac Klein, *A Guide to Jewish Religious Practice* (New York: Jewish Theological Seminary, 1969), pp. 422–23.

17. Raul-Friedman, "A Rebuttal," p. 32.

18. Daniel Landes and Sheryl Robbin, "Gainful Pain," *Tikkun* 5, no. 5 (1990): 73.

19. Ibid., p. 74. The report cited is "PedCom AAP Member Alert," 10 March 1989.

20. Michael B. Herzbrun, "Circumcision: The Pain of the Fathers," *CCAR Journal* 38, no. 4 (Fall 1991): 11. See also the response by Allen S. Maller, "Pain and Circumcision," *CCAR Journal* 39, no. 2 (Summer 1992): 70, which advocates that pain can sometimes be a virtue, and Herzbrun's retort, "Pain and Circumcision," *CCAR Journal* 40, no. 1 (Winter 1993): 61–62.

21. *Berit Milah in the Reform Context* serves as a textbook for the Reform

movement in North America. As of 1989, forty-five physicians had been certified as *mohalim/ot* (pp. 216–17). Four years later, the number had grown to sixty-three (*National Directory of Mohalim/ot,* ed. Barth and Judith Schindler [April 1993]). Graduates have formed an organization called NOAM, from the Hebrew word *no'am,* meaning "favor," drawn from Psalm 90:17: "May the favor of the Eternal our God be upon us; let the work of our hands prosper; O prosper the work of our hands." NOAM sponsors annual meetings and publishes a *Berit Mila Newsletter.* The Conservative movement operates its own program, as do liberal movements in Great Britain (for details, see *Berit Mila Newsletter,* 5 January 1991). Non-Orthodox *mohalim* are still banned in Israel.

22. See, for example, Paula Hills, "A Nontraditional 'Circumcision' Ceremony," *Mothering Magazine* 44 (Summer 1987): pp. 40–41.

23. See *Rabbi's Manual,* ed. David Polish (New York: Central Conference of American Rabbis, 1988). Two parallel services are Hachnasat Ben Labrit (Brit Milah), "Covenant Service for a Son (Circumcision)" (p. 6) and Hachnasat Bat Labrit, "Covenant Service for a Daughter" (p. 16).

24. See new wording, "covenant of our people Israel," in *Rabbi's Manual,* p. 21. The traditional "covenant of Abraham" is retained for boys, however, as a reference to the circumcision (p. 11).

25. See *Rabbi's Manual,* pp. 6–24.

Index